FLYING UNDER TWO FLAGS

FLYING UNDER TWO FLAGS

An ex-RAF Pilot in Israel's War of Independence

GORDON LEVETT

With a Foreword by
the President of Israel

FRANK CASS

First published in 1994 in Great Britain by
FRANK CASS & CO. LTD
Gainsborough House, Gainsborough Road,
London E11 1RS, England

and in the United States of America by
FRANK CASS
c/o International Specialized Book Services, Inc.
5804 N.E. Hassalo Street, Portland, Oregon 97213-3644

British Library Cataloguing in Publication Data

Levett, Gordon
    Flying Under Two Flags: An Ex-RAF Pilot in Israel's
    War of Independence
    I. Title
    358.41332092

    ISBN 0-7146-4102-2

The Library of Congress Cataloging in Publication data has
been applied for.

This book was published in Hebrew by Ma'arachoth, Israel,
in 1989, and in French by Éditions Créaphis in 1992. Edited
sections have also appeared in the following magazines:
*Aeroplane Monthly, Air Enthusiast, Air Pictorial, Aviation
News, Le Fana de l'Aviation* (France), *Flugzeug* (Germany),
A.O.P.A. (Australia) and *Aircraft and Aerospace* (Australia).
Photographs 7 and 29 are reproduced by kind permission of
Aeroplane Monthly, photograph 27 by kind permission of the
Jean-Jacques Petit Collection, and photograph 30 by kind
permission of Peter Arnold.

ISBN 0 7146 4102 2

Typeset by Vitaset, Paddock Wood, Kent
Printed in Great Britain by
Watkiss Studios Ltd, Biggleswade

Author's Note

THESE MEMORIES are based on faulty recall but no known untruth is perpetrated or perpetuated. My mitigation for any hyperbole, bias, selectivity or inaccuracy is the limitation of recall. If things did not happen as I say they happened they could have, might have and should have. Some parts of my story may be inaccurate; the sum of the parts is not. As Samuel Johnson said a man who tells a good story seldom tells the truth, the whole truth and nothing but the truth.

Contents

List of Illustrations

Foreword

MY OLD FIGHTER pilot comrade, Gordon Levett, was bitten by the aviation bug between the two world wars. Coming from a poor family, he overcame many difficulties and tribulations before he finally succeeded in getting the coveted Royal Air Force wings pinned to his chest and winning his commission. In the Second World War his heart was set on air combat but he became a flying instructor. Only when the war ended and he left the RAF was he destined to have another chance of combat, this time in the Israeli Air Force.

In 1948, the Jewish people, survivors of the Holocaust, were about to establish their own country in Palestine. Sadly, war with the Arabs was inevitable and the Jews needed experienced volunteers from abroad to help them in that war, particularly pilots. For Gordon Levett it wasn't just another adventure. Although not Jewish, he believed with all his heart in the right of the Jewish people, particularly after the horror of the Holocaust, to a land of their own, so when the telephone rang he was soon on his way to our war. He was not a mercenary; like me he was paid £6 a month.

In the critical early days of the 1948 War of Independence, he participated in the vital clandestine airlift between Czechoslovakia and besieged Israel, flying in war material, including dismantled Messerschmitt 109 fighter planes. These fighter aircraft were soon in action, flown by the pilots of 101 squadron, Israel's first fighter squadron. I first met Gordon Levett when he later joined the squadron after the airlift and joined us in the air battles against the Egyptian air force. Gordon fulfilled his wish for air combat by shooting down an enemy aircraft, possibly two. We Israelis who helped form the squadron, flying Messerschmitt 109s, Spitfires and Mustang P51s, were glad when the flyers from overseas came and joined us. Their vast experience accumulated during the Second World War helped us to eventual command of the skies and victory.

After that war the time soon came when we Israelis had sufficient experience and no longer needed volunteers from abroad to help man our air force. Most of the volunteers returned to their own countries leaving us with deep feelings of gratitude that they came to our aid in those critical early days of Israel.

Gordon Levett tells with skill the story of his life as a pilot in the Royal Air Force and, particularly, that moment in his life when his path crossed that of the Israeli Air Force. I have no doubt that pilots of today and the general reader will enjoy reading his story.

Ezer Weizman, President of Israel

PART I

PENGUIN INTO EAGLE

Chapter 1

IT ALL STARTED on 29 March 1921, Tuesday's child, Aries, at 35 Stephendale Road, Fulham, London, SW6. At that time the Stephendale Road area was a slum under the shadow of the tall chimneys and gasometers of the Fulham Gas Light and Coke Company. Pervading all was the acrid smell of gas-making and, every winter without fail, the sulphurous fog.

My father was a Merchant Navy stoker and spent his life in the bowels of steamships shovelling coal into furnaces. He travelled the world but saw little of it. Unsurprisingly he was thin and pale. Between voyages he came home, got drunk, spent five or ten minutes playing with me, beat my mother, left a few pounds and departed. My mother rarely smiled. Never laughed.

My father was frequently out of work. My parents had no money, little hope and six children of whom four died young. Two died of the Spanish influenza that ravaged Europe shortly after the First World War, another of diphtheria, another of convulsions. There were more things to die of in those good old days. That left my brother Jack, seven years my senior, and me. We were healthy but Jack was disabled for life in one leg in a motorcycle accident when he was eighteen. My father died of pneumonia in 1929, aged forty-nine and worn out, in St. George's Hospital, Hyde Park Corner, probably the only salubrious address he ever had apart from c/o *SS Mauretania, SS Leviathan, SS Aquitania, et al.* His Board of Trade log-book, stamped and signed by the captain of his ship at the end of every voyage, included an assessment of ability and conduct. To my surprise, I always imagined that my father was a bit of a rascal, he was assessed *Very Good* on both counts after every voyage. He had an anchor tattooed on his upper right arm and Vera, not my mother's name, on the left. I wonder what she felt when her eyes rested on Vera's name when they were in the throes of love-making. The log-book also mentioned that he was only 5'9" tall. It seems all wrong that he was younger and shorter than I am now when he died. He did not live long enough – I was nine when he died – to do much for me except give me his name and good health. In my memory he is the faintest of ghosts and is buried, alone, at Fulham New Cemetery, grave number Mc 188.

When I was thinking about writing this book I knew I would find it painful to write about my mother. I did not like her. She was attractive. After my father's death a series of new 'uncles' arrived on the scene. There was Uncle George, a seaman, Uncle Guy, an artist, Uncle Tom, a mounted policeman, Uncle Bill, who was unemployed and others too fleeting to remember. There were no aunts. I find it difficult even now to believe that they were lovers bearing in mind how prudish she was with my brother and me but what else could they have been? However, the uncles were a generous source of pennies and sweets.

Sex was totally taboo. I once asked her what circumcision was. Her reply was a prim-lipped frost. When I was about twelve I started masturbating. Months later, I read to my shock and horror in a nineteenth-century book written by a foolish reverend whose name I have forgotten that this vile practice makes you go mad and blind. I did not let this information put me off, but living with fear, guilt, shame and remorse was a large price to pay for such fleeting moments of ecstasy. There was nobody I could talk to because I was convinced I was the only one indulging in this solitary vice. For months I looked closely at my eyes in the mirror, compared my eyesight with that of other boys of my age and looked up the definition of madness in every dictionary I came across. Truth and relief came when I learned from an adult book circulating secretly at school all I needed to know about masturbation.

My mother's life, like millions of others in the 1920s and 1930s, was an existence of such relentless, grinding, interminable poverty that it can only be understood by those who suffered it. When my father was alive there were his wages coming in and some kind of hope, no matter how forlorn, for the future. When he died my mother was on her own. Social security was derisory.

She got a job as a charwoman in a doctor's surgery, earning eighteen shillings a week for a twenty-hour week. This, combined with her widow's pension, was her sole income. My father left nothing. Few did then. Scott Fitzgerald said the rich are different. He could have added that the poor are boring, so I won't go on too long about it. A few examples will suffice. It was my weekly job to cut up newspapers into six-inch squares for the lavatory. They were not our

4

newspapers; we could not afford them. I collected them from rubbish tips. If we had jam on our bread we would not have margarine, or vice versa. We did not have jam that often. We never had butter or books. In my childhood I never held a cricket bat or ball, or a tennis racquet, or a golf club, or rode my own bicycle. I saw the sea for the first time on my thirteenth birthday. We did not have a car. The first and last time I rode in a car as a child was at my father's funeral. We did not, of course, have a telephone. I don't think we spent much time feeling sorry for ourselves. Working-class expectancy of life was at its nadir and most grown-ups were embarrassed and hostile to those who, on soap boxes, were urging them to fight back.

To those at the front line of poverty, winters were the worst. We spent hard winters always cold, very cold, or frozen. We often went to bed early not to sleep but to keep warm. We bought coal only when we were ill and, as a special treat, half a hundredweight for Christmas Day. I wore paper cut-out vests and cardboard inserts in my leaking shoes. Aneurin Bevan was right when he said it took Tory government genius to create a situation in which so many British people were cold and hungry when they lived on an island of coal surrounded by fish. It is not surprising that the English disease then was bronchitis.

All my clothes were handed down from my older brother, most of them neatly patched. My mother was a marvellous housekeeper and cook. Our various homes, though mean, were always spotless and our bellies filled with cheap potato and offal-based food and delicious steamed suet puddings. I wore short trousers until I started work; short trousers were cheaper than long trousers. I went to the local flea-pit cinema by climbing a barbed-wire wall and sneaking in through a fire-exit. Late on Saturday nights I dredged with a stick the gutters of the street market in North End Road, Fulham, hoping to find coins. Our major treat for tea was a penny-worth of broken biscuits. My pocket money was a nominal half-penny a week. Jack's was a penny. We did not get it when there was no money in the kitty. My mother hit and swore at me only once in my entire childhood; a tribute to her stoicism. Sadly I was responsible for the lapse. I had been whining endlessly for a farthing pocket money. She angrily emptied her handbag and purse onto the kitchen table and slapped my face hard. 'Look, look, look,' she shouted, pointing at the table. 'Don't you understand, you stupid boy, there is no bloody money!' I realised years too late that my mother was a proud woman and it was the shame of poverty rather than its hardship that affected her most. She sold her engagement ring shortly after my father died. She used the pawn-shop regularly to pledge her wedding ring. She wore it on her little finger because she could not easily get it off her fourth finger, left hand. It was bad enough being a child in those good old days. It must have been crucifying being a widowed mother with two children.

North End Road market was my childhood playground. I walked its length four times a day to and from Beaufort House, LCC elementary school. It was a lucky dip. There was usually an apple or an orange in the gutter that had fallen from the market stalls. I met my mates there at night and at weekends. At night in winter each stall had a hissing butane gas lantern hanging from its roof, casting light on the wares and the costermongers standing at the back. It was like a street of tiny theatres. It seemed oddly quiet and clean on Sundays when all the shops were closed and the stalls and the shouting barkers had gone.

We lived at eight different addresses, rented flats in Fulham or Chelsea, during my youth. I do not know why my mother moved us so often. Judging by the addresses it was not for betterment. I suspect it was landlord-dodging.

In summer, I walked to the Serpentine in Hyde Park, had a swim in the free area and then watched the rich as they rode along Rotten Row. I looked at their carriages and horses and grooms and clothes more in awe than envy. How could anyone be so rich? I must have looked a forlorn, wistful waif because once a carriage stopped and a woman reached out and gave me a florin (10p), a huge sum. I stopped at the same place and wore the same expression for many Sundays to come, but no luck.

About this time I discovered the weekly boys' magazines *Gem* and *Magnet*. I preferred *Magnet* to *Gem*. I did not twig for many years that the two authors, Martin Clifford of *Gem* and Frank Richards of *Magnet* were the same man: Charles Harold St. John Hamilton, no less. I had a vicarious public school education at Greyfriars with Harry Wharton, Frank Nugent, the dusky Nabob and the immortal, yarooing Billy Bunter. I suffered the sneers of my mates, who preferred *Hotspur*, *Wizard* and *Boy's Own*, because *Magnet* and *Gem* had no pictures and were therefore not swappable.

6

I bless the day that I bought my first *Magnet* for it opened that glorious door to a lifetime of reading and a rare avenue of escape for those of my ilk.

Jack did not read much. He became the man that did things with his hands and was eventually a skilled electrician, painter and decorator, carpenter, plumber, car mechanic, panel beater and house builder. To beat petrol rationing during the Second World War, he designed and built an electric motorcycle powered by umpteen batteries. It worked for years.

I was ten years old when my mother suddenly announced that I was to go to an orphanage. In our social scale an orphanage was on a par with the workhouse. My piteous cries that I was not an orphan went unheeded. Apparently she had got special dispensation for me to go to a Merchant-Navy charity orphanage in Swanley, Kent. My tears were at the thought of her rejection of me. I was too young to appreciate the ruthless reality of poverty in the early 1930s.

I was there for eighteen months. Eighteen months is not that long for a grown-up, but to a child aged ten it seemed a lifetime. While there I read *David Copperfield*. I identified with David. There was no Mr Creakle at Swanley, but a team of minor Creakles, aided and abetted by the usual quota of bullies. I was a natural victim. I was not a proper orphan, I was a loner, not robustly built, a little brighter than the average and pretty. My health and sanity were saved by the house matron. She had grey eyes and the pale, flawless skin and benign expression of a nun. Her name was Miss Wilson. I loved her, totally. The only thing I did not like about her was that she was nice to the bullies as well.

It was a two-winter eighteen months. I had scarlet fever and my tonsils removed in the summer and bronchitis in both winters. I liked being ill because the sanatorium was warm and private, and it kept me away from the cane and the bullies, and Miss Wilson helped with the nursing. I often wished she was my mother instead of her surrogate. From the sanatorium upstairs window at night I could see and hear the distant London–Dover express. What dreams I dreamt as I heard the locomotive's shrieking whistle and saw the lighted carriages flashing past!

Routine was spartan. Reveille was at 6.15 a.m., followed by cold-water ablutions. We showered twice a week also in cold water. We wore short-trousered dark blue serge uniforms with a stiff white

collar and tie which I pretended I could not manage so that Miss
Wilson had to help me. We lined up on Saturday mornings for our
weekly purgative of Epsom salts from a tin mug. The only thing I
can recall about the food is that we had tripe and onions stewed in
milk about twice a week. It is the nastiest dish I know, but there was
no evading it for we had to file past a master with our plates empty
after every meal. I remember trying to swallow several times to
force each mouthful down. Weather permitting we went for walks,
Indian file, every Sunday afternoon. I envied the people outside the
front gates their nonchalant freedom. I once ran away but got caught
about a mile from the gates by the village constable who recognised
my uniform. I got six of the best across my bottom in front of the
whole school. It did not hurt very much as I had been advised by
Miss Wilson to wear two pairs of underpants, but my ego smarted.
There must have been pleasant moments during those eighteen
months but of these all I can remember was being school conker
champion – I cheated by getting Miss Wilson to bake my chestnut –
and going home for two weeks during the summer.

It was a smashing two weeks. My resentment and my mother's
guilt at my exile melted in a plethora of good things. It helped that a
new uncle, Uncle Fred, had appeared on the scene. He was a
widower and a bus driver on what was then the General Omnibus
Company's route No.73. Sadly, pirate buses had disappeared.
They had been introduced as competition, but were short-lived
when it was realised that bus-drivers, who were paid commission
on fares, raced each other to pick up the passengers at the next stop.
The language between competing drivers was interesting. It was
fun while it lasted.

In collusion with the bus conductor we travelled free on Uncle
Fred's bus. Some of the buses had open roofs and my mother, Jack
and I sat at the front of the top deck with the sun on our faces and the
wind in our hair as we free-loaded from one end of the route to the
other and back again and again. It was like riding in a posh convertible car. Fortunately one end of the route stopped at Wimbledon
Common where we sometimes deserted Uncle Fred and played
while he returned to the wheel. He liked beer and we often sat
outside the Green Man pub at the top of Putney Hill. He drank
brown and mild, my mother drank Sanatogen tonic wine and Jack
and I drank Tizer the Appetizer.

Jack started work at fourteen as an electrician's mate. For 10s (50p) he bought a Rudge-Whitworth motorcycle which he overhauled. I gazed in awe at the pile of nuts and bolts and entrails of the motorcycle, wondering how he would get them back together again. His hands were already gnarled. He had recently built a kayak canoe. During the evenings we walked with the kayak over our heads down the busy King's Road, like two characters from a Firbank novel, to the Thames at Albert Bridge and paddled up and down the river. Jack had become expert and he could roll the kayak over 360 degrees. Once, inevitably, we managed only 180 degrees and finished up heading steadily downstream suspended upside down from the kayak's cockpit. We were well on the way to the Pool of London by the time we, with the help of the river police, got the kayak upright.

Jack and I are different. Being older than me he has gone through life always being older than me. I think that irritated him sometimes. It is nice to be the younger brother, particularly when one is getting on. Being the eldest son, without a father in the family, meant that he had to assume some responsibilities. Actually I can't think what, but it must be so. I think Jack feels that I had what little luck was going in the Levett family.

The two weeks' holiday was soon over and it was back to the orphanage. My mother gave me a shilling when we said good-bye. I suppose she loved me. I loved her sometimes. We promised to write to each other more often.

My letters were resentful sagas of snivelling complaints. Hers always ended with a promise that she would bring me home as soon as she could. The economics of my exile baffled me. It was difficult for a child to understand that money was so scarce that the few shillings a week it would cost to feed and clothe me at home were beyond my mother's resources. It was only towards the end of my exile that I began to realise that I was at the orphanage through necessity and not rejection. That was no consolation. Being that poor was almost as shameful as being unloved.

Towards the end of that summer my mother suffered another turn of the screw when Jack was involved in a serious accident. His motorcycle was hit side-on by a car at a crossroads in Chelsea. The car driver had jumped the traffic lights. Jack finished up in St Luke's hospital in Sydney Street with a crushed right ankle. Part of his ankle was found in the motorcycle's gearbox. The surgeons wanted to amputate but Jack refused. He was crippled for life and still suffers pain from that mangled angle.

My career as a bogus orphan ended as suddenly as it had begun. I was playing snakes and ladders in the games room on a wet, wintry, no-walk Sunday afternoon when I was summoned to the head-master's study. Terrified, and expecting I know not what, I entered his study and to my astonishment found my mother sitting there. I was going home. Within an hour I had changed into the new civilian clothes my mother had brought with her, packed my few belongings and we were on the train to London. It was Miss Wilson's day off. I never did say goodbye to her, or thank her.

My homecoming was due to the £500 compensation Jack had been awarded for his injuries. It seemed a princely sum when at that time one could buy a new semi-detached house for £299, average wages were about £3 a week, a packet of twenty Player's cigarettes cost elevenpence-halfpenny and a pint of beer threepence. In later years in rows with my mother Jack used to call it his blood money.

Such is the resilience of youth that my rehabilitation was swift, and I was soon back at an LCC elementary school, this time at Park Walk, Chelsea. The only changes I noticed at home were Jack's new crutches hanging up in the hall and our first wireless set placed proudly in the living room. It was a new Ekco and the envy of our friends and neighbours. Domestic wireless was still in its infancy. There was no television, of course; or ball-point pens, or man-made fibres, detergents, jet aircraft, tape-recorders, helicopters, plastic, microwave ovens, computers, iron curtain, bikinis, dishwashers, legal abortions, zips, penicillin, canned pet-food, radar, filter-tipped cigarettes, aerosols, water-skiing, trans-Atlantic airlines, instant fame, motorways, overt homosexuality, videos, the Pill, electric razors, atomic lunacy, apartheid, credit-cards, instant cameras, Israel, driving tests, easy divorce, supermarkets or full-frontal nudes. I wonder how we managed.

An unexpected side-effect of my sojourn at Swanley was the discovery at my new school that I was at least a year ahead of my peers. Perhaps I should have stayed at the orphanage. I was moved up a form and became a bit of a teachers' pet and, once again, a magnet for the bullies.

Jack and I became quite close at this time, despite my being a swot. Like me he was a loner and his newly acquired handicap had cut him off from his few friends. He bought a second-hand New Hudson motorcycle – all motorcycles then had hand gear-change – and I spent most weekends riding pillion. He had become a heavy cigarette smoker and after I had suffered singed eyebrows and eyelashes we agreed that he would smoke over his left shoulder and I would peer ahead over his right shoulder.

It was the summer of 1933 and I was twelve years old when Jack took me to the Royal Air Force air display at Hendon aerodrome. It cost threepence to get in. I had read most of Captain Johns' 'Biggles' stories and the flood of pulp fiction magazines then being published about air combat in the First World War. Bishop, Ball and Richthofen were my heroes, but I had never been anywhere near an aeroplane, much less a pilot. Edging my way through the crowd I got within touching distance of those Royal Air Force demi-gods in sky-blue uniform, golden wings embroidered on their left breast, and parachutes slung nonchalantly over their shoulder as they lounged against their beautiful, sleek Hawker Furies, arguably the most beautiful aeroplane ever built.

A few weeks later Jack took me to Hanworth aerodrome for my first flight. It was in a Jubilee Monospar, a monoplane with two Pobjoy Niagara engines and an enclosed cockpit which carried four passengers. The pilot was aloof and grunted in response to my torrent of questions. I suppose piloting the madding crowd for five shilling joy-rides is not the most exciting form of flying. I sat in front in the co-pilot's seat, next to the pilot. I looked down at the void below and the tilting earth and had my first inkling of that heady cocktail of awe, disbelief and exhilaration laced with fear which, for those who love flying, is the very essence of flight.

By flying I do not mean being herded into a soulless aluminium tube at Heathrow airport and flying so high that mountains become pimples and the air stale with ennui. I write of the days when fellow-passengers were fellow adventurers and a flight was something more than a cheap shopping spree for duty-free cigarettes and booze, when an airline captain would occasionally fly low and circle to show passengers the Pyramids or the Eiffel Tower and one could order a lightly poached egg on toast from the steward.

I was nearing fourteen when one of my schoolmasters visited my mother at home to discuss the possibility of continuing my education at a grammar school. I was head of school and head monitor. I can remember the frustration on his face as he listened to my mother. He got angry but nowhere. I was to leave school at fourteen to earn my living. I did not mind then, I was looking forward to wearing long trousers and a hat. All grown-ups wore hats then. I mind now. Whenever the subject cropped up my mother reminded me of the working-class eleventh commandment: Thou shalt not have ideas above thy station. Later, when I did start getting ideas above my station, she produced another bit of working-class morality. That, if I persisted, I would come to a bad end.

When I left school, my education complete, I could read, write and do simple arithmetic and had a superficial knowledge of the British Empire. The rest of knowledge was a closed book.

I started work in 1935, aged fourteen. My mother had ignored the working-class twelfth commandment: Thou shalt learn a trade, and took the first job available, as an errand-boy at Arthur Beale & Sons, Yacht's Chandlers, Shaftesbury Avenue, in the West End of London. Yacht's chandler sounds very grand, but it was merely a superior ironmongers' shop that sold bits and pieces for small boats, mountaineering equipment, flags and bunting. I did not like Mr. Arthur Beale one little bit. He was a cold fish without the slightest idea of what it was like to be an ignorant, fourteen-year-old youth plunged for the first time into a largely hostile, adult working world. My wages were twelve shillings a week. I revelled in my new long trousers, a cap, and the new-found freedom of no longer being at school. When walking the glamorous streets of the West End, delivering invoices or other errands, I enjoyed watching the antics of the rich and felt glad to be away from the slog of rote learning and a life dominated by pen, pencil and rubber.

Both 1935 and 1936 were good years for the flag and bunting business. In 1935 it was the Silver Jubilee of King George V. In 1936 the turnover of kings was high – George V, Edward VIII and George VI. I seemed to spend most of my early working life shinning up flag-poles on top of buildings putting up more flags.

I have forgotten why I got the sack when I was fifteen and joined the three million unemployed.

My next career was as a lift-boy in an office block at No. 5, Theobalds Road, Holborn. It would seem my mother did not worry too much about my future. On the other hand perhaps she had three million reasons for taking what she could get for me.

12

In my new job I wore a uniform, got 12s 6d (62½p) a week wages, and fell hopelessly in love with Mrs Bullivant, the caretaker's wife. My love was unrequited. I hero-worshipped Mr Bullivant because he owned a speedway motorcycle which he raced at Dagenham Stadium. He rarely won a race, usually coming in second or third. He always had bits of plaster sticking to his hands or face which contrasted oddly with his immaculate dark blue uniform. My uniform did not look so good. It was made for a boy about three inches shorter than me. Mr Bullivant had a Morgan two-seater three-wheeler and a trailer for taking the motorcycle to race meetings at weekends to which I was sometimes invited. When that happened Mrs Bullivant had to sit on my lap. I did not mind one little bit.

On the fourth floor was a firm called Wright Aviation which specialised in aerial advertising, either towing banners or sky-writing. I eventually found the courage to speak to Mr Wright and ask him for a job or a flight, preferably both. He said no to a job, but that if I reported to his office on Saturday morning he would take me on a flight. He was a short, dapper man with an unnecessary pencil moustache and a curt, taciturn manner. His secretary told me that he had been a Royal Flying Corps pilot during the First World War and had won the Military Cross for shooting down several German aircraft. I stared obsessively at his eyes and hands: eyes that had looked down on the Western Front and hands that had pressed the trigger. Mr Bullivant now took second place to the man who had shared the same sky as Bishop, Ball and Richthofen.

On that Saturday morning we went down to his car parked outside. It was a Green Label Bentley with, as the sun was shining, the hood folded away. I peered along that vast leather-strapped bonnet as we throbbed bom-bom-bom-bom through London, past Arthur Beale & Sons and along the Great West Road to Hanworth aerodrome.

The aeroplane and the mechanics were waiting. The aeroplane, like Mr Wright, was a First World War veteran, an Avro 504K biplane with a huge skid sticking out in front to prevent the propeller from hitting the ground should the pilot make a bad landing. The original Le Rhone engine had been removed and a more powerful Lynx engine installed to overcome the heavy drag and weight of the advertising banner. The two cockpits in tandem were open to the sky, unlike the Monospar of my first flight. The

13

banner was laid out on the grass in the middle of the aerodrome, with one end held up high by two forked poles. It said *Players Please*.

It took a long time to get suitably dressed in a huge fur-lined Sidcot one-piece suit, black leather flying boots, heavy gloves, leather helmet fitted with Gosport speaking-tubes and sponge-padded goggles. Finally, Mr Wright tied his own white silk scarf around my neck with one end longer than the other so that it would stream back in the slipstream just like Biggles.

Mr Wright then briefed me about the flight. He was quite businesslike as he showed me the safety harness, a very flimsy affair I thought, how to connect the speaking-tubes and, with an encouraging smile, how to use the parachutes which were strapped to our bottoms and served a secondary function as seat cushions. He then explained about the advertising banner. We were to take off without it, which surprised me until he explained that after take-off we would dive low at high speed over the aerodrome and with a hook trailing from the aircraft pick up the end of the banner and climb steeply. He illustrated this with vivid hand movements. He added they were still experimenting with this new method of hooking the banner in preference to taking-off with the banner attached to the aeroplane at the end of a long rope laid out on the grass in a series of loops. These loops enabled the aeroplane to gain flying speed before the banner was snatched into the air.

Mr Wright gestured to me to climb into the front cockpit. It was awkward getting in. There were small toe-holds in the side of the fuselage and a walkway along the bottom wing on which one walked with care, otherwise one's foot went through the canvas covered wing. Everybody watched, waited and laughed as I cocked my leg over the rim of the cockpit and banged my head against the upper wing. All aircraft designers assume that pilots are, *inter alia*, dwarfs and contortionists. I eventually slid down into the bucket seat and wriggled up and down a few times until the parachute fitted snugly. A mechanic fitted my safety harness and plugged in the chauffeur-like Gosport speaking-tubes. I breathed deeply the smell of all aeroplanes of that era: a mingling of dope, burnt gases, Castrol X and petrol, with a hint of grass and countryside, which once smelled is never forgotten.

It was a dual-controlled aeroplane with the controls and switches duplicated in both cockpits. I was watching the ghost-like movements of the flying controls in my cockpit when Mr Wright's voice came down the speaking tube enquiring whether I could hear him and was I ready. I answered in the affirmative on both counts, at which he begged me not to shout.

After complicated backchat between the pilot and the mechanics the engine started with a bang and a puff of blue smoke. I was sitting close behind the engine and could see the propeller spinning and the rocker-arms hammering the valves down like a team of demented blacksmiths. The first spot of oil appeared on the tiny windscreen as we taxied out. Mr Wright remarked that it was a perfect day for flying. I nodded agreement. I would have agreed to any proposition he cared to mention. After all I was plugged in to a demi-God.

I can recall that first take-off in an open cockpit aeroplane as though it were happening now. The roar of a powerful radial engine at full throttle, the heat from the engine fanned back by the propeller, the smell of the exhaust, the vibration, buffeting and bouncing as we accelerated over the grass, the distant houses on the edge of the aerodrome getting closer and closer, then realising, a second or two after it had happened, that the ground was falling away and that we were airborne. After climbing to about five hundred feet we levelled off and circled the aerodrome. It had shrunk beyond recognition but for the white painted sign *Hanworth* on the hangar roof and *Players Please*.

We dived towards the banner, swooped along its length and climbed steeply. I hunched my shoulders in anticipation of the violent deceleration but nothing happened. We had missed the banner. We climbed up again, circled the aerodrome and had another go, lower this time. I was thrust forward against the safety straps and knew that we had hooked our fish. There was a roar as Mr Wright opened the throttle fully and climbed steeply. I looked back and could just see the banner flapping and trailing its message behind us. My silk scarf streamed horizontally in the buffeting slipstream. Mr Wright smiled through his goggles at the joy on my face. In my fourteen-year-old imagination I had taken the first step to becoming another Bishop. We levelled off and turned towards the vast inverted saucer that was London.

We followed the twists and turns of the Thames – I was surprised at how tortuous its path was – towards central London. The well-known buildings were easy to spot for at that time there were no high-rise flats or office blocks to compete on the horizon. St. Paul's and Big Ben dominated the skyline. We circled Piccadilly Circus and several football stadia where matches were in progress and thousands of tiny white faces looked up at our message, before turning back for home.

Flying low over the aerodrome we dropped the banner. The old Avro leapt forward eagerly at being released from the undignified weight and drag of the banner. Mr Wright enquired whether I would like him to do some aerobatics. I said yes please. For the next few minutes, in a mad maelstrom of three-dimensional motion, all logic fled. The earth was where the sky should be, or spinning madly in front of the nose, my head was being pushed into my spine by positive gravity, or feeling as though it wanted to fly off on its own with negative gravity. The airframe groaned in protest and showered me with dirt and dead flies as we flew upside down. I looked down between my legs at the flimsy ribs of wood and canvas that separated me from eternity and clung unnecessarily to the safety-straps, one moment terrified, the next in ecstasy. When the earth disappeared completely for a few seconds and then magically reappeared from behind my head I realised that we had just looped the loop. I felt as though we were stationary and it was the earth that was carrying out these extraordinary manoeuvres around us.

There came the moment when what goes up must come down. Mr Wright, who by now had assumed heroic proportions in my eyes, throttled back and with the engine popping and the slipstream sighing through the wings glided smoothly towards the aerodrome and landed. After we had taxied to the hangar and switched off we lifted our goggles and looked at each other. We looked like minstrels, our faces streaked with oil and dust apart from the large ovals around our eyes where the goggles had been. I imitated him and slung my parachute nonchalantly over my shoulder as we walked to his office in the hangar. While we were taking off our flying clothes I held out his white silk scarf but he bade me keep it.

I went to bed that night resolved that one way or another I was going to get a job where I could mess about with aeroplanes. Not fly them of course, I could not hope to do that, but as a mechanic perhaps, or a rigger or instrument-maker, anything so long as I could see and hear and smell and touch those wonderful flying machines.

16

Chapter 2

I T WAS TWO years before I was able to fulfil that resolution but I did it then in an emphatic manner by joining the Royal Air Force as a trainee aircraft mechanic.

I sent off a recruitment advertising coupon in the *Sunday Express*. My mother intercepted the reply requesting me to report to Adastral House, Kingsway, London, for an interview and a medical examination. In the row that followed it transpired that she was cross, not because I wanted to leave home and join up, but because I had not confided in her. After token resistance she agreed. By now we were living in a new semi-detached mock Tudor-style house in a vast jerry-built estate in Worcester Park, Surrey, dominated by a huge gasometer at the end of our road. It had been bought in Jack's name for £299 cash. I had got a new job as a trainee upholsterer with the John Lewis partnership in Chelsea and had been commuting eighteen miles each way by bicycle.

The RAF interviewers and doctors were busy. It was January, 1939, shortly after Munich. The interview and the medical were perfunctory. I received a letter a few days later informing me that I had been accepted and telling me to report to the recruiting depot at West Drayton, on the edge of London.

I was petrified as I walked through the depot's stern iron gates past the armed sentries. Had I realised then that it was not too late I would have turned and fled. It might have helped if there had been a hint of an aeroplane somewhere, but it was three months before I saw an RAF aeroplane, six months before I touched one, nine months before I worked on one and a year before I flew in one.

There was still 'please' and 'thank you' as we were shunted through the induction machine. These courtesies lasted until we had completed the swearing-in ceremony. It was a simple ceremony during which, on oath, I committed myself to six years' service in the Royal Air Force, extendable by mutual agreement. I also swore unswerving loyalty to King and Country and total obedience to my superior officers. I was then given my rank and service number. Henceforth I was to be known as 635686 Aircraftman Second Class

U/T Levett, Gordon Robert. U/T meant under training. There is no lower form of life in the RAF. Officially my rank was Airman, unofficially it was erk. I have never discovered why all RAF other ranks are called erks. It has a suitably derisory sound. I was seventeen, 5′ 9″ tall and weighed 128 pounds.

The moment the swearing-in ceremony was completed our bridges were burned. There was no turning back now. Requests became orders. For the next six years it was going to be 'you will' rather than 'will you'.

The following day our intake of about seventy recruits was driven in a convoy of RAF buses to the basic training camp at Cardington, near Bedford. It was here that recruits were processed mentally and physically into uniformity and conformity. Fittingly it was raining and bleak when we arrived at the gates. The camp was dominated by the vast, cavernous airship hangar where the tragic R101 airship was built in 1930. We were herded into a large hall for a reception speech by an officer. I was disappointed that he did not wear wings. We were not invited to sit down, and the speech was long and intimidating. It could be summed up that if we obeyed, worked hard for our King and Country – both always referred to in capitals – and kept our noses clean we would stay out of trouble. He did not specify what kind of trouble.

After the speech we were split up into flights of twenty-four recruits. Each flight was allocated to a hut and a corporal. Our corporal, Corporal Harker, was short, pot-bellied and wore the mass issue Pip, Squeak and Wilfred medals of the First World War.

The huts were solidly built of timber. Our beds were lined up like tombstones, twelve to each side, heads to the wall, feet to the centre. Corporal Harker had a room partitioned off at the entrance end. At the other end, in an annexe, were lavatories without doors, two baths and wash-basins with cold water only. In the middle of the hut was a round stove with a cast-iron chimney going up through the roof. We soon discovered that the stove and the bottom part of the chimney glowed beautifully red if encouraged and made an ideal toaster. Each airman had a metal bed and clothes locker, a plain deal bedside table and a black-painted metal box that fitted under the bed for odds and ends. Highly polished plain brown linoleum squeaked under our feet. Overhead, six institutional white china shaded lights hung evenly spaced from the ceiling. We looked for chairs. There were none. There was nowhere to relax except stretched out on our beds. This may explain why servicemen are masters of forty winks.

We chose our beds. It was mid–winter and the older, wiser heads grabbed beds nearest the stove. For the moment we looked at each other warily. We expected the Royal Air Force to be a bully, but what of our new comrades?

After lights out that night, our first night at Cardington, the desultory whispers soon petered out. Twenty-four islands tried to sleep. The beds were hard, the linen coarse. We were tired but none slept well. I woke frequently to the cacophony of snores, coughs, creaking bedsprings, groans, flatulence and the defenceless sighs of men who were lonely, vulnerable and apprehensive of the morning.

Reveille was announced at 6 a.m. by a bugle call, followed by Corporal Harker, fully dressed, walking up and down the hut banging a saucepan with a wooden spoon, shouting 'Wakey-wakeeey'.

The shaving habits and ablutions of twenty-four men are complex. Some had safety razors, others stroked their cut-throats slickly to and fro on leather strops, others slip-slapped their noisy, self-sharpening Rolls razors. The icy cold water brought shudders and groans as adolescent pimples were beheaded. We were reluctant to use the open lavatories but needs must. It was an unnecessary humiliation to be so watched.

The corporal then issued us with our personal knife, fork and spoon. He called them irons. They were issued to all other ranks and remained with them throughout their service career, or until they were promoted to sergeant or above. We carried them to and from the mess halls of the world. No irons, no food. It was an odd service quirk.

The mess hall was steamy, greasy and smelly. The porridge was thick enough to cut like a cake, the one slice of bacon and fried egg swam in a sea of tinned tomatoes, the bread was sliced an inch thick and the tea was tepid and grey, but the food was ample and to most of my new comrades that was all that mattered.

First on that day's agenda was a haircut. A civilian barber sheared us like sheep, leaving about half an inch all over our skulls. He had no need of scissors. The floor was littered ankle deep with

mute testimony of past vanities. Looking like death's heads we
scuttled back to our huts to hide. The process of uniformity had
begun.

Next was an FFI medical inspection. FFI meant free from infec-
tion. Corporal Harker lined us up stark naked in two rows in our
hut. Self-conscious and goose-pimpled cold we tried hard not to
look at each other's supine thingumajigs. The corporal, standing by
the entrance, suddenly ordered attention. The medical officer and a
sergeant entered the hut, strode furiously up and down one row
front and back and then the other row their eyes scanning our
bodies, and disappeared out of the hut without a word. Taking less
than a minute it happened regularly and was a simple, effective
method of keeping check on contagious diseases. Whenever I saw
that phalanx of naked male flesh I was glad that I was not a woman.
On one such occasion an erk got an erection. His face was suffused
crimson with embarrassment and the effort to control himself. The
MO and the sergeant did their best to ignore what was happening;
after all you can't charge a man with involuntary insubordination.
Inevitably after that the erk was nicknamed Horny.

The day ended with inoculations. We lined up in sick quarters,
right sleeves rolled up, to be punctured for smallpox, typhus,
typhoid, tetanus and yellow fever. There was no bedside manner or
finesse in needle technique. I went to bed that night thinking my
body was not my own. Of course it wasn't, I had sold it, and my
soul, to the RAF. Most of us spent the next day in bed, excused
duties, with post-inoculation fever.

Towards the end of the week we marched to the equipment
stores to be issued with uniform and kit. Two uniforms, greatcoat,
pullover, overalls, two pairs heavy, metal-studded boots, one pair
plimsolls, two pairs non-stretch braces, three pairs thick woollen
socks, two sets Long John underwear, three head-first blue shirts,
three loose collars, collar studs, black tie, peaked cap, forage cap,
cap badges, webbing, back packs and belts, singlets and shorts,
safety razor, shaving brush, canvas housewife to hold sewing
things, button-stick, tin mug and dinner plate, and five cleaning
brushes. With kit-bags bloated we moved next door to the tailor's
shop. The uniforms were off the peg but to our delight they were
the new tunic style instead of the old neck-chafing dog-collars. An
avuncular and surprisingly conscientious civilian tailor supervised

the fitting. I was nonplussed when he asked me whether I 'dressed' to the left or right. Everybody guffawed when I nervously felt myself and answered in the middle.

The day came when our uniforms were ready and we were to wear them for the first time. We had spent the previous evening polishing brass buttons and badges, buffing boots and rubbing soap on the inside of our trouser creases before ironing them to a knife edge with Corporal Harker's iron. We shaved with extra care that morning. Some were up before reveille, so eager were they to slough off their civilian skins. The Long Johns itched and the uniforms were crudely cut and made of coarse flannel but we did not mind; none of us had been weaned on Savile Row. We looked brashly new but good. The beginnings of military pride straightened our backs and the eagles (the erks called them shitehawks) embossed on the brass buttons and sewn onto the upper sleeves of our tunics brought aeroplanes a little closer.

With the advent of our uniforms the softly, softly period ended and the RAF bared its fangs. New orders appeared on the hut notice board, including a copy of the Riot Act, the last paragraph of which mentioned the death sentence. There were pages of standing orders listing dire dos and don'ts, supplemented by Station Daily Orders most of which were incomprehensible for we were not yet familiar with RAF vernacular.

The next ten weeks were devoted to instilling discipline and obedience, mostly through drill, physical training and aptly named fatigues. We were given work which was transparently pointless, like washing coal, to illustrate that it was not for us to reason why but merely to obey. In addition to routine duties we had extra fatigues three evenings a week, usually guard duties, kitchen duty, or skivvying in the officers' mess. The RAF closed down and the hangars were shut world-wide on Wednesday afternoons for compulsory sport, usually football. Apart from church parade, Sunday was a rest-day. Any spare time we had was devoted to cleaning our equipment, rifles and huts for weekly inspections and unannounced spot checks. At lights out we collapsed onto our beds like felled trees.

Every morning before breakfast, wearing only singlet and shorts, we had thirty minutes' physical training, usually in rain, sleet or snow. Within three weeks we were fit. We could run, jump, bend, swivel and contort without a gasp in our breath, a hitch in our pulse or an aching muscle. Except one recruit who coughed up blood and was discharged.

There were specialist PT and drill instructors at Cardington. They were all senior NCOs and old lags, masters of their craft and superb in their peacock example of show and self-pride. Their power seemed absolute. Some were disliked and feared. Our squadron was lucky, we had the best two drill instructors at Cardington. One, Shorty, was tiny, wizened and trim. He was a Warrant Officer, the highest non-commissioned rank in the RAF. The other, Lofty, was ramrod tall, curiously elegant when he demonstrated drill, and a Flight Sergeant, one rank below Shorty. They were clearly good friends for they took the mickey out of each other as much as they did out of us. We argued in the hut who was best; perhaps, being complementary, they were both best.

We were microscopically inspected for imperfections at the beginning of every drill parade. Punishment, usually extra fatigues, was meted out for dull boots or brasses, badly blancoed equipment, untidy hair, sloppy tie-knots, a speck of dust in our rifle barrels, or just because.

Shorty had the gift of inspiring us to obedience and respect, of making us want to please him. A tiny cynosure (he must have been well below official minimum RAF height), he stood on a box in front of the squadron, nearly a hundred airmen, all watching like rabbits as he demonstrated, cajoled, raged or praised. Perhaps it was his voice that captivated us as he ordered: 'Chests out, bellies and bums in, back straight, fists clenched, thumbs on top.' His voice, clear and Welsh lilted, reached us all without shouting and was warm with love of his job and affection for the airmen clay he was moulding. We knew when we had had a good drill session and pleased him for instead of giving the command: 'Squadron . . . Dissssmiss!' at the end of the session it would be: 'Squadron . . . Buggerrrr off!'

Once we had discovered where our feet and arms were we began to enjoy drill. It was a strange liking but we realised that drill was the alchemy that transformed amorphous clods into proud, homogeneous airmen. It was daft, of course, grown men playing toy soldiers, learning a new Pavlovian language of command and response.

We were content when after a few weeks Shorty and Lofty had done their job. When our ears told us that our drill rhythm was perfect and we presented arms: one-pause-two-pause-three with sensual slickness. When at the command: 'Squadron Halt!' our skill was lauded by the instant silence of a hundred men stopped simultaneously in their tracks. And when we marched, all peacocks now, our swinging arms were synchronised and the music of our studded boots rang out left-right-left-right-left-right in proud and perfect unison.

By now cliques had formed in the hut. It was acquaintanceship rather than friendship. There was, of course, a pull-together *esprit de corps* among us, but the forced, dormitory intimacy of service life and sudden postings elsewhere does not breed close relationships. Anyway, once we were broken in, the Royal Air Force was our best friend. It fed us, housed us, clothed us, thought for us, worried about us and paid us. All it wanted in return was loyalty and obedience. A small price to pay for such munificence.

In the weeks during which the cliques were consolidated and natural leaders emerged in the hut, I discovered to my chagrin that I was being excluded, the odd man out. It was a repeat of the orphanage period. I was a loner again whether I wanted to be or not. It was a bit of a shock having signed on for six years, for there are few moments in a serviceman's life when he is alone. There was not an instant in our three months at Cardington when we could do something unseen or unheard. There was nowhere to hide, no secrets.

We had no side, it would have been laughable if we had, for we were all low creatures, runts from the urban kennels of the unemployed 1930s. Volunteering for the RAF in peacetime was usually an admission of defeat by civilian life. Most of us were the unemployed, the unemployable, the tradeless, the defeated. Few joined for love of flying and aeroplanes. I never met an erk who spoke with feeling of flying except when I was talking to myself. Neither had we joined up for King and Country. There was little patriotism among the ranks. We left that to the officers. The Second World War was only eight months away but we were no more warlike than sheep.

I do not know myself well and I find it difficult to see myself as others see me. I tried hard to discover what it was that isolated me

23

from the natural, relaxed matiness and *bonhomie* of my comrades. I wondered whether I had BO. I did not lie, cheat at cards, boast, crawl to NCOs, or skive. I remembered to swear lustily and often. I cultivated a loud laugh, soon dropped. I then tried a fixed smile until my jaw ached. As a last resort I tried agreeing with everything anybody said about anything but that did not work either. My intellect was a fraction above hut par, but as our conversation usually consisted of a series of categorical arguments like 'it fucking is', 'it fucking isn't', 'it fucking is', recurring, that did not exactly make me a polymath. I was opinionated, but who isn't at that callow age? I had my head in a book more often than most and did not have to read with a moving finger. I was introverted, had a thin skin, an inferiority complex and a poor sense of humour; heavy crosses to bear in my new communal life. Neither did I have any skill at banter, the erks' substitute for conversation. Fatally, I did not have the unfair gift of charm. Few disliked me, but few sought my company. I have learned to live with it since and rely on respect, but then I badly wanted to be popular and it hurt that I was not.

After eight weeks of being confined to barracks we were let loose on the public. It was a Saturday night when we were let off the lead. The pubs and women of Bedford were our target for that night, my eighteenth birthday.

Bedford was unimpressed. They had seen it all before. Brand-new airmen, light-headed with freedom, swaggering and showing off their uniforms as they staggered from pub to pub. Bedford was not much of a change of scene. We were not welcome in several pubs and there were erks everywhere, roaming the streets, shadowed by RAF police. In the last resort we went to a dance hall, but the women of Bedford were not susceptible. Only the wallflowers would dance with us and they at arms' length.

We caught the last bus back to camp, singing furiously in defiance of a disappointing evening. We held up the legless past the surprisingly tolerant guards, they too had seen it all before. Back in the hut we banked up the fire until the chimney glowed red and belched smoke like Blake's satanic mill, made toast, told lies about our conquests and talked about civilians. They were another race now. It was, almost, good to be back in the bosom of the RAF.

We knew we were nearly home and dry when arrangements were made towards the end of the course for reshodding our boots with rubber sole and heel to prevent sparks and a fire hazard when we worked on aeroplanes in the future. Our footsteps at drill became oddly quiet and the envy of newcomers who were frequently told by us old lags to get their numbers dry.

The final week was a plethora of inspections and parades. Hut inspection, kit inspection, final passing-out parade, final P.T. parade and medical examination. The hut inspection was by the commanding officer. He wore white gloves, his fingers sliding under as well as on everything. Woe betide us if his gloves were not spotless when he had finished. But we were old lags now and knew the pitfalls. Under the coal scuttle, behind the lockers, underneath the wash basins, the barrels of our rifles. 'No sweat,' said Corporal Harker. No sweat indeed, we had learned to look both ways in a one-way street.

Our postings appeared on the notice board. After seven days leave we were to report to our technical training camps as trainee aircraft mechanics, riggers, electricians, instrument-makers, armourers, signálmen, drivers, medics, equipment and administrative clerks, RAF police and cooks. The long tail of the RAF. I respected only those who were going to work on aeroplanes. I thought it odd to join the RAF and do otherwise. After a week's leave I was to report to No. 4, School of Technical Training, St. Athan, South Wales.

Lofty, Shorty and Corporal Harker joined us at a farewell party in the NAAFI canteen on our last night. We were glad of the opportunity of saying goodbye and thanks to three great men, unsung Hampdens. Lofty took me to one side during the evening to tell me that if I kept my nose clean I would do well in the Royal Air Force. I do not know what provoked this compliment – I thought I had passed unnoticed – but as it came from him I was in seventh heaven.

Chapter 3

AFTER ONLY a day or two at home I was bored. There was an even chance that I knew exactly what my mother or Jack were going to say next. Showing off my uniform around Worcester Park soon palled. I went occasionally to the local pub with my mother and Jack. Jack did not drink and my mother drank little. They both looked at me as though I were perdition-bound when I casually ordered pints of beer and downed them with a swagger.

Regulars in the pub asked me whether there was going to be a war. It was late spring, 1939. It was a fair question for a civilian to ask a serviceman. After all, war was now my trade. I answered by trying to look knowing and arcane. Quite difficult. The head held at an angle of thirty degrees, lips pursed, eyebrows raised and eyes looking into the middle distance. Some thought the eagles on the upper arms of my tunic were the coveted Royal Air Force pilots' wings. I did not disabuse them.

Money still overshadowed everything at home. My mother asked me what arrangements I had made to send her some of my RAF pay. I curtly answered none. My pay was eight shillings and sixpence a week (42½p). By the time I had bought sixty Woodbine cigarettes (24p), one visit to the front seats of the cinema (2½p), cod and chips (2p), a paperback book (2½p), and a pint of beer a day (5p) there was not much left for mothers, toothpaste, metal polish, tea and a wad at the NAAFI canteen, bus fares or courting. But being a pauper in the RAF did not matter. Most of us, half the time, did not have a penny in our pockets, but we were all paupers together and mother RAF provided the essentials.

That first leave was a disappointing anti-climax. I felt alien and could not wait to get back to the RAF, to my new comrades at St. Athan and to find out how aeroplanes work.

When I boarded the train at Paddington for St. Athan I felt my travels had started. It was an uncomfortable journey. Erks carry their life on their back like Bedouins when moving from base to base; there are no RAF removal vans. I was wearing or carrying everything I possessed. Full kit-bag, full back-packs, webbing, full water-bottle, gas-mask and my cardboard suitcase. My naked weight was under ten stone. It was probably double that in full paraphernalia. I was not welcome as I squeezed along cramped and crowded corridors looking for a seat. I found sanctuary in the guard's van. The guard was proud of his Great Western Railway uniform and his train. It once held the world's speed record. My nose was close to the window as we sped at furious, cinder-specked speed through the Chilterns, the White Horse Hills and under the River Severn. I discovered at eighteen that England was indeed a green and pleasant land. Wales too.

St. Athan seemed vast. It had an aerodrome, but there was rarely an aeroplane in sight. There was an old Vickers Wildebeest and a Gloster Gauntlet for teaching erks ground handling but neither was airworthy and their ribs were showing. Only occasionally did we see a pilot officer. At such visions our salutes were perfection, to be answered by a casual flick of fingers towards the forehead. I soon discovered that it is a sentimental myth that pilots, RAF or otherwise, are particularly appreciative of ground staff.

The aircraft mechanic course lasted five months. Discipline, though firm, was not heavy-handed, and we responded with growing confidence. Most of us were beginning to like being in the Royal Air Force.

The first three weeks of the course were devoted to wrestling with metal. We each had to make a complex box-like object of mild steel into which we made and fitted steel cubes of various sizes, rather like a cubist jigsaw puzzle. It was an infernal device so designed that a tiny error in one place would be exaggerated a hundred-fold elsewhere. We filed and hacked away using micrometers, set-squares, calipers and spirit levels and spoke in a new language of thousandths of an inch. I was hopeless, and my corporal instructor usually shook his head sadly as he passed my work-bench.

After the metalwork we put our tools away with relief and listened to lectures for the next three months. As an aircraft mechanic I was taught only about the bits and pieces of an aeroplane at the sharp end; the engine and propeller. The rest, wings, rudder, fuselage etc., were the province of lowly creatures called riggers. In practice the mechanic and the rigger work together as a team on their aeroplanes, with other specialists, armourers, wireless mechanics, instrument-makers, as required.

The late 1930s saw, with the stimulus of threatened war, the introduction of more sophisticated aeroplanes. In addition to the internal combustion engine, we studied constant-speed propellers, retractable under-carriages, flaps, automatic boost control, super-chargers, and brakes no less! It was not until that period that much thought had been given on how to stop aeroplanes after they had landed. Until then few aeroplanes had brakes and relied only on mind-boggling tail-skids to help them stop. Self-starting engines were also being generally introduced, much to the relief of mecha-nics who risked decapitation every time they swung the propeller by hand to start engines. Similarly, designers were belatedly concluding that it was unreasonable to subject pilots to freezing temperatures and winds of 150 mph or more, and were introducing enclosed cockpits and cockpit heaters several years after motorists had been brought in from the cold.

As I recall those curious hiccups in aeroplane development it is a shock to realise that when I was at St. Athan in 1939 flying was a new science almost in its infancy. The first flight in history had taken place only thirty-six years previously.

RAF training was thorough and first-rate. Every night in the huts we questioned and answered each other in mock tests. There was a total keenness. Ignorant though we were from our past, we all coped and were the better for it. Better in knowledge and better in our pride of knowledge. We erks were blooming.

It was about this time that I made the compensating discovery that I got on better with women than men. There was a tiny pub in St. Athan village, but most of us headed for Barry or Cardiff when we had time off. I preferred Cardiff. It had a better library, better pubs and prettier girls.

Jennifer was a senior librarian. During my first few visits to the library she returned my look with only a glance, but I persisted until her glances too became looks. She soon realised I was a didactic librarian's dream, a compulsive reader, but totally undiscriminating, veering from shelf to shelf, author to author and subject to subject like a rudderless boat in a squall. She was about thirty, attractive rather than pretty, with a slow smile, a quiet librarian's voice, a patronising intellectual arrogance, and stunning breasts. Her arro-gance made me hesitate but after several visits I asked her for a date. I knew she was married because a little plaque on the counter in front of her said 'Mrs Jennifer . . .' and she wore a plain gold wedding ring. Her eyebrows shot up for a moment or two before she said yes. I floundered when she then asked where and when. She was upper–middle class with an expensive voice. My Cardiff haunts were not quite. Seeing my hesitation she suggested that we drive into the country for a drink. Her car, she added, was parked outside. Car, if you please. We arranged to meet outside the library when it closed at seven–thirty. 'Dutch', she said firmly.

The car was an almost new MG saloon. It was my first experience of a walnut dashboard, the rich smell of leather seats and the shapely sheen of a woman's silk–clad legs showing liberally beneath the steering wheel. She lived near Neath, the other side of St. Athan and suggested that we drive towards St. Athan so that she could drop me off at the camp gates afterwards. I hoped there would be erks watching as I got out of her car.

We talked mostly about books and authors. After we had dated a few times she drew up a gruelling reading list for me, with Wodehouse and some contemporary American authors for light relief. She had wanted me to write essays but with my other studies I had little time to spare, so we made do with talk. She was a graduate and mocked my banality in a slightly harsh manner, as though she harboured guilt in our relationship. She forbade any discussion about her marriage, husband or home. She had no children.

There is nowhere civilised for an erk to further his relationship with a woman. No home, no sitting room, no sofa, no privacy. Their trysts are in fields, the back row of a cinema, or dark alleys. I had the instinct not to press those venues with Jennifer. Progress was thus agonisingly slow. We got curious glances in the saloon bars of pubs. Erks were expected to use the public bar and metaphorically touch their forelock, but Jennifer, with her well brushed raven hair, classic tweed two–piece suits and bossy manner was obviously a toff, letting her class down. It was, potentially, a D.H. Lawrence relationship, though I was a trifle young for the role of Mellors.

After three or four evenings together I was determined to hold her hand. It was mid-August and a warm, still evening as we walked across Welsh fields listening to the distant putt–putt of harvesting tractors. I had learned to love the countryside. I took a deep breath and took her hand. I held my breath but not only did she not snatch her hand away, she squeezed mine back. I was still young enough to think it was a lovely thing to hold hands with a woman for the first time. An innocent yet significant intimacy. What she saw in me defies imagination. Perhaps it was because I had the bloom of youth, was totally ingenuous and had a touch of wistfulness.

The declaration of the Second World War should have been a portentous day in anyone's life, certainly a serviceman's, but at St. Athan, 11 a.m., Sunday, 3 September 1939, came and passed into history quietly.

We put up blackouts, waited expectantly and watched the skies, wondering what was going to happen next. In war, of course, no-one knows what is going to happen next. I knew enough about flying to realise that St. Athan was beyond the range of most German bombers and there were juicier targets closer to German bases. London, for example, where my mother and Jack lived. I telephoned our next-door neighbour in Worcester Park and asked to speak to my mother. It was a rash thing to do on my pay. No, said my mother, nothing had happened in London. Jack was digging an air-raid shelter and making sandbags. No, she said, they could not sell up and move to Wales. She made Wales sound like somewhere in Outer Mongolia. She thanked me for my concern and asked me about the pay allotment. One could say she had the knack of putting first things first. She did say in her next letter how touched and surprised she was at my concern. So was I. Blood is thick.

The war was a week old before I saw Jennifer again. We arranged to meet outside the gates the following Sunday after church parade. I never did ask how she got away from home for our assignations.

We had beer and a ploughman's lunch before driving to the beach. It was a sweltering day and she knew of a tiny, deserted cove. We had brought our bathing costumes and put them on with eyes modestly averted. She was tanned, I was painfully white; one down. She swam like a dolphin, I floundered; two down. She was voluptuous, I was all angles; three down. I was getting desperate. There must be something, surely, at which I was better than her.

After the swim our bodies touched here and there as we lay in the high sun. I kissed her for the first time. How sublime are the kisses of youth. Not sure what to do next I fumbled clumsily with her

30

bathing costume. It was like unwrapping a very precious gift. Finally, we were naked. I was dazed with the enormity of what I was doing, of what I had already achieved. This beautiful woman was giving me herself. My hands were shaking as they discovered for the first time the incredible softness of a woman's breast, the long smoothness of thighs, the warm, so intimate slickness between, the vulnerable, appealing charm of a brace of translucent pink nipples, the delicious, endless curves and that slightly comic inverted triangle of hair. She winced when we sat up afterwards. 'You're a bony bugger,' she said.

The war was bypassing St. Athan. The occasional drone in the sky was always friendly. The only signs of war were extra guard duties and the blackout. It was difficult to believe that elsewhere people were dying for their countries.

We were revising for our final examinations. The examinations were important for upon their results depended our rank and pay. Above-average marks meant promotion to Leading Aircraftman (LAC) and new badges on one's sleeves. Average marks meant promotion to Aircraftman First Class (AC1). Below-average marks meant no promotion and staying at the rank of Aircraftman Second Class (AC2). A betting book flourished in the huts. I was hot favourite for LAC, but knowing what a hash I had made of the metalwork and how much my thoughts had been elsewhere of late, I laid a few bets against myself. When the results appeared on the notice board I was shattered. I got below-average marks and was to remain an AC2.

In 1939, the British Empire and the Royal Air Force were still far-flung. In a few days we would be heading for an RAF squadron in the UK, France, the Middle East or the Far East. Most of the erks hoped for the glamour and prestige of joining a fighter squadron in France. I hoped for the Far East, Singapore perhaps.

We rushed to the notice board when our postings were announced. There were groans and cheers. 635686 AC2 Levett, G.R. proceed to Royal Air Force Cadet College, Cranwell, Lincolnshire. I winced when I saw my lowly rank in print for the first time. AC2 U/T was all right. AC2 meant thick. The rank was like a dunce's cap. My travel hopes were dashed for the while, but I was pleased to be going to Cranwell. Future events proved how right I was.

On our last night at St. Athan I had to choose between spending

it with the erks in a farewell binge in the NAAFI, or with Jennifer. I
chose Jennifer.

After the pub it was raining and we spent the rest of the evening
in the country in the back seat of her car. There are better places for
poignant farewells, but we managed somehow. Afterwards, we
exchanged our farewell presents. She gave me a leather-bound rice-
paper Shakespeare, a joy to feel as well as to read. I have it still
today. I gave her an inexpensive RAF wings brooch. I realised afterwards it was a crass present because she could not wear it. She then
gave me a new reading-list. It was ruthless and included Proust and
Gibbon.

The next day Jennifer was waiting on the platform at Cardiff
railway station where I had to change trains. As women are wont to
do, she had made a special effort for our farewell. She looked
stunning and wore my wings. I could scarcely believe our intimacy
as I looked at her waiting for me. She had warned me the previous
night that it would be indiscreet for us to kiss at the station. As a
public librarian she was quite well-known, but suddenly she said
'Bugger it', and kissed me anyway. The railway station resounded
with erks' whistles and cheers. I was enjoying the sweet sorrow of
parting. It is always better for the serviceman. He is leaving for
distant parts, adventure, perhaps valour. She is left behind, moist-
eyed, waving forlornly at the disappearing train. I never saw her
again.

Chapter 4

To MOST OF those who have served in the Royal Air Force, particularly before the war, Cranwell, the home of the Royal Air Force Cadet College, is a special place comparable in tradition with the Army's Sandhurst and the Navy's Dartmouth – not that either would admit it. In pecking order the RAF is still considered a bit of a parvenu, despite the fact that when Armageddon does come it will come from the air.

I had travelled by fast train from King's Cross to Grantham where I was collected by an RAF lorry. For the last mile or two I had my head out of the back of the lorry looking at the sky. Hawker Harts, Furies and Hinds, Airspeed Oxfords and a hideous Vickers Vimy glinted and droned over the flat, featureless Lincolnshire landcape. A yellow windsock waved in welcome.

Dominating the station and trying hard to look older than its ten years was the self-conscious neo-classical main building and clock-tower. The parade-ground in front of it, used for the cadet's ceremonial passing-out parades, was vast. Nothing then was old in the RAF, but Cranwell, an elegant milieu, was weathering nicely, with tended shrubs and borders, impeccable lawns and maturing trees against the backcloth of the two grass aerodromes, one each side of the public road that bisected Cranwell. My new home looked good.

The timing of my arrival at Cranwell was fortunate. It was November 1939, and I had arrived to participate in the end of an era. The last of the pre-war RAF cadet courses were going through and I saw enough of the good old days of Cranwell to regret their passing. The pre-war cadet flying course lasted two years. It was leisurely, elegant and reserved almost exclusively for swells. Flying was still a bit of a sport and pilots were old sports. Aeroplanes at that time were not too demanding or unforgiving of pilots, or very lethal at delivering death and were still being judged not by how many bombs or guns they carried, but how nicely they flew. The sky was a friendly place. People got killed occasionally, but it was usually by mistake or playing the fool.

33

In the 1920s and 1930s the Royal Air Force was considered to be the best flying club in the world. It was all a bit of a lark, with royal scions as fellow cadets, elegant uniforms, formal mess functions, full dress ladies' nights, swords of honour, being commissioned as Pilot Officers and the final passing-out parade when, with families watching, the coveted Royal Air Force pilot's wings were pinned to the cadet's left breast by a visiting air marshal.

Aircraft were still being called aeroplanes and airports aerodromes. There were no concrete runways but acres of verdant, softly welcoming grass that forgave a bad landing. All aeroplanes had propellers which, when the sun or moon was shining, spun gold by day and silver by night. Windsocks were important and easy to find, and one always landed into wind. Flying in open cockpits, pilots could reach out and touch the clouds or catch a snowflake. They wore white silk scarves, smelly leather helmets and sponge goggles that made rings around their eyes. Engines were temperamental and the skill of flying was 70 per cent art, 20 per cent science and 10 per cent luck. To wear Royal Air Force wings was a rare privilege. And flying was still so novel, magical and glamorous that 100,000 Frenchmen had greeted Lindbergh in homage when he landed at Le Bourget in 1927.

After graduating at Cranwell the pilots were sent out to Mesopotamia, Afghanistan, the Sudan, India or the Far East to preserve the British Empire by dropping tiny bombs, or strafing, with a single Lewis machine-gun, the odd dissident native. Quite soon, they would become The Few.

I was happy at Cranwell. The erks benefited from the atmosphere of casual nonchalance created by the flying instructors. Away from training depots RAF officers were pilots first and disciplinarians second. They disliked bullshit as much as the erks. Keep their aeroplanes airworthy and they were content.

I was lucky in joining 'D' Flight in the Advanced Flying Training Squadron where the cadets completed the last stage of their flying course. It was mostly formation flying, night flying, advanced instrument flying and navigation, bombing and gunnery. Erks flew with cadets occasionally for they made good ballast and it saved the trouble of fitting lead ballast weights inside the fuselage.

The erks' living quarters were substantial, brick-built, two-storey blocks, dormitory style as always, with showers, baths and hot water. Fortunately there was also basic central heating. Cranwell can be a bitter winter resort.

Where possible the erks from each flight were accommodated in the same block, so we worked and lived together. The trainee disciplines of Cardington and St. Athan were replaced by self-discipline, church parade every Sunday morning, kit and FFI inspections once a month and occasional guard duty. The war was distant.

I was made instantly welcome in 'D' Flight. Within days I was more at home than I had ever been at home. There was still crudity and ignorance and a preference for the earthy, but there was a give and take and a consideration among the erks for each other that gave the lie to the horror stories I had heard about old lags. There was usually something in our close 24-hour intimacy of work, living and play that narked, but it rarely boiled over. We took care not to tread on each other's corns. Not once did I see a brawl. The erks' bed-space was sacrosanct, his tools his, his aeroplane his, his seat at the mess table his. The rare teetotaller was not scorned, the weak not bullied. There was no homosexuality, overt or covert. All this not because we were angels, but because there was a peasant wisdom among us that made us realise that we were vulnerable to authority and to each other, and our lives would become intolerable if we did not live and let live, and push and pull together. In a word, comradeship.

I cherish the memory of the day I walked for the first time down to the aerodrome and reported to 'D' Flight. It had taken a long time, but there it all was, and I was part of it. At last! All the paraphernalia of flying. Hangars, aeroplanes taking-off and landing, the roar of engines, the blast of slipstream, windsocks, erks oil-streaked and black-nailed in greasy blue overalls, cadets in spotless white flying overalls and imperious flying instructors, with the peaceful counter-point of the grass aerodrome stretching far towards the horizon.

An erk showed me the way to 'D' Flight's office. It was a cramped, wooden hut of First World War vintage. Cranwell was an odd mixture of the palatial and the primitive. 'D' Flight's hangar was a Bessonneau, an arched, canvas, wooden-ribbed dust-bowl dating from 1914.

Flight Sergeant O'Hara was sitting behind his desk. He might have been standing, such was the effect. He was nearer seven foot than six, with a rugby quarter-back physique that took up most of the hut. His physical presence was formidable and intimidating until his Irish eyes smiled. He was in charge of 'D' Flight's erks and aeroplanes, responsible and reporting to the Flight Commander, Flight-Lieutenant Hall. Standing by the desk in stark contrast was the diminutive figure of Corporal Bennet who turned out to be as misanthropic as he looked. He was responsible to Flight Sergeant O'Hara for the routine supervision and discipline of the erks both at work and in the barracks. RAF corporals have dogs' lives sandwiched between the senior NCOs above and the erks below. Unlike sergeants and above, and officers, corporals do not have their own exclusive mess and living quarters, but have to work, live and eat with the erks while at the same time maintaining authority and discipline. It is a thankless, difficult role to play and probably explains why most corporals are miserable sods. Though they have a private room in the erks' barracks they are still inextricably mixed up 24 hours a day with the erks with whom they cannot truly fraternise. It is a lonely, pariah life.

Flight Sergeant O'Hara – we called him Tiny – was a born leader who protected his erks like a militant shepherd. Flight-Lieutenant Hall was a brilliant pilot-instructor who left everything on the ground to Tiny until he was let down. Then there was hell to pay. It happened seldom, Tiny and the flying instructors saw to that, but when it did we all ran for cover. On one occasion the wind was from an unfamiliar direction and he saw one of his cadets make a poor cross-wind landing in a Hawker Hind, culminating in a spectacular, dust-raising ground loop. Neither the cadet nor the aeroplane was damaged, but F/Lt. Hall was livid. He made 'D' Flight spend the rest of the afternoon practising cross-wind landings. Nobody was released from duty until every cadet had had a flying lesson with an instructor and then completed three satisfactory solo cross-wind landings, with F/Lt. Hall sitting on a shooting-stick watching from the middle of the aerodrome. It was dark by the time flying finished. We then refuelled the aeroplanes and manhandled them into the hangar to the encouraging shouts of 'Two-six' from Tiny. 'Two-six' is a mysterious RAF exhortation used whenever anything heavy needs pushing, pulling or lifting.

After I had drawn my tool-box from stores and spent a few days settling down I was called to Tiny's office. There was another erk there, a new arrival named Brian Halford. He was a rigger and Canadian. Tiny said we were to team up and took us across the tarmac to the hangar. In the corner was a very sad-looking Hawker Audax with a covering of dust, cobwebs strung between the wings, battered engine cowlings, tears in the canvas wings and fuselage, and flat tyres. It had not flown for two years since being replaced by the Hawker Hind. Somebody had forgotten to send it to the knackers. As I climbed on to the lower wing and looked into the cockpit I discovered a litter of new-born kittens in the pilot's seat. The mother snarled at me from the top wing.

'It's yours,' said Tiny, nodding at the Audax. 'See what you can make of it.'

The first thing Brian did was to drown the kittens – Cranwell's first war casualties. I would have held up the war at least until the kittens were weaned. He then threw spanners at the mother whenever she appeared, mewing piteously, searching for her young. We gave the Audax a good wash, using soft soap, and then stripped off all the panels and cowlings and let daylight into the works. The mice fled.

We had worked on the Audax for two weeks and were on the last lap when Brian Halford deserted from the RAF. He disappeared overnight never to be seen or heard of again. It was a serious offence in wartime, theoretically punishable by firing squad. In the enquiries that followed there was a hint of my guilt by association. I had difficulty in persuading authority that I had not been privy to Brian's desertion plans. We expected his arrest any day, but he had vanished. It was difficult to escape detection in the wartime Britain of identity cards, ration books and spy paranoia. Stowing away back to Canada, if he did, was quite a feat.

After the hue and cry I carried on with the Audax. I concentrated on the engine – a Rolls-Royce 500 horse-power, vee twelve-cylinder Kestrel – while volunteer rigger erks finished doping and painting the airframe. I bought several ill-affordable tubes of Zebo grate polish to blacken and burnish the tyres and exhaust pipes.

It was New Year's Day, 1940, when the Audax was ready. All 'D' Flight's erks were there as we two-sixed her out of the Besson-neau hangar and onto the tarmac on a typical bitterly cold Cranwell day. She looked magnificent in the sharp sunlight and made the rest of the aeroplanes on the tarmac look tatty. I climbed into the cockpit as two erks prepared to turn the starting handles, one on either side of the nose. It was an anxious moment, as the engine had not run for two years. With a bang and a huge cloud of black smoke and a blast from the propeller that nearly blew the erks from their precarious perch, the engine started first time. I was elated. When the engine had warmed up, two erks sat on the tail and I gave the engine a full-throttle test. The instruments told me I had done a good job. I throttled back, switched off and as the instruments slowly slumped to zero noticed that F/Lt. Hall and Tiny were watching. As I climbed down out of the cockpit they circled the Audax several times giving it searching looks. I hovered deferentially and proprietorially before the verdict came:

'Well done, Levett,' said F/Lt. Hall.

'Wizard show,' said Tiny.

I was tickled very pink. AC2 indeed! The Audax was returned to 'D' Flight's active flying inventory and had an honourable new career towing drogue targets for air-to-air gunnery practice. A month later I was promoted to Aircraftman First Class (AC1). It made little difference except for a few more shillings weekly, but it was nice to know I was no longer officially thick, and it was one of the fastest AC2 to AC1 promotions on record.

Cranwell, although only ten minutes from the North Sea by Messerschmitt 109 or Heinkel 111 and the subject of several comments by Lord Haw-Haw, received only minor visitations from the Luftwaffe and these, mostly at night, seemed more for nuisance value than destruction.

None of us liked night-flying duty. The landing path was outlined every fifty yards or so by paraffin-filled, goose-necked flare-pots which we lit by taper and extinguished with old-fashioned snuffers. A powerful Chance floodlight stood at the beginning of the flare-path and was switched on just before the aeroplanes landed and switched off immediately after touch-down. It was unnerving when there was an air-raid warning to run the length of the flare-path after all our aeroplanes had landed, snuffing out the flare-pots, with the deliberately unsynchronised WHIRR-whirr-WHIRR-whirr of enemy bombers approaching from the east. We usually managed to get the last flare-pot extinguished before the enemy bombers arrived overhead, but not always. Cadets occasionally, in response to Aldis-lamp warning signals from the ground (there was

1   Cardington, February 1939. AC2 U/T Gordon Levett (bottom row, middle) starting his RAF career as an erk

2   The Hawker Hart trainer – 'like all Hawker aeroplanes it looked right and flew right'. Cranwell, 1939

3   A beautiful Hawker Fury awaits its lucky pilot, Cranwell, 1939

4   LAC Gordon Levett as a mechanic at Cranwell in the summer of 1940 (sitting on tractor wheel, hands clasped), shortly before starting his quest to become a pilot

no radio), would try to land panic-quickly, make a mess of their landing approach and have to go round again. This would take another four or five agonising minutes with the flare-path a perfect target in the surrounding blackout. Sometimes we lit and doused the flare-pots several times a night, but I was bombed only once and that in a desultory way.

Subsequently we used satellite landing grounds a few miles from Cranwell for night-flying. Some of the erks would fly with the instructors to the satellite field in the evening and return at dawn the next morning. We looked forward to those short, ten-minute dawn flights back to Cranwell. We flew low, in tight formation, everyone looking forward to eggs and bacon and a morning in bed, with the sun rising behind us, mist lingering in the valleys and villages flashing by below us still asleep.

About that time F/Lt. Hall's mechanic was posted abroad. There was some lobbying, as the flight commander's mechanic had some prestige, but thanks to Tiny I got the job. F/Lt. Hall's aeroplane was a Hawker Hart trainer, a tandem two-seater with open cockpits and dual control. Like all Hawker aeroplanes it looked right and flew right.

Flight-Lieutenant Hall was bored with instructing and yearned for combat in France. He occasionally vented his frustration by taking the Hart up alone and throwing it around the sky, usually just before dusk when the air is at its smoothest and the sky and wisps of clouds are lush with sunset colours. One evening when he had asked me to prepare his Hart for such a flight I borrowed a parachute, helmet and goggles from a cadet and laid them in a neat pile under the wing which he could not fail to see when he approached the aeroplane. 'You're a cheeky bugger, Levett,' he said. 'Climb in.' It was the first of several memorable flights with him. That evening he decided to check the positioning of thousands of sharp-pointed tripod stakes driven into various fields near the North Sea coast to prevent their use as landing grounds by invading enemy aircraft. After landing successfully in several fields, with the stakes flashing past inches from our wing tips, he grunted his opinion of the Air Ministry's anti-invasion precautions and climbed high for aerobatics. To the darkening east I could see the North Sea coast and a black spot in the sky. The spot grew bigger. I grabbed the Gosport speaking-tube and shouted into it:

'Junkers Eighty-Eight starboard quarter, sir.'

'What?'

'Enemy aircraft starboard quarter, sir.'

'Where the hell's that?'

'On the right, sir.'

Pause.

'That, Levett, is not a Junkers Eighty-Eight. It's a Blenheim.'

After we had landed he looked at my crestfallen face and laughed. He was kind enough to admit that he had not seen it first and that the Blenheim did look a bit like a Junkers 88.

One month after I had been promoted AC1 I was promoted Leading Aircraftman (LAC). It seemed that Lofty of Cardington might be right. When Tiny called me to his office he threw two LAC badges at me and said they were mine. He shook my hand and, like Lofty, bade me keep my nose clean. Perhaps I had an aura of imprudence to warrant so many cautions. Had his rank not precluded it we would have been good friends. I went back to the barracks, sewed the badges on the upper arms of my tunic, left off my overalls and rejoined the erks on the tarmac. There were double-takes all round. They thought I was an imposter. I did too. It was an unprecedentedly quick promotion and beer all round in the NAAFI that night.

I had climbed three places in one year. Though I could not expect to keep up that pace I reckoned that by the time the war was over, *circa* 1942, I should be a sergeant. Post-war promotion would be slower but I should make Flight Sergeant by the end of my first six years in the RAF, in 1945. If so, I would probably sign on for another ten years and reach the highest non-commissioned rank in the RAF, that of Warrant Officer. During those years I would probably spend topi-hatted sojourns abroad in India, Singapore, Malaya, Mesopotamia, Africa and the Middle East, including Palestine. I would leave the RAF in 1956 with a pension, a trade, a smattering of Urdu and still only thirty-five years old.

But the best laid schemes o' mice an' men gang aft agley.

It was early spring, 1940. The phony war was over and we were retreating towards Dunkirk. At Cranwell our routine was undisturbed. The Luftwaffe at that time had about eight hundred experienced combat pilots, the RAF two hundred, but at Cranwell and other flying training schools no aeroplanes flew on Wednesday

40

afternoons or from noon on Saturday until Monday morning. Weekends and sport were still sacrosanct.

After Dunkirk, amid rumours of Sea Lion invasion, some of our aeroplanes were fitted with bomb-racks to carry twelve-pound anti-personnel bombs and a Lewis machine-gun in the observer's seat. Top speed of our Hawkers flat-out was 180 mph, the Messerschmitt 109, precisely twice as fast at 360 mph. Fortunately they never met.

Although the guards were doubled, the arms were not and Cranwell aerodrome was guarded against airborne invasion with two First World War rifles and twelve rounds of ammunition. One wonders sometimes how the Germans snatched defeat from the jaws of victory.

We carried on womanising, drinking and gambling while waiting for something to happen. Erks are not the stuff of heel-clicking heroes. Their life in war is cushy compared with soldiers and sailors. They are not usually asked to kill or be killed, to do or die. Theirs is a nine-to-five war. After the day is over they can go to the pub. But most of us wanted a little action to dispel the air of unreality, anti-climax and boredom of those post-Dunkirk weeks. We hoped that someone, somewhere, was doing something to prepare for the forthcoming onslaught. There was, of course, no possibility of defeat.

At Cranwell during that balmy summer we were bystanders of the Battle of Britain. In Lincolnshire we were too far from the battle skies to be affected, apart from an occasional hit-and-run maverick. A few instructors left to join the battle when at one time such was the shortage of experienced pilots that the RAF was within sight of defeat. Flight-Lieutenant Hall was considered too old.

It seemed odd at such a transcendental moment of history to be flying training as usual, for the sun to shine, for farmers to harvest fields next to the aerodrome, for civilians to pursue their normal lives, for the pubs to be full. We listened to the BBC news for the number of RAF and enemy aeroplanes shot down each day. It was as well for morale we were unaware that while the RAF's stated losses were accurate, their claims of enemy aeroplanes shot down were wildly exaggerated. The RAF claimed 2,698 enemy aircraft shot down during the Battle of Britain. The true figure verified by post-war research was 1,733. The Luftwaffe also exaggerated. They claimed 3,058 RAF aircraft shot down, whereas the true figure was 915. It was not out-and-out lying by the pilots. It was fibbing born of excitement, shock, fear and sheer dog-fight confusion.

In July 1940, in the middle of the battle, a paragraph appeared in Station Daily Orders stating that suitable leading aircraftmen would be considered for aircrew training – pilot, navigator, wireless operator or air gunner. Any LAC interested was to submit his name to the orderly room. There was a buzz of cynical interest among the erks. Most decided that it was a morale-boosting exercise and nothing would come of it, certainly as far as becoming a pilot was concerned. It was rather like asking the average man in the street whether he would like to become a concert pianist or a brain surgeon. There were about a thousand erks at Cranwell including several hundred LACs. Gossip had it that over two hundred LACs submitted their names. I was one. Most of them, realists, chose air gunner. I went for broke; for pilot.

Nothing happened. Tiny told F/Lt. Hall that I had applied. He let me handle the controls occasionally. I was not very promising on the Hawker. On the Airspeed Oxford, a friendly twin-engine trainer, I was better, probably because the pilot's view was unrestricted and, having an enclosed cockpit, there was no slip-stream buffeting my head. Still nothing happened. I went to the orderly room every day for news until the sergeant told me to piss off. I was the only volunteer for pilot in 'D' Flight.

In October I was ordered to report to the Education Officer. He asked me to sit down. I did so uneasily. It was the first time I had sat in an officer's presence. He was a Flight-Lieutenant, without wings. I wondered what it was all about. After the first few questions significance dawned. It was the first fence in my quest to become an RAF pilot.

I trembled at the magnitude of my ambition, the magnificence of the prize if I won, and the enormity of failure. He explained that to be an RAF pilot required a high standard of education and asked me about mine. I fibbed at length about Swanley Nautical College but he soon elicited that I had left school at fourteen without matriculating. There was a long silence as my voice faltered to a close. He got up from his chair, gave me a mathematics paper to solve and left the office. My heart sank. He returned after about twenty minutes and looked at my blank paper. There was another humiliating silence. He asked me gently whether I would consider becoming an air gunner. I shook my head. I dared not speak for my voice would have shown tears.

He then asked me why I wanted to be a pilot. Not being a pilot himself, his eyes glazed over when I went on too long about flying and aeroplanes, but he became more attentive when I enlarged on my recent service career and my attempts at self-education. He asked me what books I had read, what authors I liked and why, and what newspaper I read, about which I lied. Erks could not afford newspapers. I said the *Telegraph*. *The Times* would have been too much.

'Heavens, man,' he said suddenly and angrily. 'You want to be a pilot and you can't add two and two. Take my advice. If you want to fly so badly, try for air gunner.' With that he gestured dismissal. I stood up, put my hat on, saluted smartly and left. I walked quickly to the farthest corner of the aerodrome away from all the erks and blubbered. I had fallen at the first fence.

On my way back to the tarmac I met F/Lt. Hall and Tiny. I averted my eyes, saluted and tried to walk on by, but they stopped me. Tiny asked me what happened with the Education Officer. I told them. 'Got something in my eye,' I added. 'Both eyes?' enquired F/Lt. Hall. I fled as soon as I could. That's put the kibosh on it, I thought. Imagine Bishop or Richthofen weeping.

A few days later I was ordered to report again to the Education Officer.

'Are you sure you don't want to be an air gunner?' he opened. I explained that if I became an air gunner I would be frustrated sitting in an aeroplane but not flying it. It was a pilot or nothing.

'Flight-Lieutenant Hall and Flight Sergeant O'Hara have been on to me. We have cooked up a plan,' said the EO. I felt overwhelmed; two Flight-Lieutenants and a Flight Sergeant talking about an erk. The EO had a close friend, a retired professor of mathematics who lived in Nottingham, who was prepared to accommodate me and give me a two-week crash course in mathematics. After the course I could spend a week or two back at Cranwell revising with the EO's help before taking the maths paper again. Flight-Lieutenant Hall would authorise two weeks' leave.

'What do you think?' ended the EO. What did I think! It needs an erk of the time to comprehend the unorthodoxy and compassion of what they were doing for me. Damn it, I thought, I want to blubber again.

The professor's car, a Lea Francis, met me at Nottingham bus station driven by his elderly chauffeur-butler-gardener-handyman, whose wife was cook-housekeeper. He bade me sit in the back seat. I did so, feeling regal but rather daft.

On the outskirts of Nottingham we drove along a twisting drive and arrived at a well hidden, classic Georgian house. The professor, an elderly bachelor, was waiting for me on the porch step as though I was a visiting air marshal, a welcoming courtesy typical of him. He was tall, thin, wore pince-nez spectacles and had exquisite Edwardian manners. The handyman took my cardboard suitcase and led me upstairs to my bedroom and private bathroom. A gong boomed softly. 'Elevenses,' said the butler. I followed him downstairs into the drawing room.

The drawing room had an Adam fireplace with a well-tended fire, mostly for the benefit of an arrogant Persian tom sitting on the hearth. Elegant antique furniture, fire brasses and silver-framed photographs gleamed a welcome.

Elevenses turned out to be a glass of Madeira served from a silver-topped decanter and warm Eccles cakes served on translucent bone china. The cake knives were silver and bone-handled. I held out my little finger delicately as I drank.

After elevenses the professor led the way to the library-study. It was like entering a small cathedral. Two rooms had been knocked into one. Books stretched from floor to ceiling, from wall to wall, with two mobile library ladders, a vast antique desk covered with more books and papers and two deep, buttoned-leather armchairs complete with side-tables, foot-stools and reading lamps. I vowed one day to have such a room.

He asked me where we should start. I suggested the beginning. 'Formidable,' he said. We soon confirmed that I had little talent for mathematics, but I was quite good at mental arithmetic. I worked all day and most of the night, stopping only for meals.

He noticed that as I had read so much and not too wisely in the last year or two, lovingly and indiscriminately collecting words, my vocabulary was riddled with solecisms, malapropisms and, with nobody to guide me, mispronunciations. He gently corrected my excesses. I wince now when I think of it, but such was his tact that we had a good laugh at me. He also begged me to tuck my little finger away. Curiously, despite being Cockney and ill-bred, the Levett family accent was not too uncouth.

On the last evening of our course we sat in the library-study after dinner and got drunk on brandy. He passed me an envelope. Inside was a new, white five-pound note and an equally new pound note. The fiver was for me, the pound was my tip for his servants. It was the first time I had owned a five-pound note. We staggered up to bed singing a popular song of the time: 'If I only had wings.' His parting advice was to read Lord Chesterfield's letters to his son.

I scraped through the mathematics paper.

The next fence was a local appraisal board by the Commanding Officer, the Chief Flying Instructor and the Chief Ground Instructor of Cranwell. The CO was a Group Captain, the CFI and the CGI were both Wing Commanders, Olympian figures of exalted rank whom I had hitherto seen only distantly. I was petrified as I marched into the CO's office and saw the three of them with wings, medal-ribbons, and stripes half-way up their arms, sitting at a long green baize table. A lonely chair stood on my side of the table. I halted smartly and gave an impeccable salute. There was a long, long pause as they all just sat there looking at me standing rigidly at attention.

'You may sit down,' said the CO. I sat. I did not know what to do with my hands and eyes. I decided to hold my hands in my lap and to focus my eyes on the top brass button of the CO's tunic. On the table in front of them lay copies of my service record. I realised that this was a critical moment of my life.

'You may like to know, Levett,' said the CO, 'that I would not like to be sitting where you are now.' It was a lovely thing to say. There were the usual questions, including those about sport. After about thirty minutes they asked me to leave the room for a few moments and wait outside in the corridor. After a long wait they called me back.

'We have decided', said the CO, 'to recommend you for pilot training.' It is very difficult to say thank you to officers in the services. Effusion is not the thing. I stood up, said 'Thank you, sir,' put my hat on, saluted smartly, about-turned and marched out of the office with some difficulty as my feet were about three feet from the ground.

In mid-November I was ordered to report to the Aircrew Selection Board and the Aircrew Medical Board in Torquay. This was the last fence. Many had fallen here. These two Boards were ruthless professionals.

I am not sure which was the worst ordeal, the selection board in the morning or the medical in the afternoon. The questions were much the same as the Cranwell board but the atmosphere was stiff and formal. Most of the applicants were civilians. I was the only erk applicant as far as I could see. The three-man board were middle-aged Wing Commanders, ex-RFC pilots. There was a similar green baize table and lonely chair but no opening remark to put me at ease. It was not going well until I mentioned Mr Wright and my flight with him in the Avro 504K. One of them knew Mr Wright and they had all flown the Avro. They forgot me for a while as they reminisced about it. After a few more questions they dismissed me without comment.

The medical examination took most of the afternoon, with a specialist for every part of my anatomy. The heart and chest specialist was a rare bird, a Flight-Lieutenant medical officer with pilot's wings. He took an interminable time messing about with the blood pressure gadget and getting me to run stationary and hop on one foot. Listening intently to my heart-beats his lips began to purse. Now what? I thought.

'We don't get many erks through here,' he said. 'How much does all this mean to you?' he asked. I told him. 'How long has it been going on?' he asked. I told him. He nodded. 'It says it all here,' he said, pointing to the twin blood pressure mercury columns. He then told me to go away and relax and come back in an hour.

The pubs were still just open. I spent most of my money on a large vodka and tomato juice. I had been told it did not smell. As I walked along the sea-front a Messerschmitt 110 nipped in from the sea, dropped a stick of bombs and strafed the sea-front. I dived down a Ladies' lavatory steps. When quiet returned I had blood pouring from a cut on my forehead where I had collided with a waste-paper basket during the dive. I got the cut dressed with an unnecessarily large dressing at a first-aid station.

The doctor laughed when he saw me. 'You have a funny way of relaxing,' he said. He got out his tools and examined me again. 'It's all right,' he announced. 'You'll do. Your blood pressure is always

46

going to be on the high side but if you watch the booze and cigarettes and don't wind yourself up too much you will be OK.' Holding out his hand, he said, 'Try and relax in life, and happy landings.'

I returned to Cranwell without the slightest idea of the outcome of my visit to Torquay. The RAF plays its cards close to the chest.

On 27 November 1940, I was told to report to the orderly room. Sergeant Piss-off was there.

'You're posted,' he said, poker-faced. My heart sank. A routine posting to another station, perhaps abroad, was the last thing I wanted at that time.

'Where to, Sergeant?'

'No. 6 Initial Training Wing for aircrew. You are now LAC Cadet Pilot Levett. Report to Aberystwyth, Wales, on the 30th.'

What a moment in my life that was. I asked him who else was going.

'Only you, clever Dick,' he replied sourly. It was true. Of the hundreds of erks who applied for aircrew training at Cranwell I was the only one that made it for pilot. All I had to do now was to learn how to fly.

Chapter 5

ABERYSTWYTH WAS an unlikely place to begin my metamorphosis from penguin into eagle. Situated in the centre of the wide, open sweep of Cardigan Bay it was, no doubt, a pleasant seaside resort in the summer. But in winter it was lashed by gales and Atlantic rollers. Only occasionally did the mists lift to reveal to the east behind the town a backcloth of gentle hills undulating peacefully and verdantly to the horizon. I wondered why the RAF had chosen such a spot. Probably because it was well beyond the range of most Luftwaffe bombers. I doubt that Aberystwyth saw or heard an enemy aeroplane throughout the entire war.

No. 6 Initial Training Wing was a grand title for a motley collection of commandeered hotels, shops and restaurants scattered throughout the town. The sea front, wet or dry, was our parade ground and where we did our daily physical training watched by the locals. I often wondered what they thought of us, mostly aliens, as we monopolised their town, pubs and daughters.

The students were all the same rank – flying cadets. Our status was symbolised by the white flash in our forage caps and white bands around our peaked caps. I awoke every morning with a flush of joy at what was happening to me.

At the reception talk given by the commanding officer in what had once been the dining room of Aberystwyth's grandest hotel he called us gentlemen. Nobody noticed except me. It was a change from a life of 'Oi you!' Within a week my hands were soft.

The course was for three months and covered navigation, signals including Morse code, meteorology, theory of flight, airmanship, aircraft recognition, instruments, engines and airframes. Being an old lag I knew some of it and was able to concentrate on the more difficult subjects, particularly navigation. I remember my horror when I glanced initially through the navigation text book and came across something like: '. . . thus we can get the cosine of the co-altitude by multiplying the cosine of the co-declination by the cosine of the co-latitude, then adding the product of multiplying the sign of the co-declination, the sign of the co-latitude and the cosine of the local hour angle . . .'. Jesus.

Our classroom used to be a tea-shop. Peace-time posters peeling from damp walls still urged us to enjoy Walls or Eldorado ice cream and Tizer the Appetizer, halcyon days. Next door was a tobacconist with most of his stock hidden under the counter and reserved for his regular customers, including us. He gave us credit in return for our watches which we redeemed on pay day. Most of the time there were several watches hanging up like scalps behind the counter. His small contribution to the war, bless him.

Apart from navigation I coped reasonably well, although I was usually the last in class to grasp anything other than the obvious. I struggled with the more sophisticated aspects of astro-navigation using the sun, the then unsullied moon and the stars.

Each day we discovered eternal verities. That Copernicus and Galileo were right and Ptolemy wrong about what orbits what in our cosmos. That the shortest distance between two points on a map or chart is not necessarily a straight line. That once lost in the air one cannot stop and ask the way. That we would all be lost without that mass of old iron under the magnetic north pole that attracts our compasses. That the stars are signposts to distant places. That our earth really is round because if you keep heading the same way you will eventually finish up where you started. And then there were the mnemonics inseparable from flying, such as variation west, compass best; variation east, compass least.

Our meteorology instructor was a Flight-Lieutenant with wings and medals from the First World War. He explained the eternal, complicated, restless antics of the sky and the hazards awaiting us in our future environment. Why winds blew, why clouds formed, what causes turbulence, thunder and lightning. How simple water becomes treacherous ice on wings. When to expect rain, fog, mist, snow, hail or dewdrops. His skyscapes were vivid as he described poetically named clouds – stratus, cumulus, cirrus and cumulo-nimbus. He recalled his brushes with cumulo-nimbus, that majestic king of the skies, sometimes towering higher than anything on earth, bursting with violence and a raging turbulence that can snap off a wing like a twig. He liked to relate weather to music and compared Brahms's majesty to cumulo-nimbus, Sibelius's serenity to mist and fog, Berlioz's violence to a cold front and Mozart's light, joyful touch to a spring day. We left his classroom after each lecture looking at the sky anew.

We went home for Christmas, the second Christmas of the war.

It was still pre-war in America, Russia and Japan. I had ceased being a civilian for nearly two years and it showed at home. I was nineteen and my chest had broadened. So had I. I felt sorry for Jack. Being left out of the war hurt him. He would have joined the navy. I caught him once or twice looking at my uniform with almost murderous envy. Though I found it more and more difficult to get along with my mother I had arranged with the RAF to send her a small monthly allotment from my pay. I could ill afford it but I now lived a life with no fixed address, where money seemed of secondary importance. Of course I wanted things that I could not afford, mostly a motorcycle, but service life had taught me to deal with money with a shrug. My surrogate mother, the RAF, supplied my needs and the future would take care of itself.

Jack was courting Joyce Morley. Conveniently for his gammy leg she was the girl next door. Jack was now twenty-six, time to get married, my mother thought. Joyce was nice, unbelievably equable and a natural doormat for Jack, who was what we now call a male chauvinist pig. To him a woman's place was in the kitchen, in bed, or in the wrong. They got married eventually and lived moderately happily ever after.

Civilian life had become alien to me. It seemed claustrophobic and stupefyingly suburban. We spent most nights sitting in the Anderson air-raid shelter at the bottom of the garden, with bombs falling and the anti-aircraft guns full of sound and fury, arguing about trivia.

I spent an evening in one of London's flesh-pots, Shepherds pub in Shepherd Market, Mayfair, much used by the RAF because the cellars made a good air-raid shelter. Outside, £2 tarts lingered in the black-out, their cigarettes glowing in the dark. A desolate way to spend a war. Inside, the bars were full of RAF pilots, most of them with the top button of their tunics undone, a fighter pilots' conceit, and DSOs and DFCs scattered like confetti. It was good to have my white flash recognised. Bombs fell regularly and were ignored. As I left the pub to catch the last train home to Worcester Park there was a colossal crash as a bomb destroyed Burtons in Piccadilly just around the corner.

I was not sorry when my leave ended to return to service life and the peaceful skies over Aberystwyth. When the course examination results were announced I got average marks and was posted to No. 19 Elementary Flying Training School, Sealand. Wales again. Aeroplanes at last!

Chapter 6

N O. 19 ELEMENTARY Flying Training School, Sealand, was more like it. It had the guarded iron gates, the parade square, the white-painted stones, the hangars and accommodation blocks and, above all else, the aerodrome of a legitimate RAF base. The setting was curiously suburban. Most RAF bases are tucked away in the countryside, but at Sealand civil life closely bordered ours. Just to the north-west was a large factory with a high, belching chimney that saved many a cadet from being lost. Overhead, yellow de Havilland Tiger Moth training aeroplanes twittered a welcome in the sky.

The course was for eight weeks at the end of which we ought to be able to get a simple aeroplane safely into the air, fly it from A to B and back again without getting lost, throw it around the sky a bit, and land in one piece.

The combination of the Tiger Moth and my particular flying instructor brought near disaster. The Tiger Moth was a lousy, over-rated aeroplane. Its sole virtue was that it was harmless. I do not know of anybody who was killed in a Tiger Moth – but there is always someone.

It was a wood and canvas biplane, noisy, draughty, uncomfortable and difficult for trainee pilots to fly accurately, with an undercarriage that encouraged bounces on landing like a trampoline and a ludicrous tail skid as a brake. The two open cockpits were in tandem with the pupil sitting behind the instructor at the back. This meant that when the cadet was looking ahead to see where he was going, or what was happening, most of what he saw was the back of the instructor's helmet. It was under-powered with a 130 hp Gipsy Major engine and did everything at 65 mph – take-off, climb, cruise, glide and land. To go appreciably faster meant pointing the nose firmly downwards. Most wartime RAF pilots were trained on it.

My instructor was a Flight-Lieutenant, an ex-Battle of Britain pilot, resting from combat. He was pencil-thin, with a hacking smoker's cough and a violent twitch of the jaw. He detested instructing and released his bile on us with a vicious, bullying tongue. We were terrified of him. He rarely briefed us before flying. A good instructor spends more time talking on the ground than in the air. He made mincemeat of me. With my inferiority complex ready to assert itself at the slightest provocation and a desperate desire to please, I thought all my difficulties were my fault. I realized later he was a rotten instructor and not much of a man either.

His first words to me when I reported to him for my first flight were 'Take that bloody lot off.' We had just been issued with our flying clothing and I proudly wore the lot. Two pairs of socks; calf length, fleece-lined black leather boots; three pairs of gloves – silk, woollen and leather; a voluminous, padded, one-piece Sidcot suit; a splendid leather, fleece-lined Irvin jacket; helmet, goggles and Gosport speaking-tubes and, finally, Mr Wright's white silk scarf knotted nonchalantly around my neck. I probably looked like the Michelin man. Anyone else would have seen the funny side of it.

Lesson No. 1 was a fifteen-minute flight on the morning of 4 March 1941. It was called Air Experience and is the first entry in my flying log-book, an accurate journal, signed and countersigned, kept by all pilots, which records the details of every flight they have made – a useful tool for the autobiographer. It was a significant flight, my first as a cadet. Although I could not see much straight ahead the view was good up, down, left and right. I sat looking at the instruments, the Dee estuary below, verdant Wales to port and the smoke and balloon barrage over Liverpool to starboard. I was too drunk with happiness to learn much on that first flight as a cadet, but it did not matter. This sky, this aeroplane, this instructor, this day was mine. Gordon Levett was up here being taught how to fly, how to become a Royal Air Force pilot. I had become a cousin, distant certainly, but a cousin of those Royal Air Force demi-gods I had seen at that Hendon air display seven years earlier.

The routine was, weather permitting, flying and ground school on alternate days. Ground school covered the same subjects as at ITW but more advanced. We usually had two flights a day with the instructor until we went solo. Day after day it was up, around and down; up, around and down; up, around and down. It should have been fun but the fear of failure – the failure rate was at its highest at this time – turned it into anxious graft. On the ground it seemed so

5   RAF Cadet College, Cranwell

6   The Tiger Moth – 'a lousy, over-rated aeroplane, noisy, draughty, and difficult for trainee pilots to fly accurately'. Sealand, 1940

7 Miles Masters pictured at Montrose, 1941 (photograph courtesy of *Aeroplane Monthly*)

8 The Harvard – 'the most successful advanced training aircraft of the war'. Kingston, Ontario, 1942

simple. Taxi out, turn into wind, open the throttle, keep straight, control column forward, tail up, takeoff, climb at 65 mph, level off at one thousand feet, trim, throttle back to cruise power, turn left 180 degrees, fly parallel with the aerodrome, turn left 90 degrees, throttle back, glide, good look out for other aeroplanes, glide at 65 mph, final turn left 90 degrees, glide towards the aerodrome, level off close to the ground, control column back, back, back, and the aeroplane will sink gently to the ground. Simple. Thesis – air; antithesis – ground; synthesis – good landing. Ha!

Most cadets achieved their first solo flight after eight to ten hours' dual instruction, some more, some less. The rapidity with which a pilot achieves his first solo is no indication of merit, but if a cadet had not gone solo by about ten hours it was worrying and he wore a haunted look. Two cadets on my course had already got the chop. One through chronic air-sickness, the other, whom I saw crying in the barracks as he packed his kitbags, through lack of physical co-ordination.

After a month or so the cadets on my course were beginning to go solo. It was drinks on them in the NAAFI canteen and stiff upper lip for the rest. My instructor's other three pupils had already gone solo. My dual hours were creeping up; eight hours, eight and a half, nine, nine and a half, ten. My instruction in the air had degenerated into one-way shouting matches, with my instructor almost gibbering with rage as I sat in the back seat in a huddle of manic depression. We landed after ten and a half hours dual, taxied to the tarmac and switched off. He got out, turned wrathfully to me, shouting 'You are no bloody good, you know', before storming off.

That night I was violently ill with vomiting and diarrhoea; I wondered whether it was psychosomatic. The Medical Officer diagnosed food poisoning and put me to bed in sick quarters. Lying in bed, with my instructor's last remark like a balloon in my head, I thought about my future and what I would do if I failed. I decided, quite seriously, that I could not face going back to being an erk and that I would desert. After five days I left sick quarters pale and wan and reported for flying. My instructor took me up for a quick fifteen-minute flight during which I managed two landings no better or worse than usual, and then handed me over to the Flight Commander, Flight-Lieutenant Lowe, for a first solo test flight. It was a thirty-five minute flight, longer than usual. I was convinced that it was not a first solo test flight at all but a Backward Progress Test, a euphemism for the chop. Even so it was a relief to hear a civil voice down the Gosport tube.

We landed for the third time, I was bathed in sweat on a cold day, and taxied back to the take-off position. With unbelieving eyes I watched F/Lt. Lowe climb out with the engine still running, tidy away his safety straps and remove the truncheon-like control column from the front cockpit. He turned to me, smiled and shouted in the slipstream: 'You are much better than you think you are. Off you go. One circuit and landing. I'll wait here.'

I was up in the air, alone for the first time, before I knew it. My hands had gone through the motions of taking off like puppets. In a state of euphoria I was levelling off at a thousand feet on my first solo flight before I truly realized what was happening and then what a shout I gave the heavens. A shout of relief, joy, gratitude to all those who had helped and a love of life that could bring happiness so total and absolute. All pilots fondly remember their first solo flight, but I had more reasons than most for remembering. Ex-slum kid, ex-orphanage, ex-erk, I was now piloting, alone over the Dee estuary, one of His Majesty's Royal Air Force aeroplanes. It was one of those days, typical after a cold front, when the sky looks washed and brushed and deeply blue, and visibility is limited only by the curvature of the earth. And what a marvellous, revelatory view it was without the instructor sitting in front. The Moth, without the instructor's weight, was even friskier and more difficult to fly accurately but the mechanics of flying seemed simple that day. As I looked down I felt the world had stopped and was waiting for me to land. It was sublime.

No bands played or crowds cheered when I landed and taxied back to where the lonely figure of F/Lt. Lowe was waiting, but a band played in my heart and I cheered myself. F/Lt. Lowe smiled when he saw my face. 'Not a bad landing,' he commented.

That night after drinks in the NAAFI with the other cadets – I was the last on our course to go solo – I wrote stilted letters of thanks to F/Lt. Hall, Tiny O'Hara, the Education Officer and the professor.

During the next few weeks as our flying hours, dual and solo, gradually built up, so did our confidence. My initial fear of flying had vanished forever. In its place was a tiny tablet of fear secretly nestling in my heart. Under control, but there. The seventh sense. Most pilots have this secret fear. It is a great life preserver. It keeps the eyes sharp, the ears cocked, the nerves tingling, the adrenalin flowing, the imagination vivid, the reflexes automatic, the responses immediate. I would not want to fly with a pilot who had no fear.

We were still chicks, but we could now cope with flying a small, elementary aeroplane in good weather. We had a long, long way to go before we could call ourselves pilots, but a certain panache was now creeping into our landings and the way we carried our parachutes slung over our shoulder. We talked shop tirelessly. The hangar doors never closed. The entries in our flying log-books were becoming more sophisticated: spinning, aerobatics, cross-countries and instrument flying. We discussed our future. Most of us wanted to be gung-ho fighter pilots rather than bus-driver bomber pilots.

None of us talked or thought much about the war except what was happening in the headlines. I did not talk about the why of the war throughout its duration. I do not think many others of my age did either. The majority of British servicemen or women of my generation, protected by a strip of water twenty-two miles wide which kept danger distant and defeat unthinkable, enjoyed the war and have not been happier before or since. The tragedies of war in British homes were on a Lilliputian scale compared with continental Europe. It was the scorched-earth Russians, the refugees from Europe, the Poles, the Czechs, the Free French, the Jews, who knew the cost of war. One cannot imagine any of them shaking hands and drinking toasts with ex-Luftwaffe pilots at post-war reunions, a regrettable RAF habit. There are some historical circumstances in which forgive and forget is an entirely misplaced sentiment.

At the end of the course I got an average assessment as a pilot and average marks in ground subjects. My log-book recorded a total of 47 hours' flying, 19.10 dual and 27.50 solo.

I was posted, with several other cadets, to No. 8 Service Flying Training School, Montrose, Scotland, for fighter pilot training. I was content. I was still holding my own and I had got the posting I wanted. Once again I packed my kit-bags.

Chapter 7

NO DOUBT, IN the mists of RAF history, there was a good reason for siting No. 8 Service Flying Training School at Montrose, between Aberdeen and Dundee, on the bleak north-east coast of Scotland. The aerodrome was a grass field situated in the narrow coastal strip between the North Sea and the dour, brooding Grampian mountains to the west. In addition to the unnerving proximity of the mountains, Scotch mist – called Haar by the locals – rolled in from the sea without warning, obliterating the aerodrome. The area was also occasionally a target for Luftwaffe hit-and-run raiders, usually Junkers 88s.

The journey from London to Montrose was one of those long, wearying train journeys so redolent of wartime Britain. It took twenty-four hours to cover the four hundred-odd miles. Time and again, night and day, we came to a halt in the silence of nowhere and waited, with just an occasional tired grunt of steam to reassure us that there was still a locomotive up front. The train was packed with soldiers, sailors and airmen and their female counterparts, the ATS, WRNS and WAAFs. The WRNS, in dark blue uniforms and cute hats, were the most fetching. Rumour had it that their underwear was sensational because sailors could buy frilly things in foreign ports, but one felt that WRNS' favours were reserved for Captains, RN, and above. The WAAFs had deliberately clumsy skirt fastenings which helped repel boarders. The WAAF high command was notoriously short of humour.

Squeezing through the crowded, smoky corridors to the tea bar I passed through the first-class compartments. It was a quiet, different world, with some unoccupied seats and freshly laundered linen antimacassars for the heads of officers and gentlemen.

When darkness came we had not got very far. The miserly blue lights were supplemented by the glow of cigarettes. Once again we came to a creaking halt. On the horizon there was the red glow of a city in torment. The betting was Sheffield. Searchlights spot-lighted the sky and anti-aircraft guns thundered distantly. I felt uneasy. Trains are easy to see from the air at night with the only

56

partially concealed glow from the driver's cab, sparks from the locomotive chimney and moonlight glinting on the railway lines. I was glad when we moved on.

Though Montrose was a pleasant seaside town, the RAF base was spartan. Fortunately it was late spring. It must have been grim in the winter. We shared the aerodrome with a Spitfire fighter squadron resting from more arduous duties in the south. Their dispersal huts and aeroplanes were in the north-west corner of the field. A red Very flare was fired into the air when the Spitfires were scrambled to intercept enemy raiders. We scattered like startled chickens when the Spitfires were scrambled and, seeking Tally-ho, took off in all directions. They did not fuss about the niceties of wind direction. On one occasion when I was taking-off solo to the north-west I found myself on precisely the same path as a Spitfire taking off to the south-east. Our combined speed was approaching 200 mph when fortuitously – there were no rules of the air covering this situation – I went under and he went over. I heard his Merlin and felt his airwash as he roared overhead.

The training aeroplanes were Miles Masters, powered by Rolls-Royce Kestrel XXX engines. The Master had a dubious reputation and we approached it with some apprehension. It was a sophisticated, advanced aeroplane compared with the Tiger Moth. It had to be. It was our stepping-stone to the Spitfire and Hurricane fighters. It was a modern, single-engined, low-wing monoplane with a closed cockpit and all the gadgets that were inexorably making a science of the art of flying. It had retractable undercarriage, constant speed three-blade propeller, high wing-loading, 100 octane fuel, landing flaps, brakes, automatic boost control and a full blind-flying instrument panel. With its attractive configuration, gull-shaped wings and don't-take-any-liberty flying characteristics, I eventually grew to like and respect it.

My instructor was Pilot Officer Gulland, a quiet, patient man with a wispy attempt at an RAF moustache that did nothing for his looks. He had a chronic sore throat from shouting down the Gosport speaking-tube above the roar of the engine. He was a good instructor who, like most instructors, detested it. He got angry with me only once, when I made a hash of an instrument flying exercise. I was a seat-of-the-pants pilot, with the corollary that I was weak on instrument flying. It was months before I became competent at it, years before I mastered it.

The first take-off with P/O Gulland was revelatory. The roar and thrust of the Kestrel XXX engine pushing me back in the seat, the steep angle and fast rate of climb, the feeling of power in hand and the speed with which clouds swept by was almost frightening compared with anything I had flown in before.

After two hours dual with P/O Gulland I went solo. Several days later I flew with another instructor, Sergeant Switon, a Pole. He spoke rarely and when he did his English was elementary.

The exercise was an instrument flying cross-country, which entailed flying a triangular cross-country route underneath a canvas hood using only the blind-flying instruments. It was an eerie flight for there was not a word from Sergeant Switon sitting in the rear cockpit. I wondered whether he was still there. The object of the exercise was to fly about 150 miles, blind but for the instruments, and finish up where we started. It was an anxious moment when, at the end of the exercise, Sergeant Switon released the hood and I looked down. The aerodrome was about five miles to port. 'Is OK', said Sergeant Switon.

While we were flying, four Luftwaffe bodies were brought to the aerodrome's temporary morgue. They were the crew of a Junkers 88 hit-and-run raider which had been shot down earlier that morning by one of Montrose's Spitfires. We walked past the morgue and peered in the windows. The four bodies were neatly lined up on their backs on the floor, covered with RAF blankets. Eight naked feet, hideously white, stuck out from the blankets.

'Poor chaps,' I said to Sergeant Switon, the refugee from Poland.

'Fuck poor chaps,' answered Sergeant Switon, spitting at the window.

Each day there was something new – aerobatics, low flying, formation flying, night flying – and another rung climbed to our goal of wings. We were elated with the prospect of each day as we slipped our beds in the early morning. None of us wanted to be anywhere else. I doubt that we were complacent. We worked and studied too hard and the grim, salutary shock of the occasional fatal crash prevented that. One cadet had been killed on our course so far and the course ahead had recently lost two cadets and an instructor in a mid-air collision.

Each new exercise we tackled increased our self-knowledge and pushed back our threshold of fear. Once we had done something new two or three times we laughed at our earlier fears. After some dual instruction with P/O Gulland he sent me up solo to practise steep turns, spinning and aerobatics. I had 68 hours' flying in my log-book, of which 21 were on the Master. It was a reasonable basis for having a go for the first time alone at something fairly daunting in a high-performance aeroplane. Chaps were doing it every day. I climbed to the aerobatic height of 10,000 feet and levelled off. From that height bonny Scotland looked like an Ordnance Survey map. It was a perfect day for aerobatics. A sharp horizon, smooth air and touches of high cirrus to line up on. I circled once to ensure there were no other aeroplanes sharing my bit of the sky and did the steep turns. No sweat. I then did spins to left and right. No sweat. Now for the aerobatics.

I circled again, and again and again repeatedly before realising why. I was frightened of what I had to do next. A loop. I stopped circling, forced myself to open the throttle wide and dived steeply to build up the speed to the 240 mph required for a loop. When the airspeed indicator registered 240 mph I throttled back and pulled lamely out of the dive back to level flight. I tried again but, despite the fact that I had done several satisfactory loops with P/O Gulland sitting in the back seat, I could not do it. In the unlikely event that someone might be watching the antics of a tiny speck in the high sky, I flew out of sight of the aerodrome. I tried again but I was in a total funk. The thought of a loop, that huge Ferris wheel in the sky, terrified me. Diving for high speed, throttle wide open, engine roaring, airframe vibrating, pulling the nose up high, higher, unnaturally higher until the earth disappears and the nose is pointing vertically at the sky, then upside down over the top, the nose transcribing a wide vertical arc across the sky, the earth reappearing from behind one's head, then the vertical dive towards earth as one throttles back and pulls out. I thought of the things that could go wrong with an inexperienced pilot. Engine failure, pulling the aeroplane too tightly or too loosely around the loop resulting in a vertical stall, falling out at the top of the loop into an upside down flat spin, or a vertical tail slide which could result in a broken elevator, or structural failure caused by clumsy handling. All this with gravity waiting patiently, never giving up its fight against flying, always ready to pounce. On the ground one knew that there was little chance of any of these things happening, for the loop, though spectacular to watch, is the simplest of all aerobatic manoeuvres, but alone two miles up in the air the imagination of fear can be rampant. I could not do it. I landed and taxied to dispersal. 'OK?' asked P/O Gulland. I nodded a lie.

Failing nerve was not something I could talk or seek advice about. My self-loathing was worse when I was safely on the ground, where the reason for my funk became incomprehensible. I decided there was one man I could speak to, the lonely Sergeant Switon, and arranged to meet him in the nearest pub. He was puzzled. It was unusual for cadets to ask to meet sergeants privately.

He drank beer as though he needed it rather than enjoyed it. He spoke about ten sentences in our hour together. He agreed to honour my confidence before I explained my problem. Unsurprisingly his advice was simplicity itself. It was my problem and nobody could help me. Get up there and keep trying. As we got up to leave he added encouragingly that he had had a similar problem with spinning when he was learning to fly.

The next day I asked P/O Gulland if I could do some more solo aerobatics. He looked at me for a long moment or two before asking whether I had any problems. I wondered whether Sergeant Switon had broken confidence and shook my head. P/O Gulland's concern probably mirrored the tension on my face. He nodded and authorised another flight of solo aerobatics and spinning.

I climbed up to 10,000 feet in a similar sky and did some slow rolls to the left and right. Then I did spins to the left and right. No sweat. I could not understand why Sergeant Switon had been frightened of spins. In fact I discovered that many of the cadets were apprehensive about spinning, but not about loops. Such was the irrationality of my own fears. I climbed back up to 10,000 feet for the loop.

I had several false starts, getting the nose up to an angle of about 65 degrees before repeating yesterday's performance. I was shouting at myself in rage and disgust as I levelled off each time. I had an idea. Instead of reaching the required speed of 240 mph in the preparatory dive before the loop I would make it 270 mph. This would give me more speed for that infernal vertical circle around the sky. Once more I dived, throttle wide open – 200, 220, 240, 260, 270 mph – 'Come on now, coward,' I shouted and pulled the control column back and back. Up came the nose, up and up and over and I had done it. I did several more before I tried one at 240 mph.

After I had landed I collapsed on my bed. It was the first time I had experienced funk and the need to vanquish it. Ten thousand loops later I can smile about it.

Chapter 8

ROYAL AIR FORCE aeroplanes were becoming more advanced but the supporting ancillary equipment was not. Communications, navigation, instrument flying and blind landings were still at the Neanderthal stage. Most RAF aircraft at that time were flying without radio. A pilot lost or in trouble with bad weather was on his own. He had no help except his parachute. The most sophisticated aid for landing in fog was a trench dug both sides of the runway, filled with kerosine, and then set alight when an aircraft was marooned in the sky, hoping that the heat of the flames would burn the fog away. Called Fido, it saved a few lives.

It was time for us to learn to fly at night. Having mastered three dimensions in the air, we now added a fourth, darkness, to our repertoire. The sky at night is a very different flying element from that of day. With high-performance aircraft, no radio, the blackout, a thousand aircraft – British and German – wandering without lights around Britain's small sky, trigger-happy anti-aircraft guns firing at anything that moved and German night-fighters lurking for prey near aerodromes, it was a hairy time to be flying in the dark.

To be less vulnerable to enemy night-fighters, night flying training took place at a satellite field near Brechin, about eight miles to the west of Montrose and that much closer to the waiting Grampian mountains. It was a large grass field in the middle of wartime nowhere.

We were subdued as we lounged on the grass awaiting the end of daylight. I watched the erks, their silhouettes eerily outlined by the flickering flames, lighting the goose-neck paraffin flares spaced along the landing path as though in some sinister medieval ritual. There was no moon and the stars sulked behind high alto-stratus cloud. It was going to be a very black night.

When we walked out to the Masters the stage was different. The Masters loomed larger and more pugnacious in the dark. Everyone spoke quietly, solemnly. Perhaps it is the quality of night itself that lowers voices and banishes flippancy when night flying. I have noticed even on the flight deck of modern jumbo-jet charabancs that flight crews' voices are hushed and subdued at night. There is in most of us a natural respect for the peace of night. But in an aeroplane there is an added touch of awe and wonder and a heightened awareness of metaphysics when one is closer to the stars and the earth has disappeared, like Hamlet's ghost, into darkness.

I sat in the front cockpit as P/O Gulland started up and taxied out. Because of the black-out he used the landing light sparingly for taxiing. Landing lights were not used at all for taking-off or landing except in emergency. Too many aeroplanes had been shot down by enemy intruders while doing so.

I was unprepared for the flames curling from the twelve exhaust stubs, six either side of the nose, just below my line of sight. Normally hidden by daylight the flames snorted and licked around the nose like a dragon as we taxied out to the take-off point. The night flying controller signalled a steady green for take-off on his Aldis light. P/O Gulland opened the throttle wide to take-off power and the long yellow flames were replaced by short cobalt-blue emissions as we accelerated past the spaced islands of light created by the goose-neck flares. I looked ahead. I could see nothing. Earth and sky were indistinguishable. It was like flying into a vast black velvet tent. Only the dimly glowing instruments gave any assurance of equilibrium. The exhaust stubs were now a deep, glowing red, a reminder that flying is powered by primeval fire.

I did three landings with P/O Gulland before he climbed out of the aircraft and casually waved me back into the sky to do three solo landings. I looked at the sky. It was still relentlessly black. Jesus.

Like my first solo I was in the air before I knew what was happening. Ah, that bravado and scorn of youth when things are done without thought or care of consequence. I looked down on a black void, a thousand feet of nothing. Man and nature had conspired to produce a perfect blackout. It was like flying under the hood. I veered around the sky, correcting and over-correcting, trying to keep the blind-flying instruments in some sort of order. It was a relief when it was time to turn 180 degrees and the tiny flickering lights of the flare-path swung into view over my left shoulder. Now that I was flying solo the L-shaped landing area outlined by the flares looked dauntingly small. I got down all right with a landing which I was glad was hidden by the cloak of darkness. The

63

second effort was better. I taxied back to the take-off point for the third time and waited for the green Aldis signal. I got a red instead which meant do not take-off and return to the dispersal area. Rain was moving in from the west and flying was cancelled. I was not sorry. Nobody knows how dark dark can be who has not flown alone on a cloudy, moonless night over a blacked-out northern country at war.

We resumed night flying a few days later. The difference was astonishing. There was no cloud, stars twinkled, the moon shone and was mirrored in the rivers and lakes, the North Sea glistened like silver lamé and even the hard-nosed Grampian mountains bathed in moonlight looked benign. The horizon was so clear there was little need to look at the blind-flying instruments. It was a light-hearted lark compared with the dour struggle of a few days before and the beginning of my affection for the magic of night flight which lasts to this day.

Next was formation flying. Being a flashy, exhibitionist part of flying it suited my seat-of-the-pants talent. I was good at it and loved it. Holding position within half a wing span of another aeroplane required total concentration and constant, three-dimensional, fine adjustments of position, using throttle, elevators, ailerons and rudder. Eyes fixed on the other aircraft silhouetted in the sky without visible means of support heightened one's perception of the basic elements of flying; space, speed, power, height and, above all else, the majestic, infinite perspective of flight. But, also, seeing a comrade sitting hunched in his cockpit up there in space, vulnerable flesh and bone, with that vast void beneath him, was a reminder that flying is unnatural, that the sky, despite its welcome, and undefiled, ever-changing beauty, is two-faced, basically hostile to man and ever ready to purge the interloper from its kingdom if one took liberties. Sergeant Switon, pale with anger and fright, once gave me a blast, mostly in Polish, after landing, for flying too closely to him. Best of all was landing in formation and the fascination of seeing things happen in the other aircraft which one never sees in one's own. The undercarriage unfolding magically like a bird, the landing flaps coming down, the ground rushing up and by, the gap between flying and not flying getting smaller, the puff of dust and rubber as the wheels touch down, the tyres shocked from zero to 90 mph in a micro-second and the smoking brakes.

On 9 July 1941, I flew a Hawker Hurricane for the first time. God, over fifty years ago! I can feel that throttle in my hand as though it were yesterday. I can expect only pilots to understand the intensity of my nostalgia when I recall that day. The Hurricane and its stablemate the Spitfire were two of the most advanced and formidable fighter aircraft of the day and possibly the most illustrious fighter aircraft of all time, certainly in British eyes. To have flown either was to have taken part in history.

There were a few Hurricanes at Montrose used for advanced flying training towards the end of the course. They were scruffy veterans of the Battle of Britain but they wore their battle scars with honour. We approached them with respect.

As it was a single-seater aircraft there was no dual instruction. It was the deep end from square one. I climbed into the cockpit while P/O Gulland stood on the wing explaining for the umpteenth time the controls and flying characteristics. He was more nervous than I was. It seemed a surprisingly big aircraft. With a Cyrano de Bergerac nose, Richard III humped back, thick wing, sensibly big inward tucking feet and rugged construction, it was a handsome, no-nonsense aircraft compared with the dainty feline grace of the Spitfire.

I felt tall as I taxied out, with flashy blips of the throttle, past watching instructors and cadets. Pilots always watch and appraise each other at work. It was a warm sunny day as I opened the throttle to take-off power. I had been briefed what to expect but it was still unexpected. The Master was a good preparatory school, but it had only 500 horse-power. The Hurricane had 1,030. The uproar of the Merlin engine and the punch in both kidneys as I took off reminded me of P/O Gulland's comment that the Hurricane had the power equivalent of 147 Austin Seven motor-cars. I could believe it as I passed through a thousand feet, climbing like a bat from hell, with the undercarriage still dangling down. For the first few minutes the Hurricane was flying me rather than the other way round.

After settling down I revelled in the unbelievable. That I was flying this magnificent machine, this Hurricane fighter. Working-class dreams seldom come true but here was one that did. I flew in wide circles over the towns, villages and moors of north-east Scotland. Over shop assistants and bank managers, housewives and schoolboys, all impervious to the frolicking speck high over their heads. Except perhaps the schoolboys. There was a chance that some of them might have recognised the unique whistling vibrato of the Merlin and the silhouette of the Hurricane.

I climbed high to do some unauthorised aerobatics. After several slow rolls I did some loops. With so much power they were easy compared with the Master. During the third loop the throttle jammed open. I pulled out of the loop much too fast as I juggled with the throttle lever but it stayed jammed. I tried inverted flying and negative gravity to loosen it. Meanwhile I was charging around Scotland as though astride a bolting stallion. I saw the funny side of it until I realised that the throttle was not going to budge. I thought of my parachute but put it in the back of my mind as a last resort. I had fuel for another hour, but the oil and radiator temperatures were near the upper limits. This particular Hurricane, unlike some of the others at Montrose, had no radio. Losing height slowly I flew back to Montrose and buzzed around the aerodrome like a wasp around a jam-pot at about twice the normal circuit speed. To indicate I had trouble I made a series of low passes across the aerodrome. I was not yet frightened, just excited. I had two options. Baling out, or a dead-stick forced-landing which meant climbing high over the aerodrome, switching off the engine and gliding in to land. A fairly difficult task requiring the judgement of a skilled, experienced pilot, and that I was not. A bizarre third alternative occurred to me. First World War pilots had controlled the power on some aeroplanes on landing by using an ignition cut-off switch on the control column. On-off-on-off as required. I decided to do the same thing using the normal ignition switches. I switched off. The airflow kept the propeller windmilling. When I switched on again there was a screech as the Merlin revved from zero to full power in a second. As an ex-erk I winced at what I was doing to that engine. I coarsened the propeller pitch as much as possible to reduce engine revolutions. It took a long time with the ignition off to lose enough excess speed to get the undercarriage and landing flaps down. I feared the plugs might oil up. I made a mess of the first attempt at landing and had to go round again in fits and starts – silence – uproar – silence – uproar – as I turned the ignition switches on and off. White faces looked up at me from the aerodrome, no doubt wondering what the hell was going on. I got it right the second time, kept the engine switched off after touch-down and came to a silent halt at the far corner of the aerodrome, brakes smoking. The fire tender and the Chief Flying Instructor's car sped out to me. I was chuffed with myself until I heard the CFI's opening remarks. They were uncomplimentary, and it was a long time before I could get a word in and explain. I was relieved when he could not close the throttle either.

The penultimate week of the course arrived at last. A week of last-minute swotting, ground examinations, flying tests, board inter-views and a medical. The RAF does not give its wings and sergeant's stripes or commissions lightly. Our future career depended to some extent on the results of that week. I had no idea of my merit. I had worked hard. Some had not. I knew that did not signify, for many of the cadets had the gift of effortless success. The zenith of my hopes was to get by. I did not presume more.

I slept badly the night before my final Wings Flying Test and got out of bed feeling jaded to face the Chief Flying Instructor – Squadron Leader Slater. His rank, title and reputation were awesome. Rumour had it he could make grown men weep. I could feel his eyes boring into the back of my helmet as we taxied out and took off in the Master. The flight took an hour and fifteen minutes. He liked my steep turns and aerobatics and the way I handled the engine but he disliked my precautionary landing technique and instrument-flying take-off under the hood. 'Curate's egg,' I heard him mutter. I thought my end had come when, having concentrated so much on each exercise, I got lost.

Between the exams and tests we played unauthorised fools in the air. We rendezvoused out of sight for mock dog-fights in the Hurricanes. To chase and be chased in that superb aeroplane in the playground of sky and cloud, to follow another Hurricane nose to tail, to see a comrade's helmeted head grinning in his cockpit, to twist and turn, dive and climb through thousands of feet at 400 miles an hour, to see the other Hurricane silhouetted against the blue and white canvas of the sky was a sublime summation of all I had learned and loved about flying.

We were tense and edgy as we awaited the results of our ground examinations and flying tests. About three-quarters of us would become Sergeant pilots, the remainder would be commissioned as Pilot Officers. Most of us would be posted to Fighter Command, some of the older pilots to Bomber Command and an elite, unlucky few to Training Command as flying instructors.

The results and postings were announced informally. Gone, for the duration of the war, were the splendid Wings Parades with aircraft flying past overhead in salute. Now the results were pinned on the notice board.

There was a stampede when they appeared. I was told later I went white with shock and disbelief. My results were: Pilot assessment – Above average. Ground school – Above average. Promotion – Commissioned as Pilot Officer. Posting – Central Flying School, Upavon, for flying instructor training.

It was weeks before I adjusted to the brew of three parts nectar and one part bile that the RAF had served me. All agreed it was rotten luck to become a flying instructor. That it almost certainly saved my life was no consolation. Like my comrades I wanted to risk my life, not save it. Becoming an instructor was, to most young pilots, a fate far worse than the possibility of being killed in action.

Choosing me to become a flying instructor was perverse. My supposed above-average flying ability then was of a meretricious, impetuous quality, always ready to break rules and a poor example for students. My awkward, uneasy relationship with people was no asset either. As it turned out I discovered that flying is basically a self-taught skill and instructors are merely safety-pilots, keeping watch to prevent sprog pilots hurting themselves or the aeroplane.

The new sergeant pilots went to the camp tailor to have their three stripes and wings sewn on their old uniforms. The new officers went to a civilian military tailor in Montrose to be measured and fitted for their new uniforms. My first made-to-measure garment.

We wore our new uniforms for the first time the day we left Montrose, 25 July 1941. I was twenty years old. There was a lot of pride in the hut when we dressed that morning. Nobody had to be dragged out of bed. But no matter how great a day it was for the others it was more so for me, the ex-erk. It was the consummation of a ten-year ambition. The frog had become a prince at last. I savoured the feel of each garment bought with the uniform allowance. The fine cotton underwear, the well-cut Van Heusen shirt, the hand-made black shoes so lightweight after years of erks' boots, and the silky feel of a fine, worsted uniform compared with the coarse flannel of yesterday. I joined the queue for the full-length mirror. Only then when I saw myself, not masquerading but of

9 Central Flying School, Upavon, September 1941. Scarcely a smile at the end of the flying instructors' course. Pilot Officer Gordon Levett standing on extreme right of second row

10 Newly commissioned Pilot Officer Gordon Levett, aged twenty, July 1941.
Sprog pilots made their hats look more worn and dashing by occasionally
sitting on them

right, dressed as a Pilot Officer of the Royal Air Force with those hallowed wings on my chest and the thin stripe on my sleeves, did the niggle of disbelief finally vanish.

We split up, the others to Fighter or Bomber Commands, never to meet again. Most of the others would be dead by the end of the war.

The train to London, and a week's leave before reporting to Central Flying School, was late so I killed time by wandering around Montrose. I found I was lifting my feet too high in my new shoes. I got lingering looks and twinkles from women. It was a good time to be wearing RAF pilot's wings for RAF prestige was at its highest. The Battle of Britain had been won and Bomber Command was now hitting back with raids of a thousand bombers over Germany. Looking back it is difficult to believe it was still pre-war in Russia, Japan and America. I was about to go into the public bar of a scruffy pub when I remembered what I was wearing. Walking along further to a smart hostelry I got my first salute. It took me by surprise and the erk had passed before I returned his salute. It struck me as comic that all erks and non-commissioned ranks of the three services, millions of grown men like Lofty, Shorty, Tiny O'Hara and Sergeant Piss-off, must now salute me, address me as Sir and rise when I entered a room. We were told at Cardington that it is the uniform being saluted, not the man. Ha! In the smart hostelry I hesitated about ordering a pint of bitter. Did officers in uniform quaff pints in pubs? I ordered a large whisky and soda instead. My pay was now a heady £20 a month, all found. I wondered how long it would be before my mother would be on the financial prowl.

The train was crowded for the long journey to London. I stood in the packed corridors before remembering I now travelled on a first-class warrant. I squeezed along the corridors and found an almost empty first-class compartment. Nodding casually at the other swells I sank into the luxurious seat and rested my head against the freshly laundered antimacassar.

Chapter 9

CENTRAL FLYING SCHOOL at Upavon, on the Salisbury Plain, was a distinguished academy of instruction and the theory of flight. Air forces throughout the world sent pilots there for study. It was second only to Cranwell in prestige and to have been there was a distinction, but that did not help. I was fed-up.

Much as I had to learn about instructing, I had more to learn about being an officer and a gentleman. With the world in turmoil my biggest problem was coping with the manners, traditions and mores of an officers' mess. The opportunities for doing the wrong thing seemed endless. Since joining the RAF I had smoothed off some of my rougher edges but there are a million banana skins awaiting the class poseur in England and the English are superlative at spotting a phoney.

I had my own bedroom, an oasis of peace and privacy after years of dormitory life. I tried not to be embarrassed when my batman, a corporal twice my age, addressed me as Sir, cleaned my buttons and shoes and made my bed. I tried very hard to adopt the casual elegance and nonchalance of my new peers. It was weeks before I realised that the knot of my tie was all wrong. Gentlemen do not tie their ties in small tight knots. On the other hand only cads, pansies or artists wear large Windsor knots. The collar is never, never loosened, even in a Spitfire.

My vowels had improved although they slipped down a social scale or two whenever I got animated. I stopped foreshortening such words as telephone, photograph and bicycle. I learned to slow down, control my enthusiasms and not say sorry or shake hands too often. At bridge I remembered to say no bid instead of pass, to call Jacks knaves and threes treys and not to shuffle and deal with slick flourishes. I learned to conceal any knowledge I had about anything except sport. At table I learned not to cut bread rolls in half but to pull bits off, not to spread butter, jam, marmalade or pâté over a whole slice of bread or toast and not to pull the soup spoon. Not to scatter salt like a snowfall over my food but to arrange it in a neat pyramid on the side of the plate. Not to stir cups of tea or coffee

vigorously and not to eat peas the logical way. Not to pass the port
to starboard. Lord Chesterfield's letters were helpful, including his
definition of a gentleman as one who never unknowingly offends. I
tried hard but it was impossible to achieve in a few weeks that air of
effortless superiority the upper crust has taken generations to
acquire. In class terms I was the equivalent of a resident alien. I
wince when I look back. It was an expense of spirit in the pursuit of
trivia. In mitigation, I was twenty years old and overwhelmed by
the need to conform. I do not think I was a snob for I did not change
my political views to accord with those usually held by the class I
was aping. I liked their style and manners, not their values.

There were twenty students on each course. Half were officers,
half sergeants and all morose. Judging by the end-of-course photograph we were a young, handsome, miserable-looking lot. Not one
was smiling. We became part of the highly successful Commonwealth Air Training Scheme which trained thousands of pilots,
mostly in Canada, for the Allied air forces.

We teamed up in pairs and churned endlessly around the sky
practising instructing on each other. Our voices were hoarse, our
ears tender from shouting the standard instructing patter down the
Gosport tube over the noise of the engine. We did the elementary
stuff in Avro Tutors, the advanced in Miles Masters. The Tutor, an
old-fashioned, open-cockpit biplane, was a joy to fly, one of the last
links with the already nostalgic flying of the 1930s. CFS had flown
them tied together, upside down at pre-war Hendon air displays.
CFS's Masters were the Mark III version, fitted with the Pratt and
Whitney Twin Wasp Junior radial engine, giving it a better performance than the Kestrel version. The Wasp engines were supplied,
for cash, by America.

It did not help that the two aeroplanes were nice to fly, or that it
was a glorious summer, with endless golden acres of the Salisbury
Plain cornfields rippling and waving up at us. We vented our spleen
at becoming instructors with dangerous, unauthorised mock dog-
fights. I was second best. The best was my team-mate, Hal Brown.
His recklessness terrified me when I flew in dog-fights with him. If
anyone got on our tail he would, regardless of our speed, slam the
throttle shut, drop full flap and undercarriage and side-slip, leaving
it to the pilot on our tail to take violent avoiding action to prevent a
mid-air collision. Hal, shouting defiance, would then pounce on his

tail as he shot past. He would have made a good fighter pilot, but he and the deputy chief flying instructor, Squadron Leader Scott, were killed at the end of the course during Hal's final flying-instructor test. Their Master spun-in while they were carrying out a forced-landing exercise. It was an incomprehensible crash, for Hal was a good pilot, Scott an even better one. It was a salutary reminder that flying has severe statutes of limitations and is no respecter of persons if they are exceeded.

The war was two years old and we were out of it and likely to be so for some time. A bunch of us were drinking heavily at The Bear in Devizes trying to cheer ourselves up when for the first and last time in my life I hit a man, a brother officer of similar rank. We were listening to the BBC nine o'clock news on the wireless, read by Alvar Lidell. Barbarossa was two months old and Kiev had just fallen. The first million of Russia's twenty million Second World War dead were totting up. I hit him when he said in a loud voice that we were on the wrong side fighting the wrong enemy. We should be on the German side fighting the Russians. It was not the first or last time I heard that remark during the war.

At the end of the CFS course I was posted as an instructor to No. 5 Service Flying Training School, Ternhill, near Shrewsbury. There was some consolation that it was an advanced flying training school. In my log-book I had been assessed as a below-average instructor, with intelligence and ability. I was peeved about the below-average indelibly stamped into my log-book until I discovered that most of my comrades had been assessed similarly on the reasonable supposition that salad-green pilots who have never instructed before must be below-average instructors. I had 206 hours' total flying time.

I started to grow up at Tern Hill. My wife and two daughters say I have not finished yet. I hope they are right. I have rarely felt or looked my age, but nobody thinks they look as old as they are.

Tern Hill was tucked away in pleasant Shropshire countryside. It was a standard pre-war RAF base with vast, cavernous hangars, sturdy brick-built dormitory blocks for the erks and neat, tree-lined roads. The aerodrome was grass and on foot seemed endless. A long drive encircling an immaculate lawn led to the officers' mess, a building in a style and setting that clearly stated important people

live here. My single bedroom overlooked tennis courts, squash
courts and a croquet lawn. The officers' mess servants were WAAF
batwomen who did all the chores. Their presence and the flowers
they put up here and there added a slightly risqué feminine touch in
a man's world. It was nice to be woken with a 'Good morning, sir',
a cup of tea and sometimes a kiss by a pretty WAAF in uniform. By
privileged selection most officers' mess WAAFs were attractive.
The rule about non-fraternisation, a court-martial offence if
broken, was discreetly ignored by the full-blooded on both sides.

As a change from the mess we occasionally used the pub just
outside the gates, the Stormy Petrel, for a quick pint. Officers used
the saloon bar, erks and WAAFs the public bar, flying cadets the
lounge bar. We acknowledged each other across the bar counters
but only the brave or the drunk crossed the demarcation lines. For
an evening out and secret liaisons with WAAFs we drove the fifteen
miles to Shrewsbury. It was a long drive back in the blackout, with
only slits in masked headlights, cat's eyes not yet invented and an
occasional lonely searchlight seeking nuisance raiders. Petrol was
rationed but we pooled our rations, topping up sometimes with
blue-tinted aircraft petrol; another court-martial offence.

To my surprise I enjoyed instructing for the first few months. It
was a relief to have finished training, though not learning. To be my
own boss in the air, at last the puppeteer rather than the puppet. It
was nice being God to flying cadets, nursing them to wings
standard. Each course lasted three months. I took a vicarious
pleasure when I saw them wearing their wings for the first time at
the end of each course. The aircraft were again Masters I and III.
Masters were dogging me. Thank God there were a few battered
old Hurricanes as well.

Instructing improved my own flying. Having to set an example I
had to curb my flashy instincts and fly by the book. It was tiresome.
Like F/Lt. Hall at Cranwell, I became true to my own self only
when I grabbed a Hurricane after a day's instructing and played the
fool out of sight.

It was some time before I acquired the confidence to let the pupil
fly himself into trouble and not take over the controls too soon.
Instructors sat in the back seat behind the pupil, hands and feet
poised over the flying controls and throttle ready to pounce at the
last moment. I was still uneasy about loops and sweated it out when

73

I knew a pupil was looping too tightly or too loosely. It took an effort to keep my hands and feet to myself when hanging upside down at 10,000 feet at the top of a bad loop, with nothing on the airspeed indicator but the maker's name, waiting for the inevitable stall.

An average of about one fatal crash and three or four minor accidents a month kept instructors from being too sanguine about their work. The thrill of tragedy swept briefly throughout the base when somebody was killed, but most of us got used to the suddenness of death in flying, of comrades sharing the breakfast table and being dead by lunch time. There were many ways of getting killed. A Master landing at night crashed into a bulldozer parked on the edge of the aerodrome. There was nothing left of the Master airframe bigger than a matchstick. Instructor and pupil killed. I watched one of my pupils killed when his engine failed shortly after take-off on his first flight in a Hurricane. In horror I shouted 'No-no-no!' as he tried to turn back, stalled and dived in vertically on the edge of the aerodrome. After the wreckage had finished burning I found a filled shoe. During his training he must have been told a dozen times: never turn back but crash-land straight ahead if the engine fails on take-off. A pupil dropped a wing shortly after taking off on his first solo night flight. His speed built up and he pulled back on the control column without first levelling the wings. This tightened the turn and he spiralled into the ground and blew up. The only bonfire that Guy Fawkes night. A Master flew at a gentle angle into trees at night on the cross-wind leg before the final landing approach. Instructor and pupil killed. It was assumed that each thought the other was flying the aeroplane. Two Hurricanes collided playing the fool over the aerodrome, killing two senior instructors. We minded when somebody was killed, but we minded more when it was an instructor; he was kith and kin. We minded for them all that they were killed on active service rather than killed in action.

I well remember my twenty-first birthday, for on that day, 29 March 1942, I flew a Spitfire for the first time. Jaded instructors were occasionally given a treat by being sent to an Operational Training Unit for a few days to fly operational type aircraft.

I went to No. 53 Spitfire OTU at Llandow, near Swansea, nerves tingling and hands itching in anticipation. The Hurricane was a magnificent machine, but the Spitfire was the ultimate fighting aeroplane. The queen of the skies, a dream to fly and beautiful. There was not a pilot alive who did not yearn to fly it.

The pilot who showed me the Spitfire's tits and knobs seemed oblivious that this was the greatest moment of my life, so far, as I climbed awkwardly into the cockpit of one of the greatest aircraft of all time. It was not a fat man's aeroplane; the cockpit fitted snugly like a welcoming embrace. Like most British aircraft of the time the cockpit was an untidy mess, cluttered with afterthoughts. Ergonomics was not part of British designers' vocabulary. The undercarriage handle was on the right-hand side, like the Hurricane. It was perverse of both designers, Camm and Mitchell, to put the handle on the wrong side, necessitating changing hands on the controls at the critical moment of take-off. Richard Hillary was right when he said the white enamel handle looked like a lavatory plug. The Spitfire was, of course, a single-seater. There would be no dual instruction. It felt much smaller than the Hurricane. It was an odd adjective to apply to the most formidable fighter of its day but I wanted to call it dainty. The long nose completely obscured the view forward for it did not droop at the end like the Hurricane's. With a last few words of advice and a smile of encouragment from the instructor I taxied out to the runway. People watched as I taxied past. Nobody ignores a Spitfire on the move. The Spitfire's undercarriage retracted outwards giving the wheels a very narrow track of only 5' 8½", making the long nose sway and curtsy alarmingly as I zig-zagged along the taxi-track to see where I was going. It would have been an even better aircraft had the wheels retracted inwards like the Mustang's. The Hurricane had prepared me for the Spitfire but I was astonished at the acceleration and lightness of control as I opened the throttle to take-off power and roared down the runway. With that long nose it was a game of blind man's buff and sideways spatial vision until the tail came up and I could see along the nose. It was unnerving to recall the instructor's comment that in the take-off position the tips of the three-bladed propeller are only 9½ inches from the ground.

I knew half-way down the runway that everything that had been said about the Spitfire was true. It was so easy to fly I swopped hands during the take-off run and flew with my left hand, poising my right hand over the undercarriage lever so that I could retract the wheels the moment we were airborne – a fighter pilot's conceit.

Climbing high over the Bristol Channel and with the sun shining a welcome on a perfect early spring day, I felt the exultation that perfection in any form brings. I gambolled and frolicked and looped and rolled and sang alone with the clouds in the sky on my twenty-first birthday. I would not have changed places with anybody on earth. The Spitfire, nonpareil, responded as though it was anthropomorphic. I have flown over a hundred different types of aircraft but none surpassed the Spitfire for the sheer joy of flight.

I suddenly remembered where I was and turned east towards St. Athan, just down the road. It was a poignant moment when I looked down from 5,000 feet in this glorious aeroplane on my AC2 U/T past. I could not resist it. With throttle wide open I dived and shot across St. Athan flat out at nought feet, pulled up into a vertical victory roll and disappeared over the horizon before anybody could take my number. Another court-martial offence.

Of course, as I was to discover later, the Spitfire had its failings. The narrow undercarriage track made it tricky for inexperienced pilots when landing in a cross-wind. It was very heavy on the ailerons at high speed. The flashy fighter-pilot landing approach, though very satisfying, wasn't all show either. With that long nose a steep gliding approach and final turn was essential to keep the runway in view for as long as possible when landing. It is also a fair-weather-only aeroplane. Its renowned sensitivity on the controls, particularly the elevators, was a drawback when flying on instruments, especially in turbulence. It is the worst aeroplane I have flown in such conditions. It was a poor night flyer too with its narrow undercarriage and exhaust flames blindingly just below the line of sight.

It was a twenty-first to remember, particularly when on my return to Tern Hill I discovered that I had been promoted to Flying Officer and recategorised as an average flying instructor. Half a century later I visited the RAF Battle of Britain museum at Hendon and quite by chance saw that same Spitfire, No. X4590, in the static display with several other veteran aircraft. I stroked the wing-tip in an overwhelming surge of nostalgia and was sharply told by an attendant to take my hand away. I did not bother to explain.

Chapter 10

I HAD BEEN instructing for nine months. It should not be long now before I got a posting to a fighter squadron. With America and Japan now in the war it had become a true world war. There was a lot for a fighter pilot to do. I could almost feel the mauve and white DFC medal ribbon on my chest.

A month later I was posted to Canada, as an instructor, a posting as divorced from combat as it was possible to be. My CO sympathised but there was nothing he or anybody could do. Military wheels in motion are inexorable. Going to Canada meant instructing for at least another year. I felt like shooting myself in the foot.

It rained as we sailed down the Clyde in the troopship *SS Batory* and met the rest of the convoy off the Isle of Arran. We were glad of the rain and the poor visibility as we headed into the U-boat infested North Atlantic. There were about fifteen ships in the convoy, mostly merchant ships and tankers. Our escort was two toy-sized navy corvettes. Each ship trailed a canvas cone at the end of a long rope to help the ships keep station in poor visibility.

The *Batory* was a comfortable Polish ship not yet stripped down to troopship standards, at least on the first-class deck. We played bridge in the reflecting sheen of mahogany panelling. The dining tables welcomed us with huge blocks of butter, roast beef and steaks and eggs and cream and bananas, things we had not seen for two years. The bar was stuffed with cigarettes and drinks on display rather than under the counter. We ate and drank and smoked our way across the Atlantic in between submarine alarms.

I stood for hours at the ship's rail watching our agonisingly slow progress across the grey immensity of the Atlantic Ocean. The two corvettes would have been no match for a U-boat pack. Hour after hour, day after day we ploughed through either heavy seas or fog. I thought of Lindbergh fifteen years earlier flying alone in the opposite direction on and on and on as though to eternity over this vast, lonely ocean.

No. 31 Service Flying Training School, Kingston, Ontario, was

77

an RAF station recently established to train Fleet Air Arm pilots under the Commonwealth Air Training Scheme.

If one had been in the mood to appreciate it, Kingston was delightfully situated among the aptly named Thousand Islands at the north-east corner of the great Lake Ontario where the St. Lawrence river begins its long journey to the Atlantic. At the other end of the lake was the Niagara Falls. Only ten miles to the east was the border bridge that crossed the St. Lawrence into the USA. The United States of America! What a thought that was for a working-class chap whose horizons would normally have been limited to the boundaries of Fulham and Southend.

It was a shock to discover that Canada was prim. Liquor was stringently rationed and women were not permitted in bars in most Canadian provinces, including Ontario. It was a fact of Canadian life at odd variance with its rugged, masculine image. It did not affect us on base for we had booze and female visitors galore in the officers' mess and yacht club on the lake, but it was not surprising that we spent our weekend leaves in the flesh-pots of Montreal, Quebec, where the restrictions did not apply, rather than dull, Presbyterian Toronto where they emphatically did.

When flying north the narrow, horizontal, populated belt of Canada soon petered out to be replaced by the magnificent, endless, virgin forests, rivers and lakes of the then uncharted north. In autumn, when we flew low-level cross-countries, the view from the air of the untouched and uninhabited forests changing from green to endless hues of russet and copper lent moment to that lovely Canadian expression, the fall. In winter, mighty Lake Ontario froze for several miles out from its shores and the smaller lakes and rivers froze over completely. Sky and land became blinding white with snow and glare and we wore sun-glasses when we flew. As I looked down in the depths of winter on the snow-covered forests and frozen lakes I knew, sitting behind the roar of the engine, that down there was a private, infinite silence, stillness and peace. I was seeing more of Canada's unsullied secrets than do most Canadians. In summer I was surprised to discover it was so hot we wore khaki tropical uniform.

The pupils were Fleet Air Arm cadets and wore ratings' uniform. The flying instructors were RAF. Some of the ground instructors were Royal Navy. Though cadets always treat their flying instructors with huge respect, the naval cadets, being part of the senior service, managed a hint of patronage towards the parvenus of the RAF. On graduation they were all commissioned, unlike the RAF, as Sub Lieutenants and wore their wings on their right sleeve; a daft place to wear them, I thought.

The aeroplanes were American-built Harvard AT6s, the most successful advanced training aircraft of the war. It was a rugged, stubby, two-seater in tandem monoplane, fitted with a Pratt and Whitney Wasp radial engine. It was hideously noisy owing to the propeller tips exceeding the speed of sound. I felt sorry for civilians living within ten miles of the aerodrome, particularly those incarcerated in the huge penitentiary below our normal take-off path. The Harvard had a tendency to ground loop on landing. Compared with the Master it was ugly and lacking that design charisma that great aircraft possess, but it was exceptionally reliable and trained thousands of Allied pilots. For light relief we were able to fly an old Fairey Battle and a Westland Lysander used for towing drogues when the comedian Jimmy Edwards, the tower-in-chief, was not flying them. His job was even more boring than ours but he had the last laugh. He soon got a posting back to England and combat and won the DFC. There was also a veteran Supermarine Walrus amphibian for air-sea rescue duties. It was like flying a pram and could often be seen anchored in the middle of Lake Ontario with fishing rods sticking out of the cockpit windows.

A New Zealand instructor, Johnny Pierce, was killed with his pupil mock dog-fighting at nought feet. He had been the officers' mess librarian in his spare time. Tempted by a budget of 100 dollars a month to buy new books, I volunteered for the vacancy. It coincided with my discovery of contemporary American novelists. With Hemingway, Scott Fitzgerald, Dos Passos, Thurber, Steinbeck, John O'Hara, Marquand, Faulkner and Sinclair Lewis in their prime, it was a good period of American literature to have 100 dollars a month to spend. I re-organised the library from Aristotle to Zola around that marvellous Modern Library series published by Random House. Unsurprisingly I was very welcome at Kingston's only tiny bookshop. The owner was intrigued by the dichotomy of my passion for and relative ignorance of literature. He carried on where Jennifer had left off, including correcting my pronunciation of Proust, Pepys, Donne, Goethe and Nietzsche. There were complaints from my brother officers that my choice of books and magazines was too cerebral. In deference I added Peter Cheyney, Raymond Chandler and Wodehouse to the bookshelves and *Esquire* and *Life* to the *New Yorker* magazine.

Chapter 11

IN THE SUMMER of 1943, having saved up 700 dollars – Canadian and American dollars were par and the pound was worth four dollars – I arranged three weeks' leave and set off on my grand tour of the United States of America. My immediate target was New York. My ultimate destination was Hollywood, California, 2,500 miles away. I had been in love with Deanna Durbin for years.

For the sheer fun of it I walked across the Thousand Islands bridge into America. I was bubbling with excitement as I took my first step on the soil of the USA. The American immigration officials were very suspicious, despite my uniform. Only ne'er-do-wells walk in America. I caught a Greyhound coach for New York and sat up front next to the driver. The coach was fast and comfortable. While the other passengers snoozed, my eyes ached with looking at America. I did not want to miss a thing.

It was dark when we approached New York. I saw it glinting on the horizon like a vast floodlit glacier long before we arrived. Every light in every office in every skyscraper seemed to be on. Several of the higher buildings wore their own toupée of cloud. As we entered those canyon streets up to a thousand feet deep, the scarcely believable height of the skyline was not oppressive, for the streets were parallel or at right-angles to each other and looking down the long straight blocks of streets one could see the distant horizon. It gave a feeling of light and space lacking in higgledy-piggledy London. I got off the coach near Times Square and walked around in circles, mouth agape at the sheer audacity of the skyline.

America did not seem like a country at war. No black-out, no weariness, no shortages, no rationing, no fear of the sky. Shops were full and stayed open late. There were many men of my age not wearing uniform and few recognised mine. America's Second World War was, like its first, being fought at arm's length. I found a small hotel off Times Square. It was the first time I had stayed in an hotel and I made my bed. Cute, thought the chambermaid.

I did the usual things, but for me they were not usual. I whooshed up and down elevators for fun; their rate of climb equalled a

Spitfire. I looked down from the then highest building in the world, the Empire State building. I climbed up 152 feet inside the tortured copper of the Statue of Liberty, pausing to catch my breath at the forehead viewing platform, before finally reaching the top of the raised arm and the magnificent view of New York's waterfront. I smoked Camels and Lucky Strike and drank bourbon poured with a liberal flourish into ice-filled glasses. There were no licensing hours. I drank cold beer in warm bars after years of drinking warm beer in cold bars. It felt odd to be able to get a drink at four o'clock in the morning or the afternoon. The pavements were spattered with flattened chewing gum. Everybody seemed to smile widely as if to show off excellent teeth. Most men, young or old, had crew-cuts and wore kipper ties. All teenage girls wore bobby-socks, had plucked eyebrows and looked incredibly healthy and knowing. Busts were in fashion and emphasised. I was astonished at the number of coloured people. There was no doubt that at that time they were considered, and considered themselves, second-class citizens.

I went to Carnegie Hall and listened to Beethoven, to Radio City to watch Hoagy Carmichael at the piano and the incredible Rockettes chorus line. I clip-clopped around Central Park at midnight in a reproduction brougham. I went to the Algonquin Hotel on W-44th Street and gawped at Thurber, Dorothy Parker, John O'Hara, Lillian Ross, Henry Miller and others from the *New Yorker* magazine sitting at their round table. I went to Harlem and listened to inspired jazz in seedy basements.

Everybody loved the British and Churchill and seemed to have listened to Ed Murrow's broadcasts from the blitz in London, and I rarely paid for my drinks. I did not have the heart to disappoint them when they asked whether I had fought in the Battle of Britain. They thought I was very young to have been so brave. I looked and felt a wide-eyed seventeen. Everybody just luuuved my accent. I was tempted to stay on in New York, but the West beckoned.

By courtesy of the American Army Air Corps I hitch-hiked on a DC4 Skymaster the 2,500 odd miles from New York to Los Angeles. The weather was good all the way as we flew steadily west. States with evocative names slid past underneath the wings like a travelogue: Pennsylvania, Ohio, Indiana, Illinois, Missouri, Kansas, Colorado, New Mexico, Arizona, Nevada. I was bleary-eyed when we finally crossed over the Sierra Nevada mountains and slid down to California and the shores of the Pacific Ocean.

I got a room with bath at the Roosevelt Hotel in Hollywood. Almost opposite my bedroom window was the Grauman Chinese cinema where film premières were held and the stars of Hollywood imprinted their hands and feet in concrete for posterity. Prop-lagged, I ordered bourbon on the rocks from room service and had a bath. Despite the fact that I was in the glamour capital of the world I dozed off. When I woke up I looked in the telephone directory but Deanna Durbin was ex-directory. I had an inspiration and tele-phoned the British Consulate in Los Angeles. An amused woman's voice regretted that she did not have Miss Durbin's telephone number, but she gave me the name and telephone number of one of several Hollywood residents who offered hospitality to visiting British servicemen. The name was Richard Day. His wife answered the telephone. She told me to pack my bags, pay the bill and wait in the hotel lobby. She would be there in thirty minutes. I confirmed that I would be wearing uniform.

Carole Day was a youthful, middle-aged woman, not a beauty but with the warmth, openness, generosity, vivacity and curiosity about others which I was discovering everywhere in America. She was also a chatterbox and an Anglophile. The car was a huge, pillar-box red Packard convertible, with a bonnet even longer than a Bentley and immaculate white-wall tyres. The hood was down in the warm, exotic Californian sunshine. Carole drove a roundabout way home to give me a brief introductory tour of Hollywood. That is Beverly Hills, she pointed out. That's Paramount studios, this is Sunset Boulevard, there's Santa Monica beach, that is Ronald Colman's house, Greta Garbo lives down there, Constance Bennett over there, that's 20th Century Fox where Richard works, that was Humphrey Bogart driving that car, this is Hollywood and Vine, the crossroads of Hollywood. Wait here and you will see everyone. Trees and shrubs I had never seen before lined the boulevards: olive, palm, eucalyptus, jacaranda, orange, lemon and tamarind. On a hill a large, tatty, wooden sign proclaimed HOLLYWOOD. The D was crooked. I told her about Deanna Durbin. She laughed and said no problem. Richard Day was a distinguished art director at 20th Century Fox, with endless major screen credits to his name, the yardstick of Hollywood success. He and his wife were on first-name terms with most of the luminaries of Hollywood, including directors and writers.

We twisted and turned to the top of Laurel Canyon where their Spanish style bungalow overlooked Hollywood. Britain and the war were on another planet.

Richard Day was a cultured, quiet American. Sadly I saw little of him. The producer of the film he was working on had decided at the last moment to change the period in which the film was set and Richard was urgently re-doing the art work – everything from architecture to clothes, *objets d'art* to haircuts – accordingly. Art directors have nightmares about anachronisms. Autobiographers too.

I stayed with them for ten days. They loaned me their third car, a chain-driven Fraser Nash open sports car. It stood out even among the Rolls-Royce, Packards, Dusenbergs and Cadillacs. With RAF cap at a jaunty angle I drove for hours up and down Sunset and Main, Hollywood and Vine. Carole thought I looked hollow-cheeked and fed me the whole gamut of Spanish, Mexican and American food, including T-bone steaks topped with sunny-side-up fried eggs for breakfast. I have never eaten so much before or since. In Britain, food rationing was down to 4 oz. butter, 4 oz. cheese, 8 oz. sugar, 4 oz. tea, 1s 10d of meat and half an egg per person per week. I probably ate a week's rations at one sitting at Carole's table but I refused to feel guilty. I would have gone back to the UK like a shot given the opportunity. I sent food parcels to my mother and Jack but they never arrived. Victims of U-boats, no doubt. It added to the air of unreality to sunbathe on the patio listening to the news on the radio, interspersed with commercials. The Russians were on the offensive in southern Russia, the Americans had started their island-hopping offensive in the Pacific, the Germans had been kicked out of North Africa and the Allies had returned to Europe with the invasion of Sicily. God forgive me but I did not want the Allies to do too well. Save some of the war for me.

During those ten days I had dinner tête-à-tête with Susan Hayward at the Ambassador Hotel, danced with the enchanting Ann Miller and Ann Sheridan, the oomph girl, to the music of Xavier Cugat and his band at the Coconut Grove night-club – at that time perhaps the most glamorous spot on earth and a long way from Fulham. I got drunk on rum and coke with William Bendix,

Alan Ladd, Lili Damita and Errol Flynn on his yacht. I had lunch at the Brown Derby with Sir Charles Aubrey Smith and, of all people, Gracie Fields. I expected Gracie to burst into 'Salleeee, Salleeee, pride of our alleeee', at any moment. Aubrey Smith was disappointed that I was not a cricketer. I had drinks and played poker with James Cain, John Huston and Ben Hecht at a stag party. Hecht was an Anglophobe, with strong views about Zionism and Palestine. I met Howard Hughes and was to fly with him to San Francisco as his co-pilot, but his private Lockheed Electra aircraft became unserviceable at the last moment. I listened live to Count Basie, Duke Ellington, the incomparable Harry James, a hollow-cheeked, skinny Frank Sinatra, and the hilarious Spike Jones and his City Slickers band, whose instruments were mostly saucepans and kitchen implements. I had my hand crushed by Jack Dempsey and played squash with Mickey Rooney at the Beverly Hills Sports Club. I was introduced on a film-set to a devastating, twelve-year-old Elizabeth Taylor, with a tame jackdaw sitting on her shoulder. Her violet eyes were exquisite, her bosom outstanding even then. Whenever I had an idle moment I drove to the Beverly Hills Hotel, sat at the bar and gawped at the faces from the silver screen. More than fifty years later, my youthful visit to Hollywood, at the peak of its glamour as a purveyor of dreams, seems a dream itself.

I was invited by a mega-star to spend the weekend at his beach cottage in Mexico. It was a splendid drive south in his yellow Dusenberg with the sun shining, the hood down and the aptly named Pacific Ocean within touching distance on our right most of the way. Romantic place-names rolled by: Long Beach, Laguna Beach, San Clemente, Oceanside, La Jolla. The dramatic impact of the US Navy base at San Diego with grey, battle-scarred men-o'-war at anchor reminded me that there was a war on somewhere. We crossed the Mexican border at Tijuana and continued south through Rasarito and El Descanto to his cottage at Todos Santos Bay, south of the border, down Mexico way.

We spent the evening in the local village eating Mexican food and getting blind drunk on tequila. The penny dropped half-way through the night when he barged into my bedroom stark naked, with an erection. I fled and spent the rest of the night in the Dusenberg. He apologised the next morning. He is still alive and as he has not stepped out of the closet it would be ungallant to name him.

I did not meet Deanna Durbin. She was on holiday at home, in Canada.

I hitch-hiked by air back to Kingston, via San Francisco, Chicago and Detroit. During my absence I had been promoted to Flight-Lieutenant, appointed a Flight Commander and recategorised as an above-average instructor. I would happily have forgone the lot for a posting back to England and combat.

I did get a posting six months later. Not east back to England but west, far west, to Medicine Hat, Alberta. Medicine Hat! I was outraged. Instructing again. I had been instructing for over two and a half years, far longer than most, except those considered too old for combat. Going to No. 34 Service Flying Training School at Medicine Hat probably meant the war would end before I could see any action. It was grossly unfair and unusual. It was not as though I had committed a misdemeanour demanding penance. Trembling with rage at the injustice I stormed out of the adjutant's office after he had told me the news, grabbed a Harvard and made my protest in the sky. I beat up Kingston town at nought feet and then the aerodrome. It was a spectacular, noisy protest, for I had flown the Harvard for 1500 hours and could make it talk, and did not really care whether I killed myself or not. I saw a crowd of officers including the diminutive figure of the commanding officer standing in front of the officers' mess watching my antics. To finish off I dived at them, I was told they ducked, and zoomed up into a vertical climbing roll, topped by an ozzle-twizzle, a spectacular vertical flick manoeuvre forbidden in a Harvard. I had taken off trembling with anger, I landed trembling with apprehension. Christ, what had I done! It was a serious court-martial offence.

The Chief Flying Instructor was waiting for me on the tarmac after I landed. Without a word he drove me to the CO's office. They both listened to my explanation. I knew the CO, Group Captain le Poer Trench, had a soft spot for me since I had taken over the library for he was widely read and approved of my additions. He had, of course, been unaware of the details of my instructing career. I detected a gleam of sympathy in their eyes. The CO picked up the telephone and spoke to the Senior Medical Officer. It was arranged that I should see the RAF psychiatrist at Group Headquarters in Toronto. The CO was trying to save my bacon.

The psychiatrist, having shown much interest in my relationship with my mother, decided I was sane and wrote a sympathetic report recommending that I be posted back to the UK as a fighter pilot. The RAF could not let me get away with that. The CO put it to me that it was either Medicine Hat or a court-martial. I caught the train for the 1500 mile journey west to the prairies.

Medicine Hat, in the province of Alberta, was then a classic one-horse, one-road town in the middle of nowhere. Before the arrival of the RAF its sole *raison d'être* was as a watering-hole for the great, thirsty, Canadian Pacific Railway locomotives snorting their way between the Atlantic and the Pacific. I arrived in a blizzard at three o'clock on the morning of New Year's Day 1944, Medicine Hat's coldest night on record, some 55 degrees below zero. When I got off the train, the only passenger to alight, I was mush-mushing towards a dim light when a vicious gust of wind and snow toppled me down some iced steps. Limping blindly in deep snow with a strained ankle that grounded me for two weeks and carrying two large suitcases, I found a Good Samaritan station master who thawed me out in his den. There was, he said, no chance of my getting to the aerodrome that night, the roads were blocked and the telephone lines were down. After painfully taking off my shoe and sock we looked at my hugely swollen ankle and decided there was nothing we could do about it except give it the Indian snow treatment as he called it. I dozed in front of his log fire with a mug of tea, my foot in a bucket of snow, feeling sorry for myself. Fate was unkind to plonk me down in the middle of the remote Canadian prairies on a blizzard night, with a busted ankle and only more bloody instructing to look forward to. What a way to fight a war.

I was stuck at Medicine Hat for nine endless months, critical months that covered the Allied invasion of Europe and the beginning of the end of the European war. I had mixed feelings as I pushed the coloured pins forward on the war-map in my bedroom. The aeroplanes were Harvards again. There was some mild consolation when I was appointed examining officer and now sat monosyllabic in the back seat, testing RAF cadets for their mid-course progress and their final Wings test, instead of shouting endless patter down the Gosport speaking-tube. I had come a long way. I had become a demi-god. The erk from Cranwell was now deciding who would wear those golden wings. I usually examined four cadets a day, two in the morning, two in the afternoon. The job became stupefyingly routine unless I came across an exceptionally gifted cadet or a borderline case. In between making notes on my knee-pad I looked down, sometimes up, on a lonely, prairie landscape that was an endless, muffling, blanket of fathom-deep snow in the arctic winter and a limitless, rippling golden sea of wheat in sub-tropical summer. Winter and summer the only features on the ground were isolated villages, with massive, white-painted granaries and the single railway line and telegraph poles that linked them straight as a die. In a world at war it was a peaceful scene. Remarkably peaceful, bearing in mind that in addition to my own paltry 150 mph in the Harvard, I was spinning with the earth at 1,000 mph, and orbiting the sun at 66,000 mph. With so much fury and motion it is surprising there is any peace and quiet on earth.

In the sixth year of the war, November 1944, my posting to combat finally came through. I doubt if any pilot of similar age who joined the RAF before the war had to wait so long for action. It is extraordinary that I had spent my entire RAF career so far in Training Command. I deeply resented it at the time, though it almost certainly saved my life. I riffle through my log-books sometimes, looking at the names of the sixty-odd RAF and Fleet Air Arm pilots I taught to fly, wondering what deeds they have done, what happened to them. There were scores more who passed through my hands as Flight Commander and examining officer. Over three years of flying instructing, over 2,000 instructional flying hours in wartime. Chaps have got the AFC for less.

'Well I'm buggered,' I said, when details of my posting came through. I could scarcely believe it. Instead of returning immediately to Britain and Tally-ho on Spitfires, I was to travel yet another thousand miles further west to No. 6 Operational Training Unit, Comox, Vancouver Island, for a conversion course on Dakota aircraft, before joining Transport Command in England. Transport Command! Flying bloody great pantechnicons around the sky without a gun on them. Moving troops and supplies and chucking out paratroopers, when I had been training fighter pilots for over three years. I felt paranoic.

One cannot get much farther west than Comox. It was a Royal Canadian Air Force base on the north-east of Vancouver Island. The Rocky Mountains flanked it to the east, the Yukon to the north and the Pacific Ocean to the west. Siberia was closer than Britain.

I finished the conversion course with an above-average assessment as a transport pilot and navigator and at last turned 180 degrees and headed back east for England. A bunch of us caught the Canadian Pacific train for that magnificent 5,000-mile train journey across Canada from Vancouver to Halifax, from the Pacific to the Atlantic. We spent four fairly drunken days, feet up in the observation car or sleeping in our bunks, happy that we were going to war. We crossed eight of Canada's nine provinces as we wound through the Rockies, along the Prairies and skirted the Great Lakes before reaching the Eastern Seaboard. At Halifax that grand old lady of the seas, the four-funnelled *SS Aquitania*, waited for us for a quick, unescorted, six-day dash across the Atlantic. During the voyage I was given permission to climb down five flights into the ship's bowels to see the furnaces where my father once worked. It was like descending into Dante's inferno. We docked at Liverpool on 9 May 1945. VE Day. The day the European war was officially over. I was consoled that the Second World War still continued in the Far East against the Japanese.

Chapter 12

I HAD BEEN abroad for three years. There was much to notice, old and new, in Britain. Inevitably, after the New World, everything looked old and worn-out. It was only in the countryside that Britain still excelled. It was good to see from the air the patchwork fields and the inconsequential hedges and woods after the vast, hedgeless prairies and compass-straight roads and borders of North America. London felt and looked like an old sock, battered and darned but still warm. Nettles and poppies grew among the tragic rubble of bomb-sites, like wreaths on a grave. The blackouts were coming down, the lights were coming on. Every cinema had long, extraordinarily patient queues. All cars were old. The gas-masks and menacing skies had gone but the civilian adult population looked haggard and tired, nearly six years of war etched on their faces. I would not have liked being a civilian in those years. Unlike servicemen they had no uplifting moments of victory, travel or adventure in their war. The children looked pink-cheeked, saucy and fit; a side-effect of food-rationing and the shortage of rich food and sweets. And war is fun at that age. Newspapers had only four pages but still carried advertisements for things one could not buy. There was less forelock-touching; everybody was 'luv' or 'mate'. I was not surprised when the Labour Party won a landslide victory in the first post-war general election. The continuing Japanese war seemed distant, a nuisance rather than a menace.

I soon realised when I arrived unexpectedly at home in Worcester Park for two weeks' leave that it was no longer home to me. I felt and was a stranger to my mother, Jack and the neighbours. I was treated royally, of course, for after all I was a young Flight-Lieutenant pilot named Levett, but it was soon noticed that I was not wearing medal ribbons. Some also commented on how fortunate I was to have spent the last three years in lands of milk and honey when their backs were to the wall.

But it was the mind-boggling provincialism of English suburbia that alienated me. Identical houses, identical lace curtains, identical privet hedges, identical tiny lawns, identical cats and yapping dogs and, worst of all, identical inconclusive conversation. When I was trapped in my mother's cramped living-room, listening to endless platitudes, my eyes would glaze and I would think of the Pacific Ocean lapping the coast at La Jolla, sunset over the Rocky Mountains or kissing Susan Hayward goodnight. I found it difficult to believe that my mother had lived through two world wars and Jack one, so unchanged were they. It made me realise that winning or losing a war makes little difference to ordinary people. It was callow and unloving, but I could not wait to get back to my true home, the Royal Air Force and the officers' mess.

After leave I was posted to No. 233 Squadron, based at Odiham, Hampshire. An operational squadron at last. I was delighted to discover on arrival that the squadron was preparing for departure to the Far East and the Japanese war. There was still time for heroics, though it would be difficult being heroic in a Dakota.

I joined up with my first crew: Pilot Officers John Hardstaff, co-pilot, George Thomas, navigator and Jack Burridge, wireless operator. They were all sprogs with new uniforms and, as I was an experienced pilot, pleased to have me as their skipper.

After a few days of painful inoculations and graphic lectures on tropical diseases, hygiene and jungle survival, the Squadron took off and set course on the 8,000-mile flight to Imphal, near the Indo-Burmese border. Our task would be to supply logistic support for the 14th Army on its push through Burma and Malaya and on to Japan.

I began to enjoy flying the Dakota. After years of flying single-engined aeroplanes, tightly strapped into a cramped seat, doing all the work – pre-flight calculations, navigation, map-reading, engine-watching, worrying about fuel, etc. – I now had a crew to do the chores, with sophisticated radio compasses and radar to point the way and an automatic pilot. What is more, I could get out of my seat, stretch my legs and drink a cup of thermos tea. It seemed a strange thing to do in an aeroplane. I still kept a cynical eye on things. With more engines, more equipment and a crew, there are more things to go wrong.

That long flight was an astonishing confirmation of the size and might of the British Empire. It had not yet started to disintegrate and, as we flew steadily eastwards, the red blobs on school maps came to life. I had already seen one of the biggest blobs of all, Canada, but for hour after hour, day after hotter day, we flew east at

145 mph over, and landed on, territory ruled directly or indirectly by Great Britain: Malta, Cyprus, Egypt, Palestine, Jordan, Iraq, Mesopotamia, the Persian Gulf, what is now Pakistan, India and Burma and on and on around the world. We soon began to think it normal to land throughout the Near, Middle and Far East and hear only English spoken as the lingua franca and to be called Sir, Sahib, or Bwana by the natives. The sun then truly did not set on the British Empire.

We were about half-way to Imphal when we heard the news about Hiroshima and Nagasaki. By the time we arrived at Imphal the Japanese had surrendered and the Second World War was over. God forgive me, but the only thing I could think of to say was: 'Oh, shit!'

What did you do in the war, Daddy?

Imphal is tucked away in Assam, in the north-east corner of India, a few miles west of the Burmese border and not that far from China. It was the gateway to India from the east and the scene of bitter and protracted fighting when the Japanese were at last halted in their advance westward. Had Imphal fallen India might have followed.

It was good to have travelled so far that everything that met the eye was exotic, foreign and different. We lived primitively in ram-shackle, straw huts and slept on straw palliasses on simple wooden frames strung with flax. Mosquito nets were *de rigueur*. We shaved and washed in cold water in canvas bowls and showered using pierced petrol cans. The locals were friendly and became our servants for two rupees a day. Cholera and malaria were rampant, the water was boiled tasteless, the food inedible, the Indian bottled beer weak and flat, the cigarettes in round cans of fifty. We swallowed six Mepacrine anti-malarial tablets a day, two after every meal, giving us complexions like the Chinese. Rumour had it that Mepacrine was an aphrodisiac and also brought on temporary sterility, an ideal combination, but the Medical Officer said the wish was fathering the thought. It was academic anyway. For it was thought that if officers had relations with native women the British Empire would disintegrate, and the nearest white women were 400 miles away in Calcutta. We wore open-necked shirts, shorts and sandals under the ever-present sun. Lizards the size of dogs dozed tamely in the dusty heat. Twigs turned into insects at a touch. The surrounding jungle echoed with grunts, snarls, mating calls, bird-song and the gossip of monkeys. At night the air was crowded with whining, blatantly bloodthirsty, malarial mosquitoes the size of horse-flies, and bug-eyed moths with three-inch wingspans, buzzing and hovering around the candle and hurricane lights like manic autogyros. And then there was the elemental drama of the monsoon period, when the rain was so heavy it stung when it hit bare skin, when peaceful, small rivers became mile-wide muddy torrents and we watched the sky in awe as mighty electrical storms turned night into day. During the month of September we sloshed about in 61 inches of rain – UK average rainfall is 30 inches a year.

It turned out there was something for us to do. The long Chindit campaign behind Japanese lines and the final battles of the war had destroyed most of the already sparse communications, railways, bridges and roads. Northern Burma was virtually cut off. In addition, the Japanese in their final death-throes had adopted a scorched-earth policy. To make matters worse the rice crop was poor. For the first time in Burmese history there was famine in the isolated jungle and mountainous areas of the north.

233 Squadron saved the situation with an emergency airlift. For five months we flew in food and essential supplies. Our twenty-five Dakotas and fifty crews, based at Imphal, flew some thirty sorties a day, seven days a week. We landed on short strips hacked out of the jungle, or dropped the loads by parachute or free-fall on almost inaccessible dropping zones marked out on the ground by Gurkhas. They had a penchant for choosing sites in narrow, deep-gorge valleys with mountains blocking the far end. I came back twice with twigs wrapped around the tail wheel. I managed to persuade myself half-way through the campaign that what I was doing was better than killing people in combat. Burmans whom we would never meet waved thanks from the dropping zones as they dodged the falling sacks. Many sacks burst on impact but we were assured by the Gurkhas that every grain was gathered.

We averaged 65 tons daily, mostly hundredweight bags of rice and salt, supplemented with cooking oil, medical supplies, ambulance work, troops and mail. One load I flew to Katha baffled me: 5,508 pounds of soap. Nowhere or nobody could be that dirty. Our maximum load with full tanks was 7,000 pounds, though we rarely carried the maximum when dropping loads, for we needed full manoeuvrability.

We lost three Dakotas and crews during the monsoon period, all by flying into clouds stuffed with mountains. Although there wasn't the wartime imperative to press on, accidents of this nature were almost inevitable during the monsoon period when we were forced to fly up narrow valleys under cumulo-nimbus thunderheads, massive cathedrals of violence that stretched from near ground-level to 30,000 feet. We all had narrow squeaks as we climbed and dived and steep-turned to keep out of cloud around the dropping zone.

We brought manna to the people of Bhamo, Lashio, Swebo, Ledo, Homalin, Tamanthi, Kohima, Katha, Muse, Hsipaw, Kengtung, Shadazup, Myitkyina, Pangsao Pass, Sumprabum, Fort Hertz and on into the foothills of the Himalayas. It was a glorious feast to be flying every day over that beautiful and dramatic landscape of jungle, rivers and majestic mountains. We got to know every curve of the three major rivers of Burma, the Salween, the Chindwin and the Irrawaddy. At sunset and sunrise scores of golden pagodas, perched on hilltops, glinted the love of Buddha and always the northern horizon was high with the white-capped Himalayas.

Myitkyina was the American Army Air Corps base for their supply flights over the Himalayas to Kunming in China, popularly known at that time as flying over the Hump. They used C46 Curtiss Commando aircraft for the three-hour flight. In the monsoon period it was probably the toughest flying in aviation history and they lost several aircraft and crews. I managed to scrounge a flight over the Hump when I was delayed at Myitkyina with engine trouble. I was lucky, for the weather was perfect. Though I remember little of my first visit to China and the squalor of Kunming, I remember the impact of crossing the Himalayas. It is impossible to exaggerate the awe-inspiring majesty, beauty and sombre silence of what I saw. The Canadian Rocky Mountains were miniatures compared with this. We were flying at 20,000 feet and still looked up at several peaks. Even the wisecracking, cigar-chewing American crew were silent and pensive on the return flight as we watched the setting sun play golden light and shadow on peaks and valleys and on snow that never melted. It was difficult to grasp that we were seeing only the edge of a mountain range 2,000 miles long, 800 miles wide and nearly six miles high.

Towards the end of the year the new rice crop was successful and some new roads, bridges and communications had been built and our operation began running down. On 15 December 1945, it was my sad task to carry out the last operational flight both of this supply campaign and of 233 Squadron, which was disbanded as of that date.

Despite the sadness of closing down, the end of many friendships and the sight of twenty-five forlorn Dakotas parked neatly along the runway with nothing to do, most members of the squadron, who would soon be demobilised from the RAF, felt that this last campaign of humanity, saving lives rather than destroying them, was an appropriate epilogue to their RAF careers and a monstrous war.

I stayed on, and to my astonishment was promoted Squadron Leader and posted to 194 Squadron – known as 'The Friendly Firm' – based at Mingaladon, Rangoon, for general transport duties on Dakotas.

Chapter 13

I WENT TO THE Indian camp tailor before leaving Imphal to have a third ring sewn on my uniform. They were creeping up nicely.

Squadron Leader is the equivalent of Major. Other officers up to and including the rank of Flight-Lieutenant must now address me as Sir. Promotions were almost unheard-of at this time, for the war was over and the RAF was contracting rapidly. I had climbed twelve places from the bottom in six years. Only seven more places to the top. I was twenty-four with plenty of time. Lofty's comment at Cardington years ago that I would do well in the Royal Air Force if I kept my nose clean seemed a more accurate prognostication than my mother's comments that I would come to a bad end if I had ideas above my station.

Mingaladon, just north of Rangoon, was a primitive wartime aerodrome. The single runway was made of PSP metal strips hinged together, undulating over mud and dust. There were three RAF Dakota Squadrons based at Mingaladon, including 194, all under canvas. As a Squadron Leader I had a large bell-tent to myself, a personal Jeep and an Indian servant. Burmans were too proud for such tasks. The monsoon rains were over. It was hot and dry and the skirts of the tents were permanently lifted.

The commanding officer of 194 Squadron was Wing Commander Penman, DSO, OBE, DFC. I was his number two. With unassuming modesty and total lack of military side he had the respect and affection of everyone on the squadron. I tried to follow his example but I confess I did enjoy being called Sir by junior officers and being listened to.

194 had become an odd-job squadron. We flew Japanese ex-POWs from Rangoon to Singapore on their way home to Japan and brought back British ex-POWs. There were occasional transport flights to India, Ceylon, Indo-China, Hong Kong and Indonesia. I pulled rank and took the more exotic ones.

The mood among the erks at Mingaladon was restive. British servicemen in Europe were being demobilised fast on a first in, first out basis. The war had been over for five months. Most servicemen had memories of mass unemployment before the war and to them jobs were still precious. Despite the victory by the Labour Party in the the general election of July 1945, there was little faith in the assurance of a brave new Beveridge world. The only fruit of victory a working-class ex-serviceman wanted was a good job.

But the erks and troops in the Far East were not being demobilised and repatriated on a first in, first out basis. Servicemen based in Britain and Europe who had joined up later were being released before those in the Far East. No explanation was offered. The erks were worried that all the good jobs would be gone by the time they caught the boat home.

Most of them had been in the Far East a long time. Many had children two or three years old whom they had never seen. Lonely for loved ones, they had lived for years in primitive conditions, under canvas, with monsoons, tropical disease, heat and boredom. There was no moaning while the war raged, but it was now all over. 'Sod it, why can't we go home?' said the erks at Mingaladon and elsewhere.

The answer was that Britain, France and Holland intended turning the clock back in the Far East to pre-war days. It is laughable now, after the total eclipse of the former colonial empires in the Far East and elsewhere, to recall that the Imperial Powers assumed that they could simply return to the pre-war status quo and re-colonise the Far East after the defeat of the Japanese. French troops were already passing through Mingaladon on their way to Indo-China and Dutch troops to the Netherlands East Indies, followed by civil servants, merchants, bank managers and entrepreneurs. British troops and RAF squadrons were re-grouping. Each colonial power was helping the other, for they were acutely aware of the domino effect should any of their former colonies gain independence.

The erks wanted no part of it, particularly if it meant staying on in the Far East to put down any natives who were getting uppity about the return of the imperialists. This was not why so many of them had voted for a socialist government. That landslide Labour Party victory made working-class men feel that forelock-touching and imperialism were things of the past. I agreed. Now that I was part of a respectable political majority I no longer felt it necessary to cloak my views in the officers' mess. I did not stand on soap-boxes to proselytise but brother-officers began calling me Comrade, Sir.

The British were returning and setting up shop as masters in
Burma, Malaya, Singapore and Hong Kong. Every week two or
three Japanese war criminals were hanged in Rangoon gaol. The
pukka sahib Gymkhana Club had re-opened in Prome Road. It was
an elegant, pre-war establishment, with verandahs, fans whirring
lazily in the ceiling, a long bar, tennis courts and swimming pool.
Membership was confined to the British civil service, serving
officers and vouched-for gentlemen from commerce. Burmans or
Indians were not permitted on the premises except as servants. It
was ever thus. Things had not changed since Orwell's Burmese
Days. Up-country, rebel Burmans were preparing to drive the
British out. I spent most evenings at the club quaffing chota pegs
and playing bridge in an atmosphere of total unreality. Hemingway
passed through Rangoon on his way back from Japan. He spent the
night at the club. He did not like Limeys. He got very drunk and
called us a lot of goddamned, decadent, Rip Van Winkles. He was
about right.

Rangoon, once the garden city of the Far East, was a shambles.
The only building that seemed untouched by war was the giant
Shwedagon pagoda, glinting with gold-leaf and rising over 300 feet
in the sunshine from the squalor of central Rangoon. In its jewel-
encrusted peak supposedly rest one of Buddha's teeth and a lock of
his hair.

The unrest among the erks culminated in a down-tools strike at one
of the RAF squadrons at Mingaladon. I do not know why it was
euphemistically referred to as a strike rather than mutiny. Perhaps
it sounded less dramatic for the Press at home. The strike was in
support of the erks' demand to be repatriated and demobilised at
the same time as those erks with equal seniority in the UK. Had
it not been for the popularity of our commanding officer the strike
would have spread to our squadron. There were heated arguments
in the officers' mess and the Gymkhana Club. At least there
were when I was present. I wished that some of my brother officers
would come out of the closet. Some of them must have voted
Labour. I was Comrade to everybody now. The fact that I did
not support the erks' methods went unnoticed in my support of
their case.

A few months before, while with 233 Squadron at Imphal, I

had formally applied for a permanent commission in the RAF. I had no idea whether I would be accepted, but as far as I knew there was nothing on my RAF record that would have precluded the possibility. Quite the contrary. I had heard nothing. Of late, however, I was beginning to doubt the wisdom of my application. These doubts were heightened when 194 Squadron was disbanded and I was posted to Group Headquarters in Rangoon. It was a staff job with a resounding title: Squadron Leader (Air) to the Senior Air Staff Officer, but it was a penguin job. I was grounded.

I sat behind a desk, swatting flies, with In-Out trays, a field telephone, a corporal and not the foggiest idea of what I was supposed to do. The few bits of paper-work that did appear in my In Tray were dealt with by the corporal. The Group Captain SASO and I loathed each other on sight. The corporal overheard him refer to me as 'Bloody Comrade Levett'.

The strike petered out. But the mould of blind obedience had been broken and the erks were treated with more care and respect. The repatriation and demobilisation procedure was reviewed and the more flagrant injustices removed. None of the striking erks or their leaders was punished and the squadron concerned was disbanded.

After months at my new desk, without touching an aeroplane, I formally cancelled my request to be considered for a permanent commission and requested release from the Royal Air Force as soon as the exigencies of the service permitted. As I was a regular RAF officer and an ex-erk my discharge from the RAF would not be routine.

It was a complex decision of heart and mind. I had been a part of the Royal Air Force for more than seven years. Seven years is not a long time in a life's span, but it is a very long time at the age of twenty-four. There had been little else but the RAF in my life. But things were beginning to go awry. If I stayed on I might be desk-bound for the rest of my career. I had become restless with instant obedience. Leftish views and a growing measure of pacifism are awkward baggage for a career officer to be carrying. I was uneasy about my involvement in the attempted re-colonisation of the Far East and elsewhere. The RAF was already engaged in military action against 'rebels' in Malaya – the same rebels who had helped

us defeat the Japanese – as were the French in Indo-China and the
Dutch in the East Indies. Inevitably there would come, sooner or
later, an order which I could not obey. It was better that the Royal
Air Force and I part amicably now.

The night I irrevocably made up my mind I got maudlin drunk
on Tom Collins at the Gymkhana Club and played Culbertson
bridge very badly. It was late but still oven-hot when I drove back
in my Jeep, windscreen down, to my tent. Under the mosquito net,
in the middle of soft Burmese night, with two candles, a rare half-
bottle of Haig and self-cremating moths for company, I held a
solitary wake for my RAF career.

With drunken brilliance I reviewed events. I worked out a tortured
analogy between my brother Jack and his crushed ankle. Jack had
clung to his ankle and had suffered ever since. I was going to
amputate myself from the RAF before suffering the same fate.
Though my leaving the RAF was not a denunciation I felt pangs of
disloyalty. The RAF had nurtured me to maturity. Had fed, clothed,
housed and paid me for seven years. Had promoted me. Had commissioned me. Had given me three thousand glorious hours in the
air. Had let me fly its Spitfires, its Hurricanes, its Mosquitoes, its
Dakotas. It had denied me the opportunity of becoming a hero, but
that was more muddle than conspiracy. It had sent me travelling
throughout the world. Had metamorphosed me from penguin into
eagle, from guttersnipe into gentleman. After all that, it was
ungallant to walk out but we had outgrown each other. The just
war was over. Unjust colonial wars loomed. The enchantment had
faded and the time had come to put the RAF away in the book of
memory.

That night my Jeep was stolen by rebels from outside my tent.

The wake was premature. The following week I was posted again,
out of harm's way. Group headquarters and the SASO had had
enough of Comrade Levett.

My new post was Commanding Officer of RAF Staging Post,
Mergui, Burma. It sounds impressive but this was the sort of
posting that pilots and erks dread. A staging post is usually a half-
way halt in the middle of nowhere, where the occasional aircraft
pops in if it is running short of petrol, or has problems. They have
no aircraft of their own and are usually desolate, lonely places,

somnolent with boredom. I was banished. I wondered if I would ever fly again for the RAF.

In other circumstances Mergui would have been idyllic. It is in southern Burma, on the west coast of the long, beautiful archipelago that stretches from Rangoon to Singapore, flanked by the Indian Ocean on one side and the Gulf of Siam on the other and not that far from the Equator. It was so hot at times that one felt one could reach out and touch the sun. Off the Mergui coast a score of exquisite islands beckoned like paradise. The River Kwai was just across the border in Thailand.

The aerodrome, a mile or two inland from the coast, was built by the Japanese during the war, with a single concrete runway and thatched straw buildings. Wild orchids, giant petunias, purple bougainvillaea, frangipani, tamarind and golden mohur trees rioted wildly everywhere against a background of impenetrable jungle. It was like a vast, extravagant Chelsea Flower Show. Banished with me and under my command were about eighty erks, several NCOs, three officers and over a hundred Japanese prisoners of war who were as baffled as I was as to why they should still be there, six months after their war was over. They saluted and bowed interminably whenever I appeared. It was infectious and I found myself bowing in return. Most of us had prickly heat or athlete's foot. I had both.

The small, sleepy port of Mergui had not changed since the nineteenth-century days of King Thibaw. Progress had passed it by. Thatched straw huts on stilts juxtaposed with more substantial, timbered dwellings under the punctual sun. Fishing and smuggling between Burma, Malaya and Thailand, with contraband flowing each way, and a tin mine were the major industries. Tiny, black-sailed fishing boats dotted the horizon. The boats moored in the small, natural harbour scarcely rocked, so gently were they lapped by the warm sea. Gold-tipped pagodas and temples topped every vantage point, their bells tinkling quietly. Saffron-robed, shaven-headed Buddhist monks loitered everywhere, begging bowls at the ready, waiting for Nirvana. The men wore check *longyis* and open-necked shirts. With betel-stained teeth, green cheroots sticking upwards from their lips and Trilby hats perched cheekily on the back of their heads, they looked extraordinarily spiv-like. Their custom of squatting on public roads and urinating underneath their *longyis* was disconcerting. The women too wore *longyis*. Wearing simple sandals they walked flat-footed from swaying hips with their black, uncut, shiny hair coiled high. Under their bodices their breasts were bound flat in deference to Buddhist belief that women's breasts are symbols of sin. Occasionally, in contrast, young, bare-breasted native women from jungle villages, breathed deeply and held their breath as they passed by me. White skin was still prized by the primitive.

On the hill overlooking the port was the centre of power, the British Deputy Commissioner's residence. A Union Jack hung limply from the flagpole.

By now I had not flown for months. I looked at the sky like an addict in need of a fix. My suggestion to Group headquarters that a small aircraft based at Mergui would be useful for communications and the odd case of peritonitis was turned down unreasonably flat. There were several hundred aircraft sitting around the Far East gathering dust.

I discovered that the erks' canteen had not received any supplies since the RAF had taken over Mergui from the Japanese Air Force months before. The erks were relying on the Mergui black market for everything from soap and toothpaste to alcohol and cigarettes. I sent an urgent radio signal to headquarters in Rangoon requesting that canteen stores be airlifted immediately to Mergui. It was ignored. A week passed. I sent another, stronger. It also was ignored. My adjutant informed me that a delegation of erks wished to see me. I told him that commanding officers do not receive delegations from the ranks. I was, however, prepared to see their representative. He was an old lag who knew how to get his message across without insolence. The message was blunt. Get canteen stores, or else. He mentioned, *inter alia*, that some of the erks at Mergui had been with the mutinous squadron at Mingaladon.

I sent a third signal to headquarters. I remember every word: 'No canteen stores received this unit since its formation. This is my third signal regarding this subject. I cannot be held responsible for morale at Mergui unless canteen stores arrive immediately.'

It was an impertinent signal, possibly fateful. A serving officer does not send signals to the corridors of power saying what he will or will not accept. I knew that my deliberate use of the word morale would cause consternation at headquarters. Since the strike at

Mingaladon and minor fracas elsewhere, the RAF's top brass were highly sensitive to matters of morale and bad publicity. Particularly with their new socialist masters. The canteen stores arrived within 36 hours by Dakota from Rangoon.

Most of the erks got drunk that night. I visited the canteen during the evening to be met by a chorus of 'For he's a jolly good fellow'. The text of my signals had become common knowledge among the erks. I was aware that I would not be considered a jolly good fellow at headquarters. I was not keeping my nose clean.

The Deputy Commissioner often invited me to dinner at his residence. We usually dined alone except for the servants and two cross-eyed, arrogant Siamese cats. A strikingly beautiful young Burmese girl hovered in the background. The DC said she was his living-in cook. I never did discover whether she was also his mistress. Judging by the soft look in her eyes whenever she glanced at him it would have been a sad waste were she not. The DC was a middle-aged bachelor, shy, tall and cadaverous, with a Winchester, Oxford and Indian Civil Service background. He was a solitary man but we became friends. He told me that as commanding officer of RAF Mergui I would be his deputy in the event of civil disturbance. I smiled at the thought of carrying the white man's burden. It was all very Kiplingesque. We spent many evenings on his verandah under the squeaking fan, drinking local fire-water, smoking Burmese cheroots and playing chess, or content to watch the lights in the harbour 150 feet below and the glittering sea beyond. He smiled and wagged an admonishing finger whenever he caught me eyeing his cook.

He was part of the great Maurice Collis★ tradition of liberal enlightenment towards those he absolutely ruled. I occasionally went to his magistrate's court to see him in judgment. His efforts to find the accused not guilty, unless it was a heinous crime, were

---

★The author Maurice Collis served before the war in the Indian Civil Service in India and Burma, including a spell as Deputy Commissioner at Mergui, in 1932–34. He wrote several books based on his experiences in the Far East, including *Siamese White* and, aptly titled, *Trials in Burma* – a moving and beautifully written account of his difficulties as the Chief Magistrate in a sensational trial in Rangoon, of a British Army officer who had killed a Burmese woman while drunken driving, a trial that finished up as a battle between the besieged Collis and the entire British establishment in Burma.

endearing. His homilies were apt and brief, his sentences light. He was respected and liked, perhaps loved, by the Burmans. He was a tiny cog in a far-flung bit of the empire. But a great man. Had there been more like him and Maurice Collis we might still have had a bit of empire left.

Chapter 14

B ASED AT MERGUI harbour under my command was a magnificent, rakish, 70 foot RAF air-sea rescue launch. Fitted with bunks and a galley and powered by the Spitfire's Merlin engine, it had a top speed of over 30 knots. It lay at anchor in the harbour, in sleek contrast to the native fishing boats, awaiting emergency calls that never came. The skipper was a young RAF Pilot Officer with a crew of two erks and a zest for the unauthorised. I outranked him plentifully except at sea. The launch had several radios for communications with passing aircraft and air-sea rescue control in Rangoon and Singapore.

With nothing to do – I had a workaholic adjutant – and nothing to fly, I spent most of my time on the launch exploring the off-shore islands, swimming and sunbathing. Dolphins escorted us wherever we went, as fascinated by us as we were by them. I salved my conscience at such hedonism by always taking two erks from Mergui aerodrome with me, or the DC. The radios kept us in touch with land, sky and duty. Occasionally we spent a night at anchor off one of the islands, nights of incomparable moonlit beauty and peace. Had I not chosen the sky for my life I would have chosen the sea. Two unspoiled elements, for the ship's wake and the aeroplane's vapour trail are ephemeral and nature soon wipes clean these scars of man's passing.

For the erks the days at Mergui passed in a haze of 100-degree heat and boredom, waiting for the boat home. They had nothing to do but sleep and eat. They were too long in the service tooth to be fobbed off with sports and other bogus contrived activity. It was as though we were forgotten men. There was no news of my release from the RAF.

The routine was broken only once when we were signalled to expect the arrival of a French Air Force DC4 transport aircraft from Paris. It was to stay the night at Mergui for servicing and refuelling before continuing to Saigon, French Indo-China, now Vietnam. The passengers were, the signal added, to be given VIP treatment. On board was General Juin and his staff, to take up his position as Commander in Chief of the French forces in Indo-China.

The adjutant and I could not think of any VIP treatment we could offer. He suggested a guard of honour but none of us knew how. I sent an erk into Mergui to find a red carpet without success. I begged help from the DC. He offered beds and a curry dinner at his residence, followed by Burmese folk-dancing.

I saluted the general as he descended from his aircraft and stepped onto the brown matting I had borrowed from the orderly room. He looked battered and had a withered arm. Neither of us spoke the other's language. I shook his good hand.

General Juin was a demanding guest. Fortunately he liked curry, particularly when it was laced with French hors d'oeuvres and champagne from the DC4's refrigerators. His *aide-de-camp* and the DC were bilingual in French and English.

After dinner, five very young Burmese girls appeared for the folk-dancing. They looked enchanting in oyster silk nineteenth-century court dress, heavy white make-up and long nails. As they were not nubile the general soon became restless. When his eyes began to glaze I signalled to the DC to call a halt. We then played bridge. The DC and I thrashed the Frenchmen. The general was a bad loser and in a bad temper when we settled up in French francs. He was even more bad-tempered when he discovered there were no women available for dalliance. He informed us testily there would have been had Burma been part of the French Empire. He settled for brandy and Burmese cigars. We talked well into the night on the verandah. Tongues soon loosened with the brandy.

It was unnerving to listen to the general's prognostications about the future of Indo-China. As far as he and the French government were concerned the future meant a return to the *status quo* of the past. Indo-China was part of the glorious French Empire and would always remain so, despite the interregnum of the Japanese occupation. The general dismissed my comment that the Indo-Chinese might now prefer to rule themselves and might fight for independence if necessary. He replied he would soon suppress the isolated outbreaks of rebellion fomented by a few Moscow-inspired communist terrorists.

When the general detected a certain self-righteousness in his English hosts' arguments he bade us remove the beam from our own eyes before casting out the mote of his – his *aide-de-camp* had some difficulty in translating this – reminding us that fighting had already started against the British in Malaya next door and against the Dutch down the road in the Netherlands East Indies.

It is poignant to recall that Burmese night nearly fifty years ago. I can see that rumpled French general now. Lounging on a vast sofa under the creaking ceiling fan, relaxed, insouciant, armpits awash, confident that he was dealing with a little local difficulty and without the slightest conception of the tragedy and defeat in store for France, and America, in Vietnam.

In March, the air-sea rescue launch was due for a refit in Calcutta, a thousand miles away. It was an opportunity not to be missed. I gave myself three weeks' leave, handed over to the adjutant and invited myself aboard. We stowed extra drums of fuel aboard to make the voyage non-stop.

The weather was perfect. The monsoons were not due for another few weeks. Our 15-knot cruising speed reduced the temperature to a breezy 80 degrees. The sun shone from dawn to dusk, the moon from dusk to dawn. Sometimes they shared the sky like two spot-lights. The sea was a mirror of the sky by day and phosphorescent lace by night. We had an escort of joyful, indefatigable dolphins almost all the way. I assume we were passed on from one dolphin territorial school to another. Not to be outdone, flying fish skipped the surface like stones thrown horizontally by small boys. The de-rated Merlin engine throbbed deeply. We seldom sighted a ship, and the BBC's overseas service was our only link with the un-missed outside world.

On the third day the several mouths of the Ganges appeared on the flat, shimmering horizon. The widest was the river Hooghly leading us to Calcutta.

After docking I said goodbye to the crew, who were returning to Mergui with a replacement launch, and took a taxi to Dum Dum RAF aerodrome on the outskirts of Calcutta. I had decided that, by scrounging flights on RAF aircraft, this was probably my last opportunity of exploring India before returning to England.

With a bit of hanging around here and there I covered most of India in the next two weeks. A considerable achievement in a triangular sub-continent two thousand miles wide and two thousand miles long. My zig-zag itinerary took in Calcutta – Madras –

Bangalore – Hyderabad – Nagpur – Allahabad – Kanpur – New Delhi – Lahore – Karachi – Rawalpindi – Bombay. It was in Bombay that my luck ran out and I got stuck.

This is not the place for a travelogue of old India, the India before independence and partition, the India of the Raj. It was loved or loathed. I understood why, for it was a land of paradox. The squalor, the heat, the beauty, the smell of spice, the begging, the disease, the love-hate relationship between Briton and Indian, the parched, featureless central plains, the long, unspoiled coastline, the grim statistics of cholera and hepatitis deaths in the papers, the wild beauty of Kashmir, the mixture of bathos and pathos, the kohl-painted eyelids, the desperate poor, the cow-pats on the pavements, the flies, the tension between Muslim and Hindu, the infuriating incompetence and the innate patience and courtesy of its people, but above all else the unbelievably racist arrogance of the British.

It was days before I could get an RAF flight from Bombay to Calcutta and a further delay for a flight from Calcutta to Rangoon. I landed at Rangoon ten days overdue.

I was apprehensive when I reported to Group Headquarters in Rangoon to arrange a lift to Mergui. I knew I was not headquarters' favourite son. Getting stuck in Bombay and Calcutta would not be an acceptable explanation for returning from leave ten days overdue. My apprehension deepened when I was informed the Group Captain SASO wanted to see me.

When I was shown into the Group Captain's office he did not ask me to sit down, nor did he enquire after my health. We had exchanged such courtesies in the past.

'Where have you been?' enquired the Group Captain.

'On leave, sir.'

'Who gave you leave?'

'I did, sir.'

'Don't you know that commanding officers' leave is granted only by Group Headquarters?' His voice was icy.

'No, sir.'

'When did you leave Mergui?'

'March the ninth, sir.'

'Today is', he glanced at his desk diary, 'April the twelfth.' Put like that it sounded a long time.

'Consider yourself under close arrest.'

'What for, sir?'

'To establish whether there is a prima-facie case to have you court-martialled for absence without leave. Report immediately to my adjutant. Dismissed.'

It was the curt word 'dismissed' that brought home the seriousness of my position. I saluted and left his office with my heart thumping.

The adjutant was embarrassed and not too sure of what putting a senior officer under close arrest entailed. Erks are simply locked up. Scratching his head he looked up the *Manual of Air Force Law*. He concluded that I could not use the public rooms or the dining room in the officers' mess, that I was confined to my room and that I must have an escort of equal rank if I left the room. 'Flaming nuisance,' he muttered as he drew up the escort rota. There were not that many squadron leaders around.

The Court of Inquiry was quick and informal. I did not deny my absence and a prima facie case was soon established. I was to be court-martialled on two counts. Being absent without leave from 9 March until 12 April 1946, and disobeying a lawful command. What this command was I cannot remember and the records of the court martial proceedings have been destroyed. I assume it was a standing command of some sort, such as Thou shalt not covet thy neighbour's ass. It was as well the war was over. My alleged offences could carry the death penalty in wartime. While we awaited the court martial my acting rank of Squadron Leader was removed and I reverted to my substantive rank of Flight Lieutenant. It hurt to unpick that third stripe from my uniform. I was also released from close arrest to open arrest. This meant I could use the officers' mess and had to report daily to the adjutant. When I walked into the officers' mess brother officers looked the other way. Nobody asked me to join them for a drink. I already wore the mark of Cain.

Group Headquarters, where the trial was held, was located in the requisitioned Botataung Pagoda, an ornate Chinese palace built in the early 1920s. The Japanese had occupied it previously, leaving Japanese graffiti in the lavatories. It was built on classic Chinese lines, with a massive central tower, curled roofs covered in jade-green tiles and curlicues at the four corners of each storey. Huge stone elephants held up the ceilings and a grand marble staircase swept upwards. In the ground floor hall chairs and tables were laid out for the court martial. The weather was headachingly oppressive, for the monsoons had started early. The atmosphere was saturated, with temperatures in the nineties. Every movement brought soaking armpits. Mosquitoes thrived. The ceiling fans were useless. On the eve of the court martial there was a minor earthquake, immediately followed by a cyclone. The temple rocked. It seemed portentous.

The court room was crowded. Along the green baize top table sat the five senior RAF officers who were to pass judgment upon me. One of them was the Court President. With them sat an officer from the Judge Advocate General's office to lead and advise the court on procedure and legal matters. I sat facing them, with the defending officer on my left and the prosecuting officer on my right. To one side sat the court stenographer, an uncommonly pretty Anglo-Indian WAAF. Behind me were rows of chairs for an audience. They were packed with RAF officers. It was an open court and there was not much to do in Rangoon. We all wore our best tropical uniform.

The prosecuting officer was a Squadron Leader, a barrister from the Judge Advocate General's office. My defending officer was Flight-Lieutenant Maung Gyi whom I had chosen from the pool of officers available at headquarters. He knew nothing about law or courts martial. The RAF provides a professional barrister for the prosecution but not for the defence. I could, I was told, engage a barrister and fly him to Burma at my expense.

Maung Gyi was an administrative officer and a very rare bird, a Burmese RAF officer with a Viceroy's commission. This was not a normal King's commission and was considered by the British as a bit of a fake. I chose him because he was likeable and seemed articulate. It was a disaster. He was totally intimidated by the stiff protocol and solemnity of the court. Whenever he rose to speak he blushed a deep brown, sweated, stuttered and lost his tongue in mid-sentence. The prosecuting officer made patronising mince-meat of him. I was tempted but did not quite have the bravado to take over my own defence.

There were five possible outcomes from the trial. Acquittal, reprimand, severe reprimand, dismissal or cashiering from the RAF. As my alleged offences were misdemeanours rather than criminal I would not be imprisoned. Opinion in the officers' mess was that I would get a severe reprimand.

110

Although the issues were simple, the trial dragged on for four days. Those hours in court, so long ago that acorns have become oaks, seemed endless. I was as much self-conscious and embarrassed as anything else. There was more bathos than pathos in court. I felt that I had caused the whole weight of the Royal Air Force and all those mysterious forces behind it to halt in their tracks to deal with me. All these people had more important things to do. It was a bloody great steam-roller to crack such a tiny nut. I would rather have been dealt with summarily than cause all this palaver. The afternoon sessions were the worst. While everyone else in Burma was having their siesta we droned on with temperatures in the mid-nineties. The WAAF frequently caught me looking at her slender legs under the table. I detected a gleam of sympathy in her lovely, dark brown eyes. Being an Anglo-Indian she was, like me, an underdog. One bit of court proceedings I do remember:

'Are we boring you, Flight-Lieutenant Levett?' It was the voice of the President of the court.

'No, sir. Sorry, sir.' I had dozed off.

It was obvious by the end of the third day that I was going to be found guilty on both counts. There was now little else Maung Gyi or I could do other than to try to reduce the severity of the sentence by pleading mitigating circumstances. That evening I wrote the closing speech. It was a good speech and Maung Gyi spent most of the night rehearsing. I made several points. The most important, naive though it sounds now, was I did not realise that, though I was commanding officer of an RAF station, I did not have the authority to grant myself leave. In other words my misdemeanour was through ignorance rather than deliberate intent. I pointed out that I had received no administrative or staff training in the RAF. I had made no secret of my departure and my adjutant and staff knew that I was going on leave. I apologised to the court, of course, for return-ing late from leave. As for my character, I went on at some length – this was not the moment to be modest – about my RAF career. Finally, I emphasised that for over seven years in the RAF I had kept my nose clean and had not been in trouble before.

It should have made an effective mitigation speech but Maung Gyi made a hash of it. There was an embarrassed silence before the court retired.

In the RAF there is no court-room drama at the end of a court martial. No sword on the table pointing at the accused if guilty, away if not. At that time there was a curious procedure. The verdict was announced at the end of a court martial only if it was Not Guilty. If the accused had been found Guilty the President merely stated 'The court has no finding to announce', the inference being obvious. It was not until later, sometimes several weeks later, when the Guilty verdict and the sentence imposed by the court had been confirmed by higher authority, that the accused was formally informed of the guilty verdict and the sentence of the court. It was a cruel tease.

I knew by inference that I had been found guilty on both counts but I had to wait two agonising months in Rangoon before I knew the sentence. I was released from open arrest during this time but I had become a leper. Senior RAF officers cut me dead and my peers were embarrassed by my presence. I was politely informed I was not welcome in the Gymkhana Club. I became a recluse and stayed in my room most of the time. Although fraternisation between officers and female other ranks was forbidden, I sought and found secret solace in the arms of the WAAF court stenographer. She said I had been foolish to choose a 'Wog' as my defending officer, but she said it with a self-deprecating smile.

At the end of the two months I was ordered to report to Air Marshal Sir Hugh Saunders, at SEAC headquarters, in Rangoon, for the official promulgation of the court martial verdict and sentence. It took less than half a minute. I walked into the Air Marshal's office as Flight-Lieutenant Levett. I walked out, in silence except for the sound of my own footsteps, as Mister Levett. I had been found guilty on both counts and was sentenced to be dismissed from His Majesty's Service. At that time there was no appeal against sentence. There was a right of petition to have the verdict quashed on legal grounds but there were no such grounds in my case. The Air Marshal's aide coldly informed me I no longer had the right to wear my uniform and I was to remove the insignia immediately. Before the war, insignia was publicly ripped off at a formal ceremony. I went to the washroom and took a long, last look in the mirror at Flight-Lieutenant, once Squadron Leader, Gordon Robert Levett. I removed my wings and stripes, an easy task as they are press-studded on tropical uniform. I then looked at plain Mr Levett, shorn of wings and insignia, the apparel proclaiming the man. It was only then that I fully realised I would never fly a Royal Air Force aeroplane again. I had served in the Royal Air Force for seven and a half years, all my adult life so far, from pre-war February 1939 to post-war August, 1946. I had joined as a boy, I was now a broken man of twenty-five. My mother was right. I had come to a bad end.

Chapter 15

THE BOAT HOME from Rangoon to England was the troopship *SS Ormonde*, a slow, tired old lady. Troops and officers were packed aboard like matches in a box but nobody minded. Apart from my little island there was joy on board. They were all going home. I was going home too, but in disgrace.

I was given a tiny single cabin in the old first-class accommodation and had the run of the ship. Remembering the origins of Posh I was glad to note that my cabin was on the starboard side. I wore the same clothes as everyone else, khaki shorts and shirt but without insignia. I got puzzled looks throughout the voyage. People wondered who and what I was. I was among them but not of them. The few who knew me looked the other way.

During that long five-week voyage home I began the adjustment to a life divorced from the Royal Air Force. The steady throb and progress of the ship and the balm of sun, sea and cheap booze helped me recover a bit from the shock of the last few weeks. I kept to myself with the help of books from the ship's library. I still looked at the RAF notice boards on the ship but my name never appeared. As far as the RAF was concerned I no longer existed. It was uncanny to go through the day without an order to give or obey, or without being called Sir. I felt naked and vulnerable without the RAF's mother-love. I was free but it was an unwanted freedom, and I found it difficult to accept that I was no longer part of the Royal Air Force and its aeroplanes.

For the first time in my life I felt anxious about the future. My dismissal was ignominious. In those less permissive days my disgrace was the greater. I tried to comfort myself that I had not been cashiered. That is usually reserved for officers caught with their fingers in the till, or with sexual peccadilloes, or similar conduct unbecoming an officer and a gentleman. To a prospective employer I could perhaps explain that my offence was not rank. But without references from the RAF to cover the last seven and a half years of my life, I doubted I would be given the opportunity of explaining. Immediately after the war most job applicants were asked to provide their service discharge papers. It was as well I had decided to leave the RAF anyway. Had I not I do not care to think what I might have done. There was a moment one night on that voyage home when I was half-way over the ship's rail.

I did not feel bitter or blame the Royal Air Force for my downfall. I had joined their club and broken their rules. I was the transgressor. I was culpable, not the RAF. But, though my guilt was unarguable, I felt, still feel, that though the court martial was deserved, the sentence was harsh. Particularly as the RAF knew it would be rid of me in a matter of weeks anyway. There is no doubt in my mind that had I won medals in combat, had I not been known as some sort of socialist, had I not sent those peremptory signals from Mergui to headquarters about the canteen stores and had it not been felt at Headquarters, SEAC, that there was a need to make an example of someone after the mutiny and other disciplinary problems in the Far East, I would have been dealt with less severely. But that would have been another story. It was my own fault. I supplied the catalyst that destroyed my Royal Air Force career. I can blame nobody but myself.

We steamed up the Thames estuary to Tilbury docks on a cold, wet November day. I waited on deck amid the Tannoy announcements and the hustle and bustle of disembarkation until I realised I had nothing to wait for. I walked down the gang-plank, off the ship and out of the Royal Air Force. It felt very odd. I looked behind to see if anyone was following me. I was wearing my blue RAF uniform trousers and shirt and a heavy cream Aran sweater I had bought from a deck-hand. I had changed all my rupees into sterling on the ship and had about £20, my total wealth.

After pawning my wristwatch and silver cigarette case I caught a train to central London where I found a dry-cleaners off Piccadilly and got them to press my best-blue RAF Squadron Leader uniform from my suitcase. I waited in the back room in my underwear. Their eyebrows rose as I walked out into Shaftesbury Avenue wearing full RAF regalia. I had decided that I was not going to give my mother the opportunity of saying 'I told you so'. Yet.

I took a taxi to my mother's new address. Much had happened on the domestic front while I was in the Far East. Jack and Joyce had married and now lived in the family home in Worcester Park. My mother had married Fred Booth, the No. 73 bus driver. He was still on the same route. They lived in a *Coronation Street*-type terraced house in Fulham. They thought I was 7,000 miles away and my arrival caused a stir. Neighbours peeped through lace curtains. Working-class folk never took taxis except in dire emergencies. My shell looked good. Tall, slim, not bad-looking, a Squadron Leader's uniform and a magnificent tan that made everyone else look washed-out. By coincidence Jack and Joyce were there. During the hugs and cheek-kissing my mother asked me where I was going to stay. It was more of a statement than a question and a warning that I could not consider her home mine. It was a problem I had not anticipated. I lied, saying I would be demobilised from the RAF in a few days and could I stay with them until the RAF discharge formalities were over and I had settled down a bit. She pulled a face and said I would have to ask Fred, it was his house. I asked Fred. He too pulled a face. It was only a two-bedroomed house and Fred had a son, Ronald, aged sixteen. I think Fred found it as bemusing being my stepfather as I did being his stepson. Ronald, Ron as everyone insisted on calling him, was a good lad in total awe of his new Squadron Leader stepbrother. He frequently tried on my uniform. We put up an extra bed in his bedroom. Jack did not offer me a bed in his house in Worcester Park. That day was the nadir of my life.

Fred took my mother and me, wearing uniform, to their local pubs in Fulham, and Putney where his bus station was, to show me off to his mates. I hated it. Seeing myself in the uniform I loved exacerbated the torment inside, and I could have been arrested at any moment for impersonating an officer. But I did it for my mother's sake. There were few moments in her life when she could bask in reflected glory.

After a fortnight I spent two days away from home, ostensibly to get my discharge from the Royal Air Force, redeemed my wrist-watch and cigarette case, sold them and bought some civilian clothes. On returning home I packed my uniforms away. I did not have the heart to throw them out.

I spent the next few weeks trying to adjust to family and civilian life. It did not help that I did not have a girl. It was ironic trying to step down the social scale. I remembered to call lavatories toilets, women ladies, telephones 'phones, napkins serviettes, to drink beer from a straight glass rather than a mug, to say pardon instead of what, blimey instead of crikey and not to rise when my mother entered a room, but it did not ring true. I would gladly have taken

Polonius' advice, but which self was it to which I should be true? Try as I would to be a chameleon I found it as difficult to come down as it had been to go up. Ronald accused me of being posh. Fred accused me of being smooth-tongued. My mother just looked at me thoughtfully. She knew something was wrong.

Meanwhile I tried to get a job as a pilot. With over 3,000 hours, including 700 hours as captain on Dakotas, then the world's number one twin-engined airliner, and an RAF above-average assessment both as pilot and instructor in my log-books, I thought that getting a job would be a formality. I did not have a civil flying licence or the money to get one but most airlines were recruiting unlicensed ex-RAF pilots and training them in airline techniques to get their necessary licences.

I wrote to the chief pilots, some of them old friends, of the several old and new airlines then flourishing in the post-war flying boom. Air transport no longer had to prove itself. New trails were blazing everywhere on war gratuities and borrowed money. I always got to the interview stage but nobody offered me a job. It was something else I had not anticipated. With thousands of ex-RAF pilots on the market employers could be selective, and without references from the RAF no airline was going to offer me a job.

I received my final communication from the Royal Air Force informing me that after due consideration they had decided that I would not receive a gratuity for my seven and a half years' service. My last nest-egg had gone. It further informed me that His Excellency the Governor of Burma, no less, had directed that I should be fined £25 for permitting my Jeep to be stolen in Rangoon. Accordingly this sum, provisionally retained from my pay for this contingency, would be used to pay the fine.

I asked my bank for a loan of the substantial sum required to obtain a commercial flying licence at my own expense but they were not interested. My account did not inspire them with confidence.

I tried emigrating to Canada, Australia, New Zealand and America in that order, but they would not have me. Every door I pushed seemed locked or revolving.

I told my mother what had happened in Burma – I do not know whether the single tear that trickled down her cheek was for her or for me – and moved out to a bed-sitter in Belsize Park.

PART II

SHABBES GOY

Chapter 16

L ATE IN 1947 I got a job with the Sun White Nappy Laundry. The proprietor was Lionel Silver, an ophthalmic optician. Eyes bored him and he had become an entrepreneur. In addition to the laundry he had interests in baby photography, the then new chipboard manufacturing process and a short-lived football pool. He was not particularly rich. I helped a bit on all these projects. He and his wife were good to me. I did not talk much about myself but they sensed I was unhappy and a bit lost. He was classically Semitic-looking with a proud nose, large teeth, brown eyes and a mobile, smiling face. She was pretty and could occasionally circumnavigate his wiles. Like most Jewish married couples they were happy together.

It was months before I realised that Lionel was an active Zionist. This is not surprising. He knew that I was a Gentile and Jews do not proselytise about their religion, or Zion. There are no Jewish missionaries.

Over the months Lionel and I talked about the troubles in Palestine. The British government had got fed-up with the impasse between Jews and Arabs, who had been at each other's throats for decades, and were planning to terminate the British Mandate in Palestine and pull out. The British seem skilled at creating impasse. Jew and Arab in Palestine, Muslim and Hindu in India, Turk and Greek in Cyprus, Protestant and Catholic in Ireland, worker and management in Britain. Perhaps the conspiratorial theorists are right after all and it was not muddle that so often inspired British policy, home and abroad, but divide and rule.

Britain started off with good intentions. Britain alone among the great powers supported the Zionist movement at the beginning of the twentieth century, culminating in the Balfour Declaration by the British government in 1917 pledging support for the establishment in Palestine of a 'national home for the Jewish people'. In 1922 this declaration of intent was formally incorporated into the League of Nations Mandate which placed Palestine under British rule when the defeated Turkish Ottoman Empire was carved up among

121

the British, the French and the Arabs after the First World War.

Jewish immigration into Palestine increased in the 1920s as a result of pogroms and anti-Semitism in Russia, Poland, Hungary, Romania and elsewhere. Nevertheless, before the Third Reich, what was precisely meant by the words '. . . the establishment in Palestine of a national home for the Jewish people . . .' could be left to semantics, for Jewish immigration into Palestine was still only a tiny trickle. But the anti-Semitism of the Third Reich changed all that and the trickle of Jewish immigration into Palestine would have become a flood had the British government permitted it. It did not. By refusing to permit unrestricted Jewish immigration into Palestine in the late 1930s and early 1940s the British government was indirectly responsible for the death of many Jews trapped in Europe. Other nations closed their doors too but they had not made the Balfour Declaration, or accepted the League of Nations Mandate solemnly requiring the British to establish a 'national home for the Jews in Palestine'. What is a home if it is something you cannot go to when in desperate need?

British Foreign Office mandarins were, traditionally, lovers of Arabia, the Bedouin and T.E. Lawrence (twice an erk) inspired romantic myth. They preferred Damascus to Tel Aviv, Arabic to Hebrew, Mohammed to Moses, Arab to Jew. To this day the relationship between Britain and Israel is cold. Harold Wilson is the only major British politician to have shown warmth to Israel. Oil is no longer an explanation for this coolness. The British have their own oil now.

When, immediately after the end of the Second World War, in which most Jews but few Arabs fought on the Allied side, the full horror of the Holocaust was revealed, it was assumed there would be no further argument against permitting Jewish immigration into Palestine. But to the astonishment of the Jews, most of whom were now Zionists (the old argument that assimilation was the answer to anti-Semitism perished in the gas chambers, for German Jews were the most assimilated of all), the British government still stubbornly prevented other than a trickle of Jews into Palestine. Thousands of Jewish refugees from the refugee camps of Europe defied the British and travelled illegally to Palestine. They were turned back to Europe at gun-point. Hundreds died when they scuttled their ships in despair. Twelve thousand were caged behind British barbed wire in Cyprus in 1948. They were still imprisoned there six months after the British had given up the Mandate and were no longer responsible for Palestine. All this after the horror of the gas chambers of Europe had been fully exposed. One wonders what motivated this cold, implacable heart. Some say that neither Attlee nor his much admired Foreign Secretary, Bevin, was anti-Semitic. Others say the earth is flat. At any rate, there were no resignations from Attlee's Cabinet.

Jewish patience finally snapped. For them little had changed except the genocide of nearly 6,000,000 Jews. The message for Jewish people was stark: you are on your own once again, despite being the victim of the most unspeakable crimes in human history. Either you re-establish your nation in Palestine, beholden to no-one, where you were once before, or you, or your son, or your son's son will die in a gas-oven. Few Jews feel that the Holocaust was a one-off.

Zionists throughout the world united, with two objectives: to rid Palestine of British rule and bring the Jews home to sanctuary.

The Jews were not strangers in Palestine. They had been there since the second millennium BC, long before it was called Palestine. By the first millennium BC they had, with the help of Moses, Joshua, David and Solomon, settled and distinguished themselves from the Phoenicians and Philistines and others in the area by their own customs, culture and religion. Theirs was the first religion to worship one God, in sharp contrast to the idolatrous polytheism of the rest of the ancient world. In other words Jews had settled in Palestine as a nation in the era of the Old Testament and have been there, one way or another, ever since – a point frequently over-looked in the tortuous polemics of the Arab-Israel feud.

In the late 1930s and early 1940s civil war raged in Palestine, a war of terror and atrocity on all sides as Jews and Arabs fought each other and both fought the British. Neither Briton, Jew nor Arab can look back on that period with unabated pride. The only possible peaceful solution, the partition of Palestine into separate Jewish and Arab nations as recommended by the British Peel Commission in 1937 and the United Nations in 1947, was rejected by the British government and the Arabs and accepted by the Jews. Ironically, had partition been accepted Israel would have been much smaller than it is today.

The British government gave up. On 29 November 1947, after nearly thirty years of absolute British rule, it announced unilaterally that it would end the Mandate and pull out of Palestine not later than 1 August 1948. It later announced a new deadline of 15 May 1948, adding deliberately that it would not hand over the reins to any authority whatsoever, Arab, Jewish or United Nations. In Palestine, from 15 May, there would be no national or local government, no law, no public service, no administration, no police, no authority, nothing. That this would create a classic anarchic vacuum and an open invitation to the surrounding Arab nations to invade Palestine did not deter the British government one jot. Cry havoc! and let slip the dogs of war.

On 14 May 1948, the British flag was lowered for the last time. The last British troops (apart from a few security enclaves protected by the RAF) left Haifa and British rule ended. At 4 pm the same day, in Tel Aviv, David Ben-Gurion, Prime Minister designate of the provisional Jewish government, proclaimed the new Jewish nation and named it *Israel*. On the same day five Arab nations, Egypt, Jordan, Iraq, Lebanon and Syria, declared war on the new state. The next day all five duly invaded Palestine from the north, east and south, joining their Palestinian Arab brothers in the declared *Jihad* aim of 'driving the Jews into the sea'. Saudi Arabia and Yemen sent troops later. The Secretary-General of the Arab League announced: 'This will be a war of extermination and a momentous massacre which will be spoken of like the Mongolian massacres and the Crusades.'

Israel did not declare war on anybody and never has. The invaders, with a total population of 40,000,000 against some 650,000 Jews, were supported by the entire Muslim world. The invaders' land totalled 1,700,000 square miles. The land the Jews wanted, which had been allocated legally and formally to them in the United Nations partition plan of December 1947, totalled 7,993 square miles. David and Goliath again. Such a tiny piece of land for so much protestation. The scene was set for the Second Holocaust to finish off what the Third Reich had started. Shortly before ending the Mandate and evacuating Palestine the British government were informed unequivocally by their general staff, including the CIGS, Field-Marshal Montgomery, that if Britain evacuated, the Jews would be driven into the sea. To this day I wonder what Attlee and Bevin and their Cabinet colleagues would have said when the last Israeli Jew and Jewess had drowned off Tel Aviv. As history knows, the Second Holocaust did not happen, just.

In the months before 15 May 1948, the Jewish Agency in Palestine took on the daunting task of preparing to avoid chaos at the end of British rule. Secret shadow appointments were made covering national and local government, public services and defence. They had no authority but their own, but that, being moral, was absolute among the Jews. The Zionist Organisation throughout the world began the equally daunting task of raising funds, lobbying governments, politicians and the United Nations, organising arms purchasing missions and recruiting volunteers for the forthcoming war.

The volunteers from overseas were, of course, Jewish apart from a few Gentiles and mercenaries. Sadly, the Jewish cause did not inspire the support of the world's intellectuals as did, for example, the Spanish Civil War. In London over four thousand British Gentiles volunteered to fight for the Arabs, six for the Jews.

During the last few weeks of British rule the Jews in Palestine, normally the most law abiding of citizens, became a nation of Fagins. Thieving from the British became a moral imperative. Government cars, three tanks, lorries, small boats, important files, typewriters, small arms, rifles, ammunition, vanished overnight. Occasionally the last lorry in a British convoy turned right and disappeared when all the other lorries had turned left. Anything movable that might be useful after the British left was fair game. The cafés at night were full of grinning Jews comparing booty. It raised a few chuckles in that grim twilight world of atrocity and counter-atrocity, hanging and counter-hanging.

This land of miracles was about to produce more. This time secular. On 15 May, with British authority gone, the Jews were surprised and relieved to discover that when they turned taps on water still flowed, when they switched a light it came on, buses still ran, telephones worked, mail arrived, money kept its value, fire engines responded to emergency calls, newspapers were still published. There was no law but there was order. It was the theory of political anarchy working in practice. I was there a few days later. It was heart-warming to see the Israelis' delight in the realisation that they could manage things without the British. It was a unique

125

historical moment. More so because the British on their departure had adopted a scorched-earth policy where administration and paper-work were concerned. Similarly, any military equipment or installations that were immovable and might be useful for a people about to fight for their lives were destroyed.

'Can a country be born in a day or a nation be brought forth in a moment?' (Isaiah 66:8). The Jews' answer was: Yes.

Chapter 17

IN MID APRIL 1948, we had a major crisis at the laundry. It was late evening, the boiler had broken down and eight vans were parked outside crammed with soiled nappies. The mind boggled at the thought of several hundred middle-class babies without nappies. We eventually got the boiler going again and by working through the night Lionel and I did the whole wash. About three o'clock in the morning I told Lionel that I wanted to help the Jews in Palestine. 'It's not as bad as all that,' he said with a grin, 'we've nearly finished.'

He warned me that the British government was hostile to Zionism. Government lawyers were studying the implications of dual loyalty if British Jews fought in Palestine. It was not inconceivable that in the coming war, British preferment for the Arab cause, British mutual defence pacts with Iraq, Jordan and Egypt, and British oil interests in the Middle East, might result in a British Jew and a British soldier being in each other's gun-sights. The ugly word treason was being bandied.

A few days later I received a telephone call to meet a Mr Brown at Holborn tube station in London. He would be wearing a red carnation, dark glasses – much more sinister then than now – and carrying a copy of *The Times*. We met without hitch and went to his seedy hotel in Bloomsbury. We had two meetings. The second time he was Mr Green and his seedy hotel was in Paddington. Mr Brown-Green was middle-aged and mid-European. He did not smile once in our two lengthy meetings, whether because of hostility to me, the British or life, I could not decide.

His first question was how much. 'Board and lodging and pocket money,' I replied.

'What can you fly?' he asked.

'Anything.'

'You have proof?' he asked. 'We have many who say they can.' I passed him my flying log-books. It was obvious by the way he riffled through them that he knew nothing about flying. I pointed out the various aircraft types I had flown and my pilot assessments. He noticed the grand total of my flying hours. 'Is 3,337 hours a lot?'

he asked. I explained that it was not a lot, but that it was a lot more than a little. Few contemporary military pilots would have more.

'What do you think about having your genitals cut off and sewn into your mouth?' he asked politely. I begged his pardon.

'You are not volunteering for a war,' he explained. 'It will be *Jihad*. There will be few prisoners taken by the Arabs. Hence my question.'

'Will you take a loyalty oath?' he then asked.

'To what?'

'Zionism.'

'No.'

'When can you leave?'

'Tomorrow.'

At the end of the second interview he produced a small bottle of vodka and two tiny glasses. The toast was Zion. We knocked the vodka back Russian-style. He then gave me an open train/boat ticket to Paris, a moderate sum of sterling and francs, and a name and address in the Avenue de la Grande Armée in Paris. He reminded me that I would need a visa for France and asked me to report there as soon as possible.

'I must tell you,' he said, 'I have reported to my superiors that I think you are an agent working for British Intelligence. They have decided to play along to see what happens.'

'Surely,' I said, 'the British would not use an uncircumcised Gentile as an agent in Palestine?'

'That,' he said, 'might be disingenuous double-bluff.'

Next day I said goodbye and thanks to the Silvers and caught the Paris-bound Golden Arrow boat-train at Victoria Station. It was still an adventurous thing to do. My fellow passengers were mostly middle-aged and elegantly dressed, with braying voices and expensive luggage. It was before package tours and mass travel. Only the rich or the fugitive travelled abroad. I read my passport. Among other things it stated: 'We, Ernest Bevin . . . His Majesty's Principal Secretary of State for Foreign Affairs, Request and Require . . . and to afford him every assistance and protection of which he may stand in need.' I wondered whether, in the circumstances, that applied to me. I went through customs and immigration formalities at Dover and Calais with a delicious feeling of intrigue.

The Avenue de la Grande Armée office in Paris was the Zionist recruiting office for the whole of Europe. There was no secrecy. The French were, at that time, pro-Israel, probably just to irritate the British. The four-storey building and the pavements outside were packed night and day with male and female volunteers. There was a babel of different tongues.

Most of the volunteers were destined for Marseilles and a slow boat to Palestine. My contact, explaining that I needed a visa, asked for my passport. I asked for where but he refused to answer, explaining that my mission, as he called it, was highly secret and I would find out on my departure.

I spent several days at a small pension around the corner, awaiting my mysterious visa.

It was an austere Paris in 1948, with gas-driven cars, decrepit taxis, hefty surcharges for a bath, and horsemeat in butchers' shops. I am not a Francophile. Nor have I discovered the Paris that so many people love. I find it aloof, covetous and lonely. I spent most of my time up the Eiffel Tower drinking coffee while trying to translate French newspapers for news of Israel, in the Louvre with the Impressionists and reading Obelisk Press pornography by Anaïs Nin and Henry Miller.

Chapter 18

THE ISRAELI CITIZEN army at the start of the war initially consisted of Haganah, which became the official army of 15,000 troops, and two political private armies; Irgun Z'vai Leumi, 3,000 troops and the Stern Group, 650 troops. Conscription and volunteers from overseas, called Mahal, soon swelled these figures.

Haganah was a quasi-legal Jewish militia established in Palestine in the late 1930s, with a nod and a wink from the British authorities, to protect isolated Jewish kibbutzim from marauding Arabs. They were assisted by a British Army captain, later Brigadier-General Wingate, of Chindit fame in Burma, known in Palestine as Lawrence of the Jews. The Haganah's official position was curiously ambiguous. Some of its activities were approved by the British, some forbidden. It became even more ambiguous towards the end of British rule when the penalty for possessing unauthorised arms was death by hanging. Many of the Haganah had served in the British forces, including the Jewish Brigade, during the Second World War, and their experience was to prove vital.

The Haganah was considered moderate, even respectable, in its opposition to British rule. The underground Irgun and Stern Group, however, were extremists dedicated to the use of terrorism to drive out the British and to counter-intimidate Arab terrorists.

The skirmishes between Jew and Arab, which had lasted intermittently for decades, became a full-scale civil war in the six months up to the end of the British mandate. For the Jews the civil war was useful, if such a word can be used in the context of war and death – their casualties numbered 1,200 dead in the last six months of British rule – for it honed the Jews into soldiers in preparation for the War of Independence, as it is called by the Israelis, due to start on 15 May 1948.

At the beginning of the war the Israelis were armed with 12,000 old rifles, 5,000 Sten guns, 850 mortars, 750 light machine-guns, 200 medium machine-guns and stocks of ammunition that would last only a few fighting days. They had no heavy machine-guns, anti-tank guns or artillery, apart from four ancient First World War

130

65mm guns with colossal bangs which were towed from front to front to impress the Arabs.

In Haganah there were people who could mess about with boats and some who could do the same with aeroplanes. They could not yet be called a navy and an air force. The boat people, about 350 personnel, had spent most of their time helping illegal immigrant ships to evade the Royal Navy blockade. Secretly they had built up their fleet to a total of 7,000 tons, mostly small boats, a quarter the size of the Egyptian Navy, whose fleet included destroyers.

What was to become the Israeli Air Force started as civil flying clubs in Palestine in the early 1930s. When the troubles started the clubs became part of Haganah and, equipped with a few small civil aircraft, mostly tiny Austers, established landing strips and primitive communications throughout Palestine, particularly with isolated kibbutzim in the Negev desert in the south. During the Second World War many Palestinian Jews served with the RAF. A few served as pilots. Their RAF experience proved invaluable when they returned to Palestine after the Second World War and set up the air-arm of the Haganah. As most of their operations were illegal they soon earned the oxymoronic sobriquet the underground air force.

In the heavy fighting before the British left the air-arm carried out reconnaissance and communication flights, supply and ambulance duties, escorted lorry convoys and attacked marauding Arabs with hand grenades and bottle-bombs. Meanwhile they were slowly expanding to a total of thirty light aircraft and some thirty pilots. None of the aircraft was military. None of the pilots had combat experience.

At the beginning of May 1948, the Chiefs of Staff of Egypt, Lebanon, Syria, Iraq, Saudi Arabia, Yemen and Jordan met in Damascus to finalise their invasion plans.

Syria was to attack from the north-west to capture Galilee. Lebanon, dragged unwillingly into the war, was to attack from the north along the coastal plain towards Acre and Haifa. Iraq was to attack on the central front on a short twenty-mile advance to the Mediterranean Sea to cut Palestine in half. Egypt was to advance from the south in a two-pronged attack: one column to advance through Gaza and capture Tel Aviv, another column to attack through Beersheba and join up with Jordan's Arab Legion to capture all Jerusalem. After capturing Jerusalem, the Arab Legion and the Egyptians were to advance to capture Nablus and the central plains and press on to Tel Aviv. The forces of Saudi-Arabia were to fight under Egyptian command. Yemen did not send troops until later. Within Palestine itself there was the Palestinian Arabs' own forces, led by Fauzi el-Kaukji, of 10,000 semi-trained troops, supported by 35,000 irregulars.

All these forces, except el-Kaukji's, were regular armies, equipped with modern weapons, tanks and artillery. They were to attack simultaneously on all five fronts, supported by the air forces of Egypt, Syria and Iraq, totalling 130 fighter and light bomber aircraft. The Egyptian Navy would complete the encirclement of the Jews by blockading the Mediterranean Sea.

The most formidable of the Arab forces was Jordan's Arab Legion, with 8,000 front-line troops, commanded by an Englishman, Lieutenant-General Sir John Bagot Glubb, better known as Glubb Pasha. Mostly tough Bedouin tribesmen devoted to King Abdullah, the Legion was a British security force, equipped, trained and led by British officers and NCOs seconded from the British Army. Overnight on 14–15 May the Legion ceased to be a British security force and became Jordan's army. Simultaneously, Glubb Pasha and several of his fellow British officers and NCOs resigned from the British Army and signed up for King Abdullah.

In modern warfare it is rare that there are not enough people available to kill and be killed. It is arms that matter and this was the case with the Jews in Palestine. The British arms embargo in Palestine until the end of the Mandate played into the hands of the Arabs. Arms were smuggled across the border from neighbouring Arab countries. After the British pulled out, the United Nations well-meaningly continued the Middle East arms embargo. But the Arabs still acquired arms freely from their Arab brothers. One look at the map explains why an arms embargo in the area is in effect an arms embargo against the Jews alone. Neither did the embargo take into account that the invading Arab armies were fully equipped before the war started.

Geography was also on the Arabs' side. Palestine is long, thin and narrow-waisted, with vulnerable borders. With fifty metres of border for every square kilometre of territory it is a strategist's nightmare. There was no room for strategic subtlety or mistakes. Israel started the war with its back to the wall and the sea. The first war the Israelis lost would be their last.

What odds on Jewish survival in Palestine on 15 May 1948?

Chapter 19

M Y VISA WAS for Czechoslovakia. In the bus to Le Bourget airport I tried to recall what little I knew of where I was going. King Wenceslas, Kafka, Bohemia, St. Vitus, Dvorak, Prague and, of course, Munich. Czechoslovakia had recently been in the news with the communist coup in February. It was now firmly behind the Iron Curtain. Western newspapers said the coup had been bloody and the country was now suffering the worst excesses of the Stalin era. The only blood I saw was when I cut myself shaving.

The Air France Languedoc aeroplane from Paris to Prague was an old-fashioned, lumbering, pre-war delight. The scarlet-clad air hostesses oozed chic and care in the nearly empty airliner. Few passengers flew through the Iron Curtain in 1948. We flew east over Germany, my first sight of it. It was a clear, sunny day and in 1948 airliners still flew reasonably low. I was not sorry when for mile after mile I saw the retributive ruins of the Third Reich.

In the arrivals lounge at Prague airport armed guards with red stars on their peaked hats, huge jackboots and stern, forbidding expressions emphasised which side of the Iron Curtain I was on. I was relieved when a chauffeur held up a piece of cardboard with *Levit* chalked on it. My name was going to be a problem for the next fifteen months. Everyone assumed I was Jewish and spelt my name with the Jewish spelling. Inevitably my *nom de guerre* became *Leviticus*.

There was a Skoda car parked outside. We drove on the right-hand side of the road; always a prelude to adventure for the British. After unsuccessful attempts to communicate with the chauffeur, who did not speak English, I sat back and looked at the country that Munich had been all about. It was beautiful, apart from Klandno, a mining and steel town, where murdered men from the nearby wiped-out village of Lidice had worked. The road signs were enjoyably foreign with vowels missing between consonants: Plzen, Brno, Krkonose. Since the coup Carlsbad was now Karlovy Vary, Marianbad was Marianske Lazne.

I had no idea where I was going. It was a longish drive. The sun indicated we were driving westwards, a mildly comforting thought with the Cold War warriors on both sides hotting things up. Jan Masaryk, Foreign Secretary and the only non-communist member of the Czechoslovakia government after the February coup, had recently jumped, slipped or been pushed to his death from a window in Prague. The Berlin airlift was about to start, and I was on the wrong side of the Iron Curtain.

I had forgotten to buy cigarettes on the flight. I also wanted a drink. By miming I conveyed my needs to the chauffeur and we stopped at an inn in a tiny village. The cigarettes I bought were Russian and cough-making, with each cigarette built into a stiff paper holder. Two full, small glasses were plonked down in front of me and two more in front of the chauffeur. He said 'Na Zeravi' and knocked one drink down in a single gulp, immediately followed by the other. Not to be outdone, I said 'Na Zeravi' and, with everybody watching expectantly, did the same. They guffawed as I gasped and choked. It was slivovice, the Czech fire-water aperitif. I got my own back when the chauffeur was obliged to pay. I had no Czech krona.

In an isolated and rural area about twenty miles from the East German border we turned onto a minor road leading to a military aerodrome. Heavily armed Czech Army guards at the gate gave us and the car a thorough going-over before waving us through with a salute. The aerodrome was primitive with a control tower, a few huts and a single concrete runway. It had been used as a fighter base by the Luftwaffe during the Second World War.

When the tarmac came into view I saw an astonishing collection of American transport aircraft and several Messerschmitt 109 fighters parked neatly along the tarmac. There were six or seven Curtiss Commando C46s, a Douglas Skymaster DC4 and several smaller aircraft. A Lockheed Constellation and three B17 Flying Fortresses would be added later. Even more astonishing, the ground staff wore baseball caps and were speaking with American accents. As I watched, another C46 circled and landed. What on earth was an American Air Force base doing behind the Iron Curtain?

It was not, of course, an American base. This was Zatec, the secret Israeli base behind the Iron Curtain of a clandestine air-lift that was busting the United Nations arms blockade of Israel. The

135

then civil operation, set up almost entirely by American Zionists, was called Balak, an obscure reference to one of Zippor's sons.

Because of the British and UN arms embargo, the Jews could not buy arms legally and openly before and during the Arab–Israeli war. During those months Jewish agents throughout the world were scouring junk-yards, war-surplus dumps and thieves' kitchens for arms, ammunition and aircraft. When possible they bribed and bought. If necessary they stole. Export licences for arms are granted frugally. Certainly not to nations that do not yet officially exist or suffer an arms embargo. The American Neutrality Act, with penalties including loss of American nationality, was a further deterrent to American Jews helping to arm Israel.

Most arms dealers by their very trade are unprincipled and arms appropriation for the Israelis was a witches' brew of broken promises, lies, Byzantine intrigue, treachery and a race against 15 May 1948. D-Day for the War of Independence.

Once bought, the arms and equipment and aircraft had to be transported and smuggled into Palestine. For this purpose one enterprising Israeli agent in America bought an ex-US Navy aircraft-carrier, the *Attu*, for $125,000. Conversion work was carried out, but with the FBI showing interest and the realisation that aircraft-carriers are difficult to hide or disguise, Israel's first and last aircraft-carrier was sadly sold and broken up for scrap.

For years during the British Mandate the Palestinian Jews had smuggled arms into Palestine for the civil war against the Arabs and terrorism against the British. It was on a small scale. A few rifles here, a few machine-guns there. But it was the nucleus of the world-wide network that mushroomed when the British government announced the ending of their Mandate.

With that announcement I suppose a few Jews in Palestine sat down, scratched their heads and started making lists. Their problem was unique. There were no reference books and they had little recent experience. The last war the Jews had fought had been against the Roman Legions. What does one need to start a nation from scratch? And what else does that nation need when it will be fighting a war of survival from day one of its existence? How many guns, rifles, grenades? How many tents, blankets, boots, lorries, pilots, mechanics, aircraft, tools, flags, bugles, binoculars, tyres, field-radios, knives, forks, spoons? How much ammunition and blood plasma? How many stretchers? Their formula must have been think of a number, double it, double it again.

It was soon realised that with the Royal Navy still intercepting and searching all ships entering Palestinian waters the magnitude and urgency of the arms logistical problem would not be solved by itty-bitty smuggling. There would be no problem with the British Navy after 15 May, of course, but by then it would be too late.

Daunting though the distances were between America and Israel, the answer was a covert airlift, a novel thought in 1947. Plans were drawn up to use a banana republic in Latin America as a base, with a re-fuelling halt in southern Europe and with the flights so timed that they would arrive in Palestine at night at secret strips prepared throughout the country.

Buying warplanes and arms in 1947/48 was no problem for the legitimate. War surplus material was cached throughout the world waiting for a purchaser. Tens of thousands of aircraft, new or mission proud, awaited the knackers' hammer, or a purchaser at ten for the price of one. Dakotas at $6,000, Lockheed Constellations at $15,000, Spitfires at £500. It was a buyer's market for the tools of war. Except for Zionist Jews.

Early in 1948, Zionist agents in the New York purchasing office using bogus fronts bought, *inter alia*, ten C46 Curtiss Commandos, three Lockheed Constellations and three B17 Flying Fortresses. Jewish aircrew and ground staff were recruited. All the transport aircraft were stripped and modified for the airlift to Israel. The B17 bombers were flown to Israel after 15 May and became the nucleus of the Israeli Air Force bomber command. The cover story for the American State Department, FBI, CIA, and various other American government agencies showing interest was a company called Service Airways, supposedly a new airline to carry freight to Europe and refugees back. It was flimsy and unconvincing. It was not long before faceless G-men were seen in the middle distance watching the aircraft as they were being converted at Burbank, California, and Millville, New Jersey. It was obvious the cover had blown. Everything had to be got out quickly, but where to?

By a remarkable coincidence an American pilot had recently obtained a franchise to start an international airline in Panama to be called *Lineas Aereas de Panama, Sociedad Anonima*, LAPSA for short. Unfortunately he had little capital and no aircraft. He had a friend,

who knew a friend, who knew a chap, who had a friend who had
heard that the Jews were setting up an airline or something. Contact
was tortuously made. The Jews had aircraft and crews but no airline
as a front. In Panama there was an airline without aircraft or crews.
They met and joined forces. A perfect fit.

LAPSA was to be based at Tocumen, Panama, a recently com-
pleted white-elephant airport about thirty miles east of Panama
City. Zion's airlift would fly the flag of Panama's national airline.
The Panamanians from peasant to President were delighted. Lineas
Aereas de Panama had an imposing and reputable ring.

Meanwhile Rome-based agents were completing negotiations to
establish a secret refuelling base at a disused airstrip near Perugia,
central Italy. It had primitive facilities and was surrounded by
mountains.

Politically, Panama was a perfect cover. Logistically, with a
round trip of some 18,000 miles, it could hardly be worse. Half the
C46's payload, despite the refuelling base in Italy, would be the
dead weight of its own fuel. Every flight would be illegal gun-
running, with crews arrested and aircraft and cargoes impounded
should anything go wrong. Each return flight to Palestine meant
crossing the South Atlantic twice, via Natal and Dakar, in over-
worked, under-maintained aircraft with exhausted crews. Few of
the pilots had flown the type of aircraft to be used and there was
little time for training. A large part of the route would be near
hostile Arab territory. In the eastern Mediterranean the Royal Air
Force would be on the prowl, gladly supporting the United Nations
arms embargo. Essential secrecy would be almost impossible to
maintain. It seemed a recipe for disaster.

Panamanian logos and registration numbers were painted on the
aircraft and long-range fuel tanks fitted inside the fuselage of the
C46s. In April, just before the American authorities pounced, the
C46s and one Constellation were flown out to Tocumen, some via
Mexico, the others via Jamaica. It was a proving flight for the newly
recruited aircrews and the converted aircraft. Flaws were found in
both. One C46 crashed taking off from Mexico City, killing both
crew members, the first casualties of what would soon be the Israel
Air Force. The two Constellations left behind were seized by US
Customs and never got out.

Crews and aircraft then languished against time at Tocumen,

138

waiting for their cargo of P47 Republic Thunderbolt fighter aircraft, spares and armaments that were to be supplied by Mexico.

The P47 was a first-rate fighter aircraft but it was fat-bellied and heavy. It was planned to dismantle the wings and shoehorn them into the C46s half at a time. An 18,000 mile round trip to deliver half a fighter. It was a logistical nightmare born of desperation. It was hoped the Constellation would accommodate a whole P47.

Negotiations with Mexico dragged on. Desperation spread from Tel Aviv to New York to Mexico to Panama, but the Mexican authorities were unmoved – *mañana*. But there were few *mañanas* left for the Jews before 15 May.

The supply noose was pulled tighter when President Truman, in support of the UN arms embargo, closed loopholes on the export of civil aircraft to the Middle East. There was more bad news when a crew despatched in a C46 to inspect the airstrip at Perugia in Italy reported back that it was far too short for loaded C46s and Constellations. The C46 was held on suspicion by the Italian authorities for weeks. The crew quietly disappeared and got back to Panama. The C46 was released later. Zionist agents in Rome, using the LAPSA cover, arranged a new refuelling base at Catania, in Sicily. It was an improvement on Perugia, with a long concrete runway, fierce Sicilian independence to keep Rome inquisitiveness at bay and requiring less of a dog-leg on the flight from Panama to Palestine.

Some relief came in December 1947, with a secret offer from Czechoslovakia to sell fighter aircraft, arms and ammunition and the exclusive use of a military aerodrome at Zatec as a base. That Czechoslovakia, virtually a communist nation by this time, was the only country in the world prepared, with a nod from Russia, to help the Jews at this critical moment, is a quirky piece of history that Israelis and Jews tend to overlook or dismiss. Czechoslovakian rifles, machine-guns and ammunition were bought and smuggled into Palestine during March by merchant ships, despite the British naval blockade. Some arms were flown non-stop from Czechoslovakia by a chartered American DC4 aircraft, landing at a secret strip in Palestine at night. The offer of Czech fighter aircraft was not taken up. The P47 Thunderbolts would soon be on the way from Panama.

Or would they? By mid-April, four weeks before D-Day, it was still *mañana* in Mexico. After being informed that the Egyptian, Iraqi and Syrian Air Forces had a total of 131 military aircraft and the Jews had none, Ben Gurion, designated by his Zionist colleagues to be Prime Minister and Minister of War after the British had left, lost patience. Three weeks before D-Day he cancelled the Mexican negotiations for the P47 Thunderbolt fighters and took up the Czechoslovakian offer, with an order for ten new Czech-built Messerschmitt 109G fighter aircraft, including guns, ammunition and spares, for $44,000 each, with an option, soon taken up, for a further fifteen. The exclusive use of Zatec as the European air base for the airlift was also confirmed.

It was a politically courageous decision. Although Marxists are historically anti-Zionist, Russia and its allies had surprisingly voted in favour of partition in Palestine and a Jewish state during the important United Nations General Assembly debate in November 1947, and had been diplomatically supportive since then. But the Cold War was now at its frigid height and most of the financial aid for the new Jewish state came from American Jews. Offend them by close relations with Russia and its allies and the financial aid might dry up. Offending the American government could be even more disastrous. But the need for fighter aircraft was critical and Russia, through Czechoslovakia, was offering help. America was not.

If it was feasible to airlift P47 Thunderbolts 9,000 miles from Panama to Israel, it was more feasible to airlift the lighter and smaller Messerschmitt 109 2,200 miles from Czechoslovakia to Israel. And so it was decided. Overnight, Lineas Aereas de Panama became redundant. During the next few days it disappeared into the eastern sky, heading for Czechoslovakia, never to be seen again by the baffled Panamanians.

On 14 May 1948, without ceremony, the last British High Commissioner in Palestine, General Sir Alan Cunningham, left Haifa on board a British destroyer and the League of Nations Mandate, signed on 29 September 1923, ended with a whimper. A sad, bitter, bloodstained end to the admirable intent expressed in Britain's Balfour Declaration of 2 November 1917. And, with hindsight, a colossally tragic what-might-have-been.

Had various British governments, left and right, during the Mandate accepted the advice of its own Peel Royal Commission, the League of Nations, the United Nations Assembly, influential members and supporters of Tory and Labour governments, America and the Russian bloc, and imposed the partition of Palestine into separate Jewish and Arab states, it would have been accepted on both sides. By the Palestinian Jews immediately. By the Palestinian Arabs after the obligatory show of riot and protest.

Middle East politics were not yet dominated by oil expediency and Muslim extremism. The Arabs had not yet entrenched themselves into the position of total opposition to any form of Jewish sovereignty. If it had been necessary, in order to make the new Palestinian Arab nation economically viable, King Abdullah of Jordan would have been delighted to join with the Palestinian Arabs to create a greater Trans-Jordan embracing the West Bank, the Gaza Strip and a neutral corridor from Jerusalem to the Mediterranean Sea at Jaffa. Jerusalem would have been a free city administered by all the religions concerned. Israel would have been small but beautiful, ironically a third of its present size and quite possibly could have joined the British Commonwealth to form a stable British–Israeli sphere of influence in the Middle East. Iraq and Egypt had little interest then in the squabbles between Palestinian Arab and Jew, and anyway were virtually British puppets. Syria was too busy trying to get rid of the French and their Mandate. Lebanon, that tragic, beautiful, quasi-Christian country, would have flourished as an entrepreneurial link between the two new nations. Saudi Arabia would happily have continued a nineteenth-century way of life lubricated with twentieth-century oil. Five wars would not have been fought. Jew and Arab, remembering that they are both Semites and first cousins, would have quashed the lunatic fringe on both sides and lived happily ever after. It is my view that this could and would have happened but for one man, supported by his mandarins: Ernest Bevin.

On the same day as the British left Palestine, 5 Iyyar 5708 in the Jewish calendar, the provisional government of the Jews in Palestine, led by David Ben-Gurion, made their historic Declaration of Independence, part of which included the following:

Accordingly We, Members Of The People's Council, Representatives Of The Jewish Community of Eretz-Israel And Of The Zionist Movement, Are Here Assembled On The Day Of The Termination Of The British Mandate Over Eretz-Israel

And, By Virtue Of Our Natural And Historic Right And On The Strength Of The Resolution Of The United Nations General Assembly, Hereby Declare The Establishment Of A Jewish State In Eretz-Israel, To Be Known As The State Of Israel.

As Declarations of Independence go it was not as unkind to the British as Jefferson's. Neither did it have his pellucid prose. Perhaps it reads better in Hebrew.

Chapter 20

ON ITS ARRIVAL in Czechoslovakia Lineas Aereas de Panama
became the Air Transport Command of the Israeli Air Force,
ATC for short, based at Zatec, 2,200 miles from Israel. Most of the
Panamanian logos and registration numbers were removed from
the aircraft. In addition to being ATC's base, Zatec was to become
the secret operating and collecting centre for aircraft and spares
being covertly bought throughout Europe, including the UK.

Zatec looked like a peaceful, small town but it was used to
upheaval and the ironies of history. It was formerly in Sudetenland,
that part of Czechoslovakia annexed in 1938 by Germany, with the
authority of the Munich Pact, before Hitler then annexed the whole
of Czechoslovakia in March 1939. The Germans renamed Zatec,
calling it Saaz. So it remained until the end of the Second World War
and Czechoslovakia regained the freedom it had lost at Munich.
Saaz became Zatec once again. And now, in 1948, the final irony.
The hotels, bars and cafés in the small square which had echoed to
the sound of 'Horst Wessel' and 'Deutschland über Alles' when the
Luftwaffe were at play, and the airfield down the road where they
flew their Messerschmitt 109s into combat, was now the European
base of the despised *Juden*.

The two hotels, the Stalingrad and the Zloty Lev, were full of ATC
personnel. There were about fifty altogether – pilots, navigators,
flight engineers, wireless operators and ground staff – mostly
Americans. Exotic names rolled from the tongue; Tolchinsky,
Schwartz, Horowitz, Marmelstein, Rosenbaum, Moonitz, Katz,
Kurtz, Pomerantz, Goldstein, Applebaum, Schwimmer, Chinsky,
two Rubens and four Cohens. I got a warm smile, a hand-shake and
a 'Hi, there' from all except the Chief Pilot who gave me a cool nod.
He dismissed anything – animal, vegetable, or mineral – that was
not American.

The airlift to Israel had already started. The two hotels were like a
Second World War officers' mess. Fresh crews departed, exhausted
crews returned. There was eating, sleeping, drinking, poker and
gin-rummy going on night and day. The bedrooms were a sham-

bles, the dining-room, kitchens and bars always open, the staff happily harassed. Nobody wore a *kippa* and there was little sign of Judaism, orthodox or not, except wit, humour and *chutzpah*.

To have been a Gentile virtually alone among Jews at war, work and play for over twelve months should provoke some thought and comment but at the end of it all the Jewishness did not matter. To most of them being Jewish was not an act of faith but merely a fate. They were good, bad, indifferent, like the rest of us. No better, no worse. As Shylock said, if tickled they laughed, if pricked they bled. I realised that to be thought as good as the rest of us the Jews had to be better. It is the Gentiles who have created the belief that if there are some Jewish crooks, all Jews are crooks. If there are some Jewish usurers, all Jews are usurers. If there are some Jewish communists, all Jews are communists. If there are some Jews with big noses, all Jews have big noses. Jews must despair sometimes at being Jewish. Even the Jews' alleged guilt about the crucifixion of Christ is not the answer. Anti-Semitism started long before Christ and I find it difficult to believe that the average anti-Semite cares very much about what happened at Calvary.

The anti-Semite now wears a fashionable new cloak. He or she is not anti-Semitic, merely anti-Zionist or anti-Israel, as if they were divisible.

I had a check-flight on the C46 Curtiss Commando with the Chief Pilot. I had not told him, or anyone, that I had scarcely flown for over two years, that what little flying I had done was in toy aeroplanes, and that I did not have a flying licence. I was afraid I would be sent packing if they found out. Fortunately nobody worried about flying licences.

The C46 by the standards of the day was a big aeroplane. Two stories high and with a maximum take-off weight of 56,000 pounds compared with the 28,000 pounds of the C47 Dakota, it was one of the largest twin-engined aircraft ever built, with an undeserved reputation for killing people. With a cruising speed of 220 mph and a normal range of eight hours it carried up to 18,000 pounds of freight. Tough, rugged and capacious it was the biggest and most sophisticated aeroplane I had flown. I grew to love the great, fat, ugly beast.

It was the first time I had flown with an American pilot. He raised

144

---

his eyebrows when, after my first take-off, I requested 'Under-carriage up, please.' The Americans shout 'Gear-up' and are similarly laconic with other flight orders. Despite his eyebrows I kept to the RAF vernacular. The crews had a laugh mimicking me: 'Actually, I say old sport, would you mind tewwibly selecting undercawwiage up for me please. Thanks awfully, old boy, tewwibly kind of you and all that.'

Despite being rusty and tense under the Chief Pilot's appraisal it was a joy to fly a man's size aeroplane again with four thousand horse-power at my finger-tips.

After several take-offs and landings and some instrument flying he passed me as a captain. He had reservations but there was an acute shortage of captains and he felt I had enough experience to muddle through. On the tarmac a C46 had just returned from a successful airlift of half a Messerschmitt and arms to Israel. I heard the captain loudly telling the mechanics – all pilots spoke too loudly after landing, ears buzzing as though suffering from tinnitus, in those propeller days – that he had picked up heavy icing over the Alps. It was a language I had sorely missed.

The crew brought back news from Israel. On the southern front the Egyptians were advancing from the south towards Tel Aviv and Beersheba. Their air force was bombing and strafing at will, including Tel Aviv where 41 people had been killed by a bomb on the central bus station. On the eastern front there was bitter house-to-house fighting in Jerusalem and Jordan's Arab Legion had captured the Old City. On the northern front Israeli forces held Galilee but the Syrians were advancing down the Jordan valley. On the central front Iraqi and Jordanian forces were pushing towards the sea and were only eight miles from the coast in their advance to cut Israel in half. It was a grim picture. The Israeli forces, still without artillery or fighter aircraft, were fighting with rifles, blood and guts.

Of immediate concern to us was that Ekron, the Balak aerodrome in Israel, was under fire. (Ekron was the former RAF base Aquir.) Aircraft had been fired on when landing and taking-off. We were advised to enquire over the aircraft's radio before we landed there who it was in charge of the aerodrome. If the answer was in Arabic a short landing-strip at Tel Aviv was the only alternative.

The Arabs had the freedom of the skies. The three or four Messerschmitt 109s already airlifted to Israel were being assembled with the help of Czech engineers but were not yet ready for action. Israel's small, unarmed, flying-club aircraft were being used for supply, reconnaissance and bombing with home-made bombs. Two had been shot down by Egyptian Spitfires.

The nucleus of a fighter squadron for the Messerschmitts had been formed with a a few Israeli pilots. I felt a twinge at that news. Perhaps I could transfer later. Ex-Second World War fighter pilots, including Gentile mercenaries, were being recruited from abroad. Two had been killed – one was Buzz Buerling, a Canadian ace of Malta fame – without firing a shot when the Norseman aircraft they were ferrying to Israel crashed while taking-off from Urbe aerodrome, near Rome.

For reasons best known to the Italians the Balak airlift suddenly became unwelcome at Catania aerodrome. Perhaps leaks in the world's press about the airlift, in defiance of the United Nations arms embargo, embarrassed the Italians. France, however, was not intimidated and secretly offered the use of Ajaccio airport in Corsica as a refuelling base. This added about 500 miles to the round flight to Israel but the offer was hurriedly accepted.

On one of the first flights from Zatec to Ekron, ATC lost a C46 in the kind of accident that was to be expected. Long-range communications between Ekron and the C46s were poor. For the ten-hour flight between Ajaccio and Ekron the crews were like deaf mutes most of the way, ignorant of any change in the weather, or the war situation. Much can happen in either field in eight hours. It was only during the last forty miles or so, fifteen minutes, that the pilots were able to communicate direct with the aerodrome, using short-range radio telephone.

The C46 arrived at Ekron at midnight to a welcome of thick fog. There were no blind-flying instrument landing facilities. Captain Moonitz, ex-USAAF, who had resigned as a New York fireman to join ATC, made several attempts to land. Ground staff lit flares but the crew could see nothing. The short landing-strip at Tel Aviv aerodrome was also fog-bound. The only alternative aerodrome was at British Cyprus where the aircraft and its precious cargo would be impounded and the crews arrested. Moonitz said nuts to that. He decided to circle to burn off petrol – there was no way of dumping fuel in a C46 – hoping meanwhile, having burned his boat to Cyprus, the fog would lift.

11 Squadron Leader Gordon Levett at Mergui, Burma, a few weeks before his court martial

12 A C46 Curtiss Commando of ATC over Haifa Bay, summer 1948

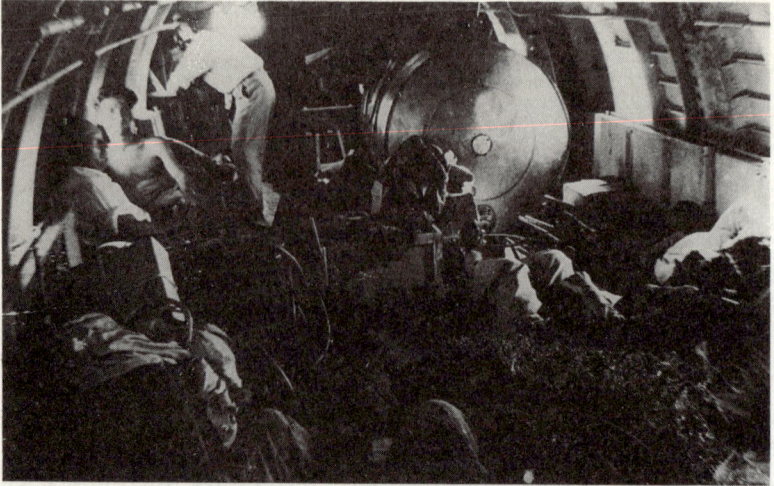

13 Exhausted aircrew taking a nap in the cabin of an ATC C46 returning to Zatec
from Ekron during Operation Balak. Note massive auxiliary fuel tank

14 This photograph gives an indication of the size of a C46 parked in a bomb-
blast shelter at Ekron, autumn 1948

With twenty minutes' fuel left the fog was worse. Moonitz rejected ditching. The C46 and cargo would be lost. He decided to let down over the sea and fly in low on a timed approach. The C46 hit a low ridge about two miles from the runway and burst into flames. The navigator was killed when the cargo shifted on impact. The wireless operator was seriously injured. Moonitz and his co-pilot suffered minor injuries. Before the ground staff were able to locate the crash in the fog, Moonitz had carried the wireless operator, a well-built six-footer, on his back to the aerodrome.

Another C46 landed safely later the same night, took off just before dawn for the return flight and was forced to land at Athens with engine trouble. The Greeks impounded the aircraft but released the crew. It was a bad night.

There was other news. To cover the final evacuation of the British from Palestine, Spitfires of 32 and 208 Squadrons of the RAF were still based at Ramat David, about fifteen miles south-east of Haifa, the main port of evacuation.

At 0600 hours on 22 May two Egyptian Spitfires bombed and strafed Ramat David aerodrome, destroying several RAF aircraft on the ground and causing casualties. 208 Squadron Spitfires scrambled but were too late to intercept. A standing flying patrol was then mounted by the RAF. At 0754 hours the Egyptians returned to the attack with three Spitfires. All three were shot down, two by the standing patrol Spitfires of 208 Squadron, the third by anti-aircraft guns. At 0915 the Egyptians returned for a third bite of the cherry with two Spitfires. They too were shot down by 208 Squadron.

The Egyptians subsequently apologised, explaining that their pilots thought they were attacking an Israeli Air Force base at Megiddo, some fifteen miles further south. The RAF thought they were defending themselves against Israeli attacks. The RAF had lost several dead and injured and several aircraft destroyed. The Egyptians had lost five Spitfires. The only people to benefit from this fiasco of mistaken identity between two allies were the Israelis, the last thing the RAF or the Egyptians wanted. To add a final irony, one of the Egyptian Spitfires was salvaged and repaired by the Israelis and subsequently shot down several Egyptian aircraft.

My first flight as captain on the Balak run was at the end of May. The airlift itinerary was, depending upon weather, an 0900 hours take-off for the three-and-a-half-hour flight to Ajaccio for refuelling and lunch. Then the ten-hour flight to Israel, arriving about midnight. After unloading, refuelling, a meal by candlelight, a smoke and a nap we took off again for the return flight before dawn and the arrival of the Egyptian Air Force. There were still no air defences and the C46s would have been wiped out had they been caught on the ground. We usually arrived back at Zatec late the same afternoon, after a day and a half without sleep and nearly 24 hours' flying time. Sometimes we slipped crews at Ekron.

I had a crew of two, co-pilot and navigator/radio operator. I scarcely knew either of them and sought them out the night before our flight for a chat. Yehuda Shimoni, the navigator, was a jocund, tubby Dutch Jew, who spoke fluent English, French, German and Italian in addition to his own incomprehensible tongue. Pesach Tolchinsky, the co-pilot, was nicknamed Pussy. Ex-American Air Force, he now lived with his family in a kibbutz in northern Galilee. With blond curls, a deep tan, blue-grey eyes, medium height and rugged shoulders he looked more like a casual Greek god than an archetypal Jew. He had served in the Haganah underground during the last year of the British Mandate. One of his closest friends had been hanged by the British for terrorist offences. He had been flying Haganah light aircraft in action before being transferred to ATC. He spoke Hebrew fluently. The kibbutz, where he lived with his wife and two children, was under attack by Syrian troops. His dislike of me was blatant. His responses to my overtures were monosyllabic; either 'Yep' or 'Nope'. It augured badly for our flight.

Later that evening I took Yehuda to one side and asked him why Tolchinsky did not like me. Yehuda explained that he did not like mercenaries, particularly if they were British. I wondered whether Yehuda felt the same.

I sought out Tolchinsky again. I had not wanted to broadcast that I was not a mercenary or a Jew, and was fighting for the same pay as any Israeli soldier (£6 a month, all found), but the cockpit is no place for a feud. After his apology we made up with slivovice and Russian cigarettes. I asked him to tell Yehuda.

Chapter 21

I FELT THE OLD wave of pride and pleasure when we arrived at the aerodrome and saw the C46, glistening, challenging, waiting. Christ, it was a big'un. The Chief Pilot had wisely given me the best crew available. Nobody in ATC knew me and I was a dark horse. Pussy and Yehuda were no doubt asking themselves whether this Limey Goy could fly. I felt their eyes on me as I went through the usual pre-flight rigmarole. The weather forecast was fair: low cloud and rain locally and a warm front between us and Corsica. At Corsica and beyond, at this time of year, the weather would always be blue and gold with only one or two isobars covering the whole Mediterranean. Balak flights eastbound to Middle East weather were not a problem apart from the risk of fog. Westbound into European weather, with no instrument landing facilities at Zatec, was another matter.

To encourage Pussy and Yehuda I did an exaggeratedly thorough pre-flight inspection of the aircraft. Our cargo was half a Messerschmitt 109, with every bit of extra space crammed with bombs, rifles, machine guns and ammunition. The long-range fuel tank in the fuselage took up the remaining space. With this extra tank we carried 1,650 gallons of fuel, eleven hours at normal cruising speed. We had to clamber over crates to get to the cockpit. We flew well in excess of the official gross weight and did not worry too much about the centre of gravity.

I had $5,000 in $100 bills in my pocket, our slush fund for bribery and corruption should things go awry. There was much that could. We were law-breakers, smuggling arms from behind the Iron Curtain across several international boundaries in defiance of the United Nations arms embargo. We were flying secretly, without communications to or from anywhere. We had no papers. Nobody knew who we were, where we came from, where we were going, what we were carrying. We could not make official flight plans, or ask for the latest weather en route, or report our position. We had no alternative destination after a long flight. Not all of us were licensed to fly. We had no oxygen, life rafts, life jackets, or instrument landing equipment. By the time we reached Ekron there was a fair chance it might be in enemy hands. Wearing assorted mufti we looked like wild-eyed brigands, particularly, unshaven, on the return flight.

It was good to climb into the left-hand seat up front. The captain's seat of undisputed authority, where one is king. A tiny kingdom on the ground but infinite in flight. Sitting in that worn green leather seat I savoured, as always, those few quiet moments while the doors were being checked and locked and the crew were settling down. My routine was always the same in this prelude to flight. Touching the controls with my finger tips, wiping a speck of dust from the windscreen, glancing at the instruments, a long look at the sky deciding whether it was going to be friend or foe, gathering my wits, concentrating my mind and establishing a rapport with the sleeping aeroplane. It was a moment of reflection and contemplation before, at the touch of a switch, the aeroplane stirs to life and generators whine, gyros whirr, hydraulic lines creak, lights flicker, instruments spring into action and radios hum. It never palled.

I was tense. We would be in cloud on instruments at five hundred feet. Nothing much to worry about if one is in practice, flying a familiar aeroplane, with a familiar crew, on a familiar route. None of these prerequisites applied. The crew knew it was my first flight as skipper and were quietly watchful as we taxied out to the runway. I had the windscreen wipers click-clacking already. I asked the flying Dutchman for the course to steer. He handed me a scrap of paper with the course written on it. I groaned. His number one looked like our seven, his seven like our four. Remembering Nevil Shute's story I asked him to Anglicize his figures when flying with me. The concentration camp numbers tattooed on his right forearm were also continental. I was impressed with Pussy. He was deft with the controls and correct with me. The cockpit is no place for larking about.

I was glad for the sake of the crew's confidence that I managed a good take-off. No singular achievement, but the C46 is a stubby aeroplane with a relatively short wheel-base and its tendency to swing on landing and take-off had troubled some of the pilots. The whites of my knuckles were showing when we entered cloud almost immediately after take-off. I had not flown blind on instruments for nearly three years and it showed. I was far too tense. Instead of being guided by the blind-flying instruments I was chasing them, my senses overloaded with their vital messages. Our airspeed, rate of climb and heading were all over the place. My arms and legs were aching with needless strain as I fought the C46 instead of coaxing it. Pride too was taking a fall. Crews are like valets, there are no secrets from them and they were watching intently. Pussy gestured towards George, the automatic pilot. At this height it would have been normal to switch it on and let George do the work. I shook my head. Somewhere lost within me was the ability to fly accurately on instruments. I had to find it. A pilot and his aeroplane fly in three dimensions; a simple matter when the sky is clear and a glance at the horizon tells the pilot his attitude in relation to the earth. Not so simple when in cloud and the horizon is hidden. The pilot then flies by reference to six blind-flying instruments that tell him, if he is prepared to trust them and not his senses, whether he is or is not climbing, diving, turning, banking, yawing, right side up and heading in the right direction. The siren call of one's senses giving messages different from those of the instruments must be ignored. They mislead to disaster. If the pilot is rusty and out of practice those six instruments are torment. Watch one too long and the other five play the fool. Get the course right and the rate-of-climb instrument tells you that you are heading for a stall. Get those two right and you are half-way through a slow roll. Add a bit of turbulence and a bit of icing and one has a diabolical brew. And always at the back of a pilot's mind is the knowledge that if he does not get it right and keep it right he is dead.

I was beginning to settle down when we hit turbulence and icing. I cursed the sly alchemy that transmutes, without warning, harmless water droplets into treacherous ice. We switched on the de-icing equipment – wings, tail-plane, propellers, windscreen and carburettors. We had not spoken a surplus word since taking-off for it was obvious I had bitten off about as much as I could chew. But slowly, humiliatingly slowly, my instrument flying improved. In recognition Pussy lit two cigarettes and passed one to me. Despite the whiff of petrol from the long-range tank behind us we inhaled deeply, the first time I had smoked in an aeroplane. Smoking was strictly prohibited in RAF aircraft. We were still climbing. The minimum safety height for crossing the Alps ahead of us hidden in cloud was 13,500 feet. At 15,000 feet we were still in cloud, our mouths gaping like landed fish from lack of oxygen. It was 18,000 feet before we broke through into blinding, brilliant sunshine. The clouds bleached white by the sun and stretching to all horizons like a soft eiderdown looked innocent of malice. I levelled off, switched on George and sat back. Yehuda gave me a new course to steer and passed cups of thermos coffee.

I proffered a brief explanation about my rusty instrument flying but the explanation was acknowledged rather than accepted. There was only one thing to do. Finishing the coffee and cigarette I switched off George and slowly let down back into the clammy, murky embrace of the clouds until we reached the icing and turbulence level. I flew for over half an hour on instruments without a word or a cigarette. By then I was as good as ever I was on instruments. Not brilliant, but sound. The point made, I handed over control to Pussy. To my delight he too was rusty. After a few minutes I grinned at him and pointed upwards. He grinned back. It was quits. We climbed back into the sunshine to see the Alps, arc-lighted by the sun, welcoming us on the horizon.

Corsica rises from the Mediterranean like a mountain. I was unprepared for the beauty of the island as we approached it from the north-east and banked around its northern tip before landing at Ajaccio on the west coast. It was exquisite. Apart from the coastal strip it was mountainous and heavily wooded, with wild Alpine flowers waving in welcome. The entire coastline was a series of isolated coves and bays edged with sun-bleached, untrodden sand, lapped by gentle ripples flecked with foam. The sea was so limpid we could see its depths as we looked down.

The airport had only one runway and was nuzzled by mountains, necessitating a tight final turn and a steep approach to the runway. With flashy blips of the throttle and a touch of slide-slipping it was light relief after the clammy embrace of freezing cloud.

A follow-me Jeep led us to the farthest corner of the aerodrome. It was good to feel that Mediterranean warmth as we switched off the engines and opened the cargo door. The airport buildings were low slung and fort-like, with the Tricolour flapping lazily from the top of the small control tower. It was all very Gallic.

While the C46 was being re-fuelled and serviced we had lunch al fresco on the airport restaurant verandah overlooking the mountains and the sea. The airport commandant, complete with Sam

Browne belt and kepi, joined us for an aperitif. He did not speak English. Yehuda interpreted for us.

I asked the commandant whether our being able to use his airport for refuelling was a little, local matter, or whether the Quai d'Orsay was privy to the arrangement. He winked hugely and made no comment. He warned us that secrecy was essential and that we should keep a low profile. That was why our C46 was parked in the far corner. There was also a suspicion of sabotage. A Halifax four-engine bomber aircraft, smuggled out of England and secretly bound for Israel, had recently crashed. Sugar in the petrol tank was one theory.

A moment or two of fear in a flight renews the appetite for life and the pleasure of simple things. I thought that day how good it was to be flying a man-size aeroplane again, to sit near where the mountains join the sea and white table-cloths and glasses sparkle in the sun. I sadly remembered that, four years before, during the Second World War, Saint-Exupéry had taken off from this island on a reconnaissance flight over southern France, never to return.

I was mildly concerned as we started our take-off. The tempera-ture was in the eighties and we had full fuel tanks. This meant a much longer take-off run than at Zatec where the fuel tanks had been half-full and the temperature lower. Half-way down the run-way with the engines at full take-off power the C46 was sluggish, the tail still down, the controls unresponsive. I opened up to emer-gency power for several seconds, changed my mind, chopped the throttles and braked heavily. The end of the runway was not that far ahead when we stopped with smoking brakes.

I taxied back to the beginning of the runway and U-turned care-fully so that we could use every inch of the runway for taking off. The windsock was hanging limply. That was no help. I lined up with the runway, kept the brakes on and opened the throttles slowly to take-off power. The C46 juddered and protested. This sort of treatment was all right for flashy, single-engined fighters, not for a stately, dignified pantechnicon. At emergency power I released the brakes and we shot down the runway like an enraged bull. It was a struggle to keep straight. The two Pratt & Whitney R2800 engines, asked to deliver more than the usual four thousand horse-power for take-off, were snarling in protest. It was uproar. I dropped 15 degrees of flap. I was glad I was not Pussy sitting there with nothing to do but sit and watch as the end of the runway drew nigh. I tried to push the throttles further forward but they were up against the stop. We had gone well beyond the point of stopping before I knew we were going to fly. We cleared the end of the runway by about ten feet.

We climbed to 8,500 feet and levelled off. It was a good height for the engines and our lungs. With the two engines sweetly on song, we set course for the long ten-hour haul to the Middle East. I flew the C46 with the confidence of a rider who had finally mastered a wilful stallion.

When we had settled down, with Italy's foot on the horizon, I handed over to Pussy and dozed and day-dreamed in the warm sun. Sitting up there, a spot and a drone in the sky, with shreds of summer clouds sailing past, I felt that life was good. This was a time when merely crossing the English Channel was still an adventure for most. When travellers were voyageurs and not tourists and 600 mph jet aircraft had not yet shrunk the globe to everyone's playground and reduced pilots to bus drivers. Aeroplanes still vibrated with life. Weather had to be fought, not merely flown over. The unexpected was expected. I was twenty-seven, a good age. Youth's acne and exaggerated cares gone. Wrinkles and dewlaps not yet harbingered. No sinister aches and pains. Teeth, despite youthful neglect, white and strong. Hirsute. Libido high, but no longer frantic. No wife, no children, no ties, no home, no mortgage, no money and earning none. In an iconoclastic way I preferred it so. Looking neither forward nor back, but enjoying today. Young, but slowly acquiring wisdom. I decided, as we crossed Italy's instep with the instruments signalling all's well, that I was, sometimes, a lucky man.

When I glanced at Pussy's brooding face I felt ashamed of my sanguine reverie. It would be another eight hours before he knew whether his family was still alive. I made him switch George off and fly manually. For practice, I said, but it was to keep him occupied.

Day was surrendering to night as we crossed Greece and the Aegean Sea. We detoured slightly to see the sun setting on the Acropolis and the islands scattered like pearls between Greece and Turkey. The sky and the sea and the islands were aflame with the sun's extravagant farewell. To the east ahead of us a daub of mauve and the appearance of a weak quarter moon heralded night. Yehuda worked out that we should cross the Israeli coast at midnight local time and arrive at Ekron four minutes later.

The thermos coffee was finished, the French bread and fish pâté long gone and there was no lavatory. We had to pee into bottles. We smoked cigarettes and played gin-rummy to keep awake. I tuned in to the BBC for news about Israel. To Pussy's disgust the BBC still called it Palestine. There was heavy fighting on all fronts. The Israelis had broken the Arab Legion siege of Jerusalem by carving a new road, the Burma Road of Israel, through the rocky hills to Jerusalem, by-passing the Legion. The Legion still held the Old City and was shelling Jerusalem indiscriminately. Jerusalem was now divided and was to remain so for nineteen years until the 1967 Six-Day War reunited it.

We saw the dogs of war long before we sensed the dim, blacked-out Israeli coast. The night sky over Israel was in torment. Tracer, flares and the blue-red explosions of shells and mortars peppered the horizon from Gaza in the south, to Acre in the north. In the Judean hills beyond there was a glow in the sky above Jerusalem. We switched off all our lights except the dimly glowing instrument lighting.

We raised Ekron aerodrome on the R/T and were cleared to land. They mentioned that there was hand-to-hand fighting a mile or two from the end of the runway. 'Which end?' I asked. 'The south,' they replied, at which I told them we would land towards the north. They switched on the dim and sparse runway lights when they heard our engines overhead. As I started our descent tracer ambled across our path. It had taken two wars before somebody fired at me in anger. Pussy poised his fingers over the landing-light switch. I shook my head and felt our way in darkness down to the runway. The runway lights were extinguished the moment we stopped. Nothing happened. I felt uneasy and vulnerable, sitting in total darkness, in a stationary aeroplane, in the middle of an aerodrome in the middle of a war in the Middle East. Pussy blasted a few words in Hebrew down his microphone. Waving torches appeared and guided us to the tarmac.

The moment we stopped the engines arc-lights flashed on illuminating the C46 and there was cheering and waving of hands. It was theatrical but gratifying. As Yehuda opened the cargo door the warm, soft wind ushered in the scent of orange blossom.

There was a babel of different tongues, with harsh Hebrew as the common denominator. There were no uniforms, but the casualness of their clothes was uniform. Open-necked shirts, shorts, sandals. Jews, I thought. All Jews and Jewesses, a majority at last. I was a minority of one. The noise of war surrounded the aerodrome but nobody took the slightest notice. Within minutes our arms were off-loaded and on their way to a critical battle on the outskirts of Jerusalem. The truncated Messerschmitt 109 was mated with its other half which had been delivered the previous night and was soon in action.

We were debriefed by Hayman Shamir, the Deputy Chief of the Israeli Air Force. Like everybody else he had a title, but no rank. He was an ex-American Israeli and had Hebrewised his name from Hyman Sheckman. (I became Gideon Levavi.) The Deputy Chief used his clout and fluent Hebrew with much force over the telephone to get through to Pussy's kibbutz 90 miles to the north. He passed the telephone to Pussy. I did not understand what Pussy was saying in Hebrew, but I did not need to. His face told me his family was safe.

Things happen and often it is not until years later that their significance registers, but on that balmy night in May 1948, I was fully aware of the historic momentousness of the time. The rebirth of the Jewish nation after an exile lasting two millennia.

Amid the bustle there was a striking equality among them all. It was not the equality of democracy, though that was to follow, but an equality sired by re-born Jewish freedom, pride and independence. No longer were they wandering Jews. They were Israelites of sovereign Israel.

From Galilee in the north to the biblical wilderness in the south and in Jerusalem to the east Jews were carving the name of Israel with pride. At last they had reached nationhood again. At last they were masters in their own land. No longer second-class citizens, a race without a nation, a barely tolerated minority. No longer the helpless target of petty bigots and powerful tyrants and the cruel jibes that Jews are heir to. No longer subjected to a thousand minor holocausts that led, finally and inexorably, to The Holocaust. It was this that gave them their equality, their swagger, their joy. No matter that the outcome of the struggle was unknown. No matter that this might be a second Masada, another immolation. No matter that the Arabs might destroy them as the Roman Legions had destroyed their forefathers 2,000 years before. They would serve their new nation with pride and would die, as their forefathers had died at Masada, rather than yield.

I had been looking forward to seeing Tel Aviv that night but Hayman advised against it. There was sniping on the Tel Aviv road and everything would be shut by the time we got there.

Hayman was a rare bird, a right-wing intellectual. We had our first political argument that night and spent the next thirty years, on my infrequent visits to Israel, continuing to argue. We argued without rancour for there was respect and affection on both sides. Among other things, he could never understand why I found it incomprehensible that Jews, history's victims, could be right-wing, and I could never understand why he could not understand. He was about thirty-two, an ex-navigator in the American Army Air Corps. Under medium height, slightly overweight, he could be formidably cold and brutal. He told me months later that he had been assigned to decide whether I was, or was not, a British spy. When I asked him what his conclusions were he grinned ambivalently. 'You are', he said, 'the only English Gentile idealist in the Israeli Air Force and just too good to be true.'

We took off for the return flight about two o'clock in the morning. Pussy was pleased when I let him do the take-off from the left-hand seat. Captains are not usually so kind. It was not a bad take-off, though the C46, now unladen except for fuel, was in a frisky mood. As I sat in the right-hand seat watching Pussy, ready to pounce if things went wrong, I felt frustrated that I had seen nothing of Israel.

It was a darkish night still, with a half-hearted moon. We could just discern the darker mass of the island of Karpathos as we flew over it. Looking down there was only one solitary light on the entire island. One lonely light in the middle of the night in our radius of view of a hundred miles. I wondered about that light and whether they were wondering about us as we droned overhead, invisible in the night. Was it an insomniac, or love, a police station, a deathbed, or had someone simply forgotten to switch off the light?

I dozed off and woke up at dawn over the Greek islands. We had timed it perfectly. From the air, dawn over the Greek islands with that special pellucid Greek light is incomparable, even with red-rimmed, bleary eyes. A mixture of saffron from the dawning sun, turquoise from the retreating night, and the glittering aquamarine of the sea with merchant ships trailing their white wash across the Mediterranean, their course as straight and true as ours. The white villas on the hills reflected the light sharply and breakfast smoke rose vertically from their chimneys.

ATC flights back to Zatec usually stopped overnight at Ajaccio. With no instrument landing facilities at Zatec, no politically viable alternative aerodrome should things go wrong, and exhausted crews, it would have been foolhardy to press on and attempt a landing at Zatec at night.

At Ajaccio two other ATC C46s, eastbound to Israel, were parked at the airport. It was certainly not a low profile. We joined the other crews in the restaurant and gave them the latest operational and other news.

Ajaccio was a short drive from the airport. It had the charm and picturesqueness of a miniature Marseilles. The waterfront was crammed with bars, bistros, fishing boats and tempting, flash-eyed tarts. The Corsican men were swarthy and sinister-looking and wore baggy corduroy trousers held up by heavy leather belts. It was not difficult to recall that Napoleon was born here.

ATC crews stayed at the Hotel d'Etranger, a pleasant, small two-star hotel, with huge old-fashioned beds, delicious food and balconies overlooking the Mediterranean. We collapsed on our beds for a late afternoon nap.

After dinner we went to the casino. I left most of my captain's slush fund in the hotel safe. The casino was dreary, functional and all male. We soon tired of it and left to sit at a bar on the waterfront, content to drink and absorb the velvet warmth of Mediterranean night. Jewish people do not drink very much; I drank three to their one. The per capita consumption of alcohol in Israel is the lowest of any country in the world, apart from Muslim countries.

Raimu, or his double, was serving behind the bar. Decades of Gaulloises, Disque Bleu and cognac had darkened the walls and ceiling. Tarts were drifting into the bar in our honour. One of them, emboldened by my admiring smile, sat unasked at our table. She looked like an apache dancer. Black ringlets, a hint of Africa in her skin, high cheek-bones, jade-green eyes, carmine lips and talons and a low-cut white silk blouse and short red satin skirt with nothing underneath either. Her breasts were breathtaking. When Yehuda

translated our united refusal she rose to her feet, looked down at us
scornfully, tossed her head and flounced off in high dudgeon, hands
on hips and her buttocks jiggling like two ferrets fighting in a sack.
She was magnificent and I mimed applause. The Corsicans grinned.
The next time I was in Ajaccio I contrived to be alone in the same
bar. Alas, Raimu informed me, she had departed for richer pastures
in Paris.

The next morning we departed early for the three-and-a-half-
hour flight back behind the Iron Curtain to Zatec. The weather was
perfect and the Alps in glorious view as, with the C46 lightly laden,
we broke the rules and flew low down valleys and between snow-
bound peaks. There was no fear of starting an avalanche at that time
of the year.

On my third flight from Zatec to Ekron I slipped crews for the
first time and spent a few days in Israel. It was during the first
United Nations imposed truce between the Arabs and Israel. Lasting
from 11 June to 19 July, it was the first of several truces and cease-
fires between the belligerents during the war. I stayed at the Park
Hotel, ATC's favourite watering-hole in Tel Aviv, overlooking the
beach.

The terms of the truce required that neither side should take any
action that would improve their military position, including the
supply and distribution of military equipment and aircraft. Both
sides constantly broke the agreement. ATC continued its airlift
throughout the truces.

To everyone's disbelief Israel was holding its own in the war. By
the first truce Israel held most of the north of old Palestine, the
coastal strip, a corridor to Jerusalem and a large, though surrounded,
pocket in the Negev in the south. As expected the Egyptians, by
sheer weight of numbers, were still a formidable threat from the
south and south-east.

The air war was slowly swinging Israel's way. The Messerschmitt 109 fighters delivered by ATC had shot down several
enemy aircraft and had stopped the bombing of Israel's cities.
Several new aircraft including five Bristol Beaufighters smuggled
from the UK, nine Norseman and several Dakotas and Harvards
had arrived in Israel. By the end of the War of Independence the
Israeli Air Force had covertly acquired over 200 aircraft despite the
United Nations' arms embargo.

Israel was also faring well on the political and diplomatic front. In the first month of its existence several countries had formally recognised the new state of Israel. Russia was the first nation to do so, closely followed by the USA. Sourly, Britain was dragging its feet and, ten months later in March 1949, was the last major power to acknowledge Israel's existence.

Chapter 22

IF YOU CAN find a quiet field in Israel, stand in it and listen carefully you will hear a low hum. It is not the hum of traffic, but the hum of Israelis at their favourite pastime. Talking. Israelis do not go through life suffering misfortune, or reaping good fortune, in stoic silence. I spent most of my leisure time in Israel sitting alone in outdoor cafés, in marrow-warming sunshine, with a book, watching the Israelis at talk; their hands and eyebrows as eloquent as their tongues. They had much to talk about. The war. Being rid of the British. Their new sovereignty. They were no longer *de facto* but *de jure*. Civilian morale had tottered a bit when Egyptian aircraft bombed their cities, but now that the Israeli Air Force had won command of the skies, morale was high.

Israeli neologists were having a field day. Lists of new Hebrew words, bringing Hebrew up to date, were being officially announced every week. The new word for taxi, *moneet*, was greeted with hilarity. No doubt there were good etymological reasons for *moneet*, but a taxi is a taxi is a taxi anywhere in the world. After a few lessons in Hebrew I gave up. I found it impossible and made do with some essential phrases: *ter dar rabbar* – thank you; *im halav* – with milk (for my tea); *schtok veshev* – Shut up and sit down, essential when flying tough Israeli troops from A to B.

Tel Aviv, which means the city on the hill, will never win a beauty contest but, in 1948, with its low-rise buildings, dominated at one end by Jaffa's minaret and the other end by a power station, and much smaller than it is now, it had a cosmopolitan, raffish charm. The eyes of the world were focused on this then capital city of Israel, a tiny nation fighting for survival.

In a land almost surfeited with antiquity, Tel Aviv is not much older than I am. The first few houses were built by Jewish pioneers, on sand dunes in 1909, during the days of Turkish Ottoman rule, as a sort of Hampstead Garden Suburb to Arab Jaffa. Half-grown palm trees and soil were brought from Tiberias to line the few streets. Over the years the architectural style has become an appalling mixture of Turkish, Arabic, British Official and Jewish Speculator, with occasional set-piece parks and gardens and tired tropical trees to salve civic conscience.

Tel Aviv is saved from perdition by its setting. At the eastern end of the Mediterranean, it looks westward over the sea 2,000 miles towards Gibraltar, giving a theatrical, uninterrupted view of the nightly performance of the sun slowly setting on the sea's horizon.

The beaches, once Arab snipers had been eliminated from Jaffa, were perfection with safe swimming and white sands lined with al fresco café society. When the winds were in a certain direction a whiff of orange, lemon and tamarind completed the transmogrification of Tel Aviv from a sow's ear into a silk purse.

On the Sabbath of Saturday, 19 June, I was lazing in the sun on my room balcony at the Park Hotel. Jewish Sabbaths confused me, rather like jet-lag. Our Fridays are their Saturdays, their Saturdays are our Sundays and, worst of all, their Sundays are our Mondays. I was wondering what to do, with everything shut, when a runner arrived with a message requesting me to report urgently to Hayman Shamir at air force headquarters. HQ was in the Yarkon Hotel, a few yards down the road from the Park Hotel.

With little preamble Hayman asked me what my reaction would be if I was asked, officially, to kill Jews. I replied that that was not quite why I was in Israel and asked him to enlarge.

He explained that having existed for only four weeks the chain of command in the Israeli military was still anarchic. Certain senior military figures were laws unto themselves. In addition, the Irgun Z'vai Leumi, the group led by Menachem Begin who had fought the British during the Mandate using terrorist tactics, was still operating with 5,000 men as an independent fighting unit, rather like a private army. It was a very odd arrangement born of anarchy and chaos following the British exodus and the immediate plunge into war. There had been no time for the finer points of command structure, organisation and administration – civil or military. However, abrasive negotiations had recently begun to disband Irgun's private army and absorb it into the army proper.

But, months before, Irgun had bought a 6,000-ton cargo ship in America. The *Altalena* sailed for Israel on 11 June, the first day of the first truce, from Port de Bouc, near Marseilles, carrying 500 American, European and North African Jewish volunteers and several hundred tons of arms and ammunition supplied gratis, curiously, by Bidault's French government.

While the *Altalena* was on the high seas, Irgun and the Israeli government were negotiating by radio the disposal of its cargo of arms and men, and the complications caused by the United Nations' truce. Irgun insisted initially that about half the men and half the arms go to Irgun units on the Jerusalem front, where the Irgun was heavily involved in the fighting against Jordan's Arab Legion. This was interpreted by the provisional Prime Minister, Ben Gurion, as a blatant bid for power which could not be countenanced, particularly as the government, sensitive at that time to world opinion and seeking further diplomatic recognition, was anxious not to break the truce quite so brazenly. Negotiations broke down and the *Altalena* stuck to its course. The seeds of tragedy and conflict had been sown.

I asked Hayman what all this had to do with me. He pointed out that the government could not permit the Irgun to defy it. The *Altalena* must surrender, or be captured, or sunk. The alternative could well be civil war. A contingency foreseen by the high command was that, if and when it came to it, Jews might refuse an order to fire on Jews. That was where I came in.

'Shabbes Goy,' I observed.

'Sort of, yes,' he grinned. Orthodox Jews are forbidden by Judaic law to do any work on their Sabbath, even to switching on a light or pressing a lift button. They employ Gentiles, colloquially known as Shabbes Goys, to do the work for them on the Sabbath.

'Can you fly a C46 without other aircrew?' he asked.

'If necessary, yes.'

'We will use one as a bomber to attack the *Altalena*.'

'We?'

'You.'

'The C46 hasn't got bomb racks or a bomb sight.'

'We have been chucking bombs out by hand from Dakotas and Austers. Why not a C46? We have two chuckers-out standing by.'

'What size bombs?' I asked.

'Hundred pounders, I think.'

'You can't sink a 6,000-ton ship with hundred-pound bombs.'

'We don't want to sink it. We need the arms. We want it to surrender.'

'Will they put up a fight?'

'Don't know.'

'If they do, what have they got?'

163

'Rifles and machine guns I imagine.'

'I'll never hit the bloody thing.'

'You will if you attack low and slow.'

'Yeah, thanks.' Low and slow in that situation was a euphemism for RIP. 'Perhaps you would like me to do a Kamikaze?'

'No,' he said, with a straight face. 'The C46 is too precious.'

'Won't the Irgun hit-men be after me for the rest of my life?'

'We will give you protection and anonymity.'

'Ha.'

'Can't the navy handle this?' I asked.

'Same problem. All Jews.'

'Why not use the Dakotas?'

'Same problem.'

'Bloody Jews get everywhere,' I said. 'When will all this happen?'

'If and when the *Altalena* refuses to surrender. My guess is Monday or Tuesday.'

'Can I think about it?'

'Yes, but not too long. Please stay in at the Park in case I need to contact you urgently.' I nodded and got up to leave.

'Shalom,' he said.

'Yeah, Shalom,' I answered. Shalom means peace be with you.

I went back to the Park, ordered sandwiches and a large jug of Tom Collins made from excellent local gin to be sent to my room and sat on the balcony looking at the Mediterranean.

Well, yes or no? It was a potentially tragic impasse. And like all tragedy a waste of life and, in this case, desperately needed arms. I thought Ben Gurion was right; nothing must be permitted to jeopardise the cause of Israel. Hayman had paid me the compliment of not trying to persuade me. He had left it to me. The whole thing was preposterous. Particularly the premise that Jew would not fight Jew. Some Jews might not but surely some, like Hayman, would. I was not worried about the risk. At that age one does not worry much about danger. I might, just might, be able to hit the ship. I would have to fly low and slow along it from stern to bow to make it an easier target. I had taught Fleet Air Arm pilots low-level bombing technique. The main problem with the C46 was that the target would disappear under the nose long before I reached it. I would have to work out distance and time and angles and use a stop-watch.

164

I said yes.

The *Altalena* arrived at Kfar Vitkin, a small natural harbour about twenty miles north of Tel Aviv, at dawn on Sunday morning, 20 June. Menachem Begin, commander-in-chief of the Irgun Z'vai Leumi, boarded the ship there to take command. Negotiations were still going on by radio between ship and government. She went out to sea again shortly afterwards to avoid being spotted by United Nations observers and returned to Kfar Vitkin that evening after dark. Most of the 500 volunteers and some of the arms were disembarked on the beach during the night with the help of the local population. At dawn the baffled volunteers were surrounded by troops, armoured cars and all the other paraphernalia of enmity. Confused arguments continued, confused terms were agreed, but communications between ship and shore broke down. Muddle reigned. The first shots were fired at the Irgun and the volunteers that afternoon. During the night the *Altalena* slipped out to sea with its crew, a few score volunteers, Begin and other Irgun leaders and most of its cargo of arms. The following morning those left on the beach surrendered and were permitted to disperse.

With the first shots fired on the beach at Kfar Vitkin my part in the affair ended before it had started. Though many refused, Jew had fired on Jew. There was no need of a Shabbes Goy.

It did not matter now where the *Altalena* went. It was doomed to surrender, capture or destruction. It was up to Begin to decide which.

On Monday night the *Altalena* beached head-on at full speed in Tel Aviv about 100 yards from the shore and directly in front of the Kaete Dan Hotel, the United Nations Truce headquarters. It is difficult to find a logical explanation for Begin's extraordinary decision to beach the ship rather than surrender. Perhaps he felt that the government would not dare to fire on the *Altalena* in full view of the population of Tel Aviv and the United Nations, and that he could continue to negotiate with the government. If so, he was grievously wrong. Mortar and rifle fire from government forces on the beach started at dawn. The whole of Tel Aviv, the world's Press corps and United Nations personnel watched in horror as the ship was bombarded all day and Jew killed Jew. I watched from the roof of the Park Hotel, a stone's throw away. Men jumping from the ship were fired on as they swam ashore. Jewish blood dyed the

Mediterranean red. Jews were crying in the streets. There was no white flag. At tea-time, mortars set the ship on fire and the ammunition started to explode. The ship was abandoned and the last survivors jumped into the sea. Begin was among the last to leave the ship.

Eighty-two Jews were killed at Kfar Vitkin and Tel Aviv. The *Altalena* burned, arms exploding, for days. It glowed red at night. The dead were buried in military cemeteries. One wonders what was written on their gravestones. The *Altalena*, a tortured, twisted hulk, rusted on the beach at Tel Aviv for several years, a playground for swimmers, before it was finally removed. It was as though all concerned wanted to keep this memorial to man's talent for muddle, mischief and tragedy.

To be fair to the Irgun Z'vai Leumi and Menachem Begin, it could be argued that it was their terrorist tactics, more than anything else, that hounded the British out of Palestine – tactics constantly under the threat of the British gallows. Having succeeded in their object, they were then snubbed by the respectable Jewish Agency. Begin was not asked to add his name to the thirty-eight signatories, mostly nonentities, who signed the Declaration of Independence. Nor was he, or his political party, invited to join the first provisional government. It is not surprising if Begin felt no loyalty to Ben Gurion and his unelected provisional government.

A few weeks later the Irgun Z'vai Leumi's private army was voluntarily dissolved and absorbed into the army proper. Some of its members formed the Herut political party. Years later it became part of the Likud Party. Later still, in 1977, it became Israel's elected government and its leader, Menachem Begin, after decades in the political wilderness, became Israel's Prime Minister. The wheel had turned full circle.

Chapter 23

B ECAUSE OF THE arms embargo, which included civil and military aircraft, the C46s were, of course, irreplaceable. Those C46s were, in military terms, some of the most precious aircraft in aviation history, certainly as far as Israel was concerned. The loss of any of those C46s was critical.

ATC's fleet started off with ten C46s. One was written-off in the crash at Mexico City airport while being smuggled out of the USA. Then there were nine. Next was Moonitz's crash in fog at Ekron. Then there were eight. One was forced to land at Athens with engine trouble. The crew were arrested and the C46 and cargo were impounded. Then there were seven. The very existence of Israel was threatened when another C46 was forced to land at Ciampino, Rome, with engine trouble. The crew disappeared underground and eventually smuggled their way back to Israel by slow boat, but the aircraft and its cargo of half an ME 109 and arms was impounded. Then there were six. The situation was so desperate it was decided that an attempt should be made to get the C46 and its cargo out of Rome.

After several days of secret negotiations by Israel's man in Rome, Danny Agronsky, suitcases of lira changed hands and it was agreed that the C46 and its cargo would be released, provided the C46 took off in total secrecy in the middle of the night, not for Israel, but for Czechoslovakia, with no publicity. If the news leaked to the media, particularly any connection with Israel and what the cargo was, the deal was off.

I was chosen for this operation because not being Jewish and therefore uncircumcised I could, if anything went wrong, deny under interrogation any connection with Israel. For similar reasons Abe Nathan, my co-pilot, was chosen because he was Indian-born, an unlikely-looking Jew and had an Indian passport.

We flew to Rome, via BEA Viking from Cyprus, arriving mid-afternoon at Ciampino where we were met by Danny. It was raining with the persistent steady rain of a warm front. In broad daylight Danny did not want us to go to the C46 parked in the far corner of the aerodrome so he drove discreetly up and down past it several times. It had been sitting there for weeks and was a very sad and disgruntled-looking aeroplane. The engine trouble had, we hoped, been cured by a change of plugs. I asked Danny to arrange for me to do a test flight. 'No chance,' he said firmly. He then drove us to an hotel in Rome for a bath, a meal and a nap. Danny would collect us at 11.30 pm that night to drive us to the airport.

When we drove to the airport it was still raining. We picked up an Italian official and drove straight out to the C46. There was no question of going to the control tower for flight-planning and clearance, or getting the weather from the meteorological office, or anything fancy like that. I looked at the weather map in Danny's Italian newspaper. It was covered with fronts and close-knit isobars all over the Mediterranean. Danny asked me not to do a test run-up because it would be too noisy. I compromised by agreeing to do a sort of run-up while taxi-ing out to the runway. The Italian official assured me there was no other air traffic at the time and we were to take off for Prague, maintaining radio silence, when we were ready. Danny winked at me behind the Italian's back at the mention of Prague. We would, of course, be heading in the opposite direction, Ekron, Israel. As we shook hands goodbye Danny begged us to take off quietly (!) and for God's sake not to land back in Italy if we had any trouble.

It was 1.30 am and raining heavily when we took off. Within a few hundred feet we were in cloud. My instrument-flying was still rusty and I did not blame Abe for looking a bit anxious. With full fuel tanks, including the long-range tank in the cabin, and over-loaded cargo as always on the airlift, the C46 was a handful. But the two Pratt & Whitney R2800 engines were running smoothly despite weeks of neglect. Over the years I had learned to respect those great engines as much as the Merlin. As we climbed up to 10,000 feet I set course over the sea to nip between Sicily and Italy's big toe rather than dice with Italy's mountains. The sky was very black, very wet and very turbulent, with intermittent icing. Abe estimated that the flight would take about nine hours. It was a relief to find that George and the ADF radio compass were working.

At dawn we were still in cloud. We hadn't caught a glimpse of land or sea since taking off. We had no communications to find out what was happening with the weather ahead of us, or in Israel. We droned on, with a few crude ADF fixes to give us some idea of where we were. There were some breaks in the cloud south of Crete but after about an hour's sunshine the clouds built up again. We climbed up and down trying unsuccessfully to find a break in the cloud. Abe and I were beginning to get concerned. We were not equipped to carry out an instrument let-down and landing at Ekron if the weather was bad. About forty-five minutes before our crudely estimated ETA I decided to lose height to try to get down under the weather. Down we went, down and down. We were fairly certain we were over sea but we had no idea what the altimeter pressure setting should be. Heavy bouts of turbulence and rain indicated cumulo-nimbus. At about 500 feet Abe started cracking his knuckles. The altimeter was reading about 300 feet but we were virtually at sea-level when we broke through under cloud. We pressed on in the narrow gap between cloud and sea. In showers the gap disappeared. At this height and in this weather the romantic Mediterranean looked more like the North Atlantic. Not suprisingly, Abe tried to persuade me to climb back up but I was damned if I was going to climb back into the cloud again. Too many pilots have died that way. I didn't envy Abe just sitting there watching the waves go by. A 25-ton transport aeroplane is not the ideal aeroplane for this sort of split-arse flying. When we talked about the flight years later, Abe said that our propellers sometimes touched the tops of the waves. Now that we had burned off most of the fuel the C46 was easier to handle. It was only because of this we managed to miss hitting an oil tanker.

The rain and low cloud stayed with us all the way. Ekron's ADF radio beacon was now sending a strong, steady signal to head us home. We were not that far off course. We peered anxiously ahead for the Israel coast and our landfall – Tel Aviv. I knew that Tel Aviv, at that time, had a low profile. There was only the power station chimney at the northern end of Tel Aviv and the Arab mosque in Jaffa to worry about, but there were some 400-foot-high sand-dunes between Tel Aviv and Ekron – the sand-dunes that had caused Moonitz's C46 crash in May. While Abe called the tower at Ekron I prepared the controls for landing. 'Ceiling and visibility poor in heavy showers,' said the tower in a heavily accented female voice. '*Mazel tov*,' she added, meaning good luck. The ADF needle was pointing encouragingly straight ahead. We saw the coast and Tel

Aviv simultaneously. We were bang on course. 'Climb, for Chrissakes,' shouted Abe as the power station chimney flashed past our port wing. 'And how the hell do we get back down again?' I shouted back. We had only about five minutes to go before reaching Ekron and I knew the landscape fairly well.

Those few minutes took a long time. The windscreen wipers were busy, the thrash of rain drummed against the fuselage and Abe's nose was pressed against the windscreen. We shot past a landscape of citrus groves, palm trees and the white blobs of upturned, startled faces. We were now among the sand dunes. If we missed Ekron the hills of Jerusalem were not that far ahead. 'There it is,' shouted Abe, pointing straight ahead at the runway, shining in the rain like black glass. We went straight in and landed in a shower of spray. Within a matter of minutes the C46 was being urgently unloaded.

And then it was back to seven C46s. And another Messerschmitt 109.

Chapter 24

AFTER THREE MONTHS the Balak airlift ended suddenly on 12 August 1948, with two versions of why. The popular version is that the Czech government, under pressure from Russia, called a halt, giving the Israelis 24 hours' notice to quit Zatec. I do not believe a word of it. At that time Russia's diplomatic and political support of Israel was total, as manifested by being the first country to recognise Israel – another might-have-been – and Czechoslovakia continued to supply arms, including forty Spitfire aircraft in the late autumn of 1948, ensuring Israel's supremacy in the skies. The alternative version, which I believe, was that the American State Department put pressure on Zionist organisations in America and on the Israelis, to stop their American boys messing about behind the Iron Curtain. The Cold War was at its height, the Berlin airlift had just begun and McCarthyism was rearing its vile head. The American crews were also under the threat of losing their American citizenship. Operation Balak was by now a poorly kept secret. Whenever we went to our favourite restaurant at the Ambassador Hotel in Prague the band played Israel's national anthem and Israeli flags were placed on our table.

Towards the end we made a few airlift flights using a refuelling base in Yugoslavia instead of Corsica, but these too were terminated abruptly and all ATC's aircraft and crews withdrew to Israel.

Statistics for that period are unreliable, but it is generally accepted that in twelve weeks Balak Air Transport Command with its nine C46s, one DC4 and one Lockheed Constellation, made nearly a hundred return flights between Czechoslovakia and Israel, airlifting twenty-five Messerschmitt 109 fighter aircraft, 300 tons of arms and ammunition and countless personnel. It was also the communications umbilical cord between besieged Israel and the rest of the world.

By modern standards the logistics are not that impressive, but this was over forty years ago. It was a covert operation, with poor maintenance facilities and few spares. With a round trip of over 4,400 miles it was probably the longest regular airlift in aviation history. The aircrew were odds and sods from all over the world, up there on their own when things went wrong. That things did not go wrong very often was a remarkable tribute to the aircraft, the men that flew and serviced them and the cause that inspired them. In a critical period of the war ATC supplied Israel with enough arms and ammunition to keep going and enough fighter aircraft to win the war in the air. Prime Minister Ben Gurion stated in his memoirs that without the Balak airlift from Czechoslovakia, Israel would not have survived.

We were now billeted at the commandeered Bristol Hotel, in Ben Yehuda Street, Tel Aviv, a short walk from the beach. It was a pleasant hotel with about sixty of us squeezed into bedrooms that normally accommodated thirty. ATC's aircraft were now based at Ekron.

During the lull I took the opportunity of getting checked-out on the Douglas DC4 Skymaster, a magnificent four-engined aircraft and also on the Douglas DC5, a rare, twin-engined, high-wing aircraft of which only twelve were made.

The first truce collapsed on 9 July. But those four weeks of relative peace had given Israel vital time to re-equip with more men, women and material from home and abroad. Equally important, it gave the Israelis time to think. Time to create civil government. Time to reorganise military command structure. Time to sort out priorities, strategy and tactics. Agreeing to that first truce was possibly the Arabs' biggest mistake of the war. They too used the truce to re-equip and re-group, but not so needfully as the Israelis fighting on five fronts.

In the ten days between the end of the first truce and the beginning of the second truce starting on 19 July, bitter fighting took place on all fronts. With *Jihad* fanaticism motivating the Arabs and a win or die situation with the Israelis little quarter was asked or given and atrocities were committed on both sides. It was not the sort of war in which to get captured.

The ten days' fighting resulted in several tactical gains by the Israelis. The tanks pinched from the British were now being used by the Israelis. The arrival at this time of the three fugitive B17 Flying Fortresses from America via Czechoslovakia, and a bombing raid over Cairo, was a tremendous boost to Israeli morale.

On the Jerusalem front there was stalemate and nothing but

blood-letting was achieved by either side. Similarly at Latrun, half-way between Jerusalem and Tel Aviv, scene of the bloodiest fighting of the war between the British-led Arab Legion and the Israelis. The Legion was poised for the twenty-mile drive to Tel Aviv but this threat was lifted when the Israelis, led by an unknown, one-eyed battalion commander named Moshe Dayan, captured Ramle and Lydda airport half-way between Latrun and Tel Aviv and blocked the Legion's advance.

On the central front the Iraqi drive to the Mediterranean to cut Israel in two at its eight-mile-wide waist near Netanya was repulsed and the Iraqis were thrown back, fully opening the main highway between Tel Aviv and Haifa for the first time in eight months. On the same front the Israelis captured Lagun, Jenin and Megiddo, site of the apocalyptic Armageddon.

On the northern front the Israelis crossed the border into Lebanon. Kaukji proved to be a man of straw and most of his irregular troops dispersed. In the north-east the Israelis captured Nazareth and relieved the threat to Haifa by pushing the Syrians back nearly ten miles.

The situation on the southern front was serious. The Egyptians had advanced to within eighteen miles of Tel Aviv and had encircled Israeli positions in the Negev desert. This siege of Israeli kibbutzim and villages in the south and the strategic stranglehold the Egyptians had on the Negev desert was the most critical fulcrum of the war.

During the second truce, a secret briefing for ATC captains was called at Air Force headquarters. As we gathered that morning at the Yarkon Hotel it was the first time we had all been at the same place at the same time. We had been passing each other in the night over the Mediterranean for months. It was moving to be all together. To see the sum of our disparate parts. There were about twenty of us, bound together by pilots' argot. I looked at us and decided it was not a myth. There is something about pilots' eyes, always seeking but never reaching the horizon. A detached, peering, expectant wariness, as though none of us would be surprised at anything. A belief born of half a lifetime at 10,000 feet hoping for the best but expecting the worst, with death as a neighbour.

There was a buzz when Hayman Shamir walked in with Aharon Remez, Commander of the Israel Air Force. It must be something big. Remez was an ex-sergeant pilot in the RAF. There was the

173

usual self-deprecatory Jewish joke going the rounds: I can understand Remez being head of the Israeli Air Force, but how the hell did
he make sergeant in the RAF? Most of his time was spent fighting
the government and the army for funds for his air force and dealing
with the American prima donnas of ATC. He had an Eisenhower-
like tact and patience. He needed it, for there were no ranks yet to
prop up those in command. After the war, he became Israel's highly
successful Ambassador in London.

Shamir gave the briefing. ATC's next task was another airlift.
This time to the Negev desert. Code name Avak, meaning Dust,
but soon amended by us to Dustbowl.

Dustbowl had three objectives. To establish an airbase behind
the Egyptian enemy lines in the Negev desert and evacuate the
exhausted and beleaguered Negev Brigade which had been fighting
the Egyptians continuously for eight months, and fly in a fresh
brigade. To fly in food and supplies for the besieged kibbutzim and
villages. Finally, to fly in military equipment and troops in preparation for a major offensive to break out of the Egyptian stranglehold
and capture that part of the Negev allocated to Israel under the
United Nations' partition plan.

We would use the C46s and the DC4. The operation would be at
night to avoid Egyptian fighter aircraft. Arabs did not fly and rarely
fought at night. A flat bit of desert near Ruhama, fifteen miles east
of Gaza and twenty miles behind enemy lines had been selected as
our landing strip. The flight from Ekron to Ruhama would take
only twenty minutes each way, less if we did not bother to climb to
normal cruising height. We would be down as soon as we were up.
There would be light anti-aircraft fire. It was top secret, top priority
and maximum effort. All ATC's resources were to be used and each
crew was expected to complete at least two round trips a night,
possibly three. The truce would be ignored.

I enjoyed that briefing. The words used were an overture to
action. Night flights, desert landings, behind enemy lines, pass-
words, break-out, troop movements, the enemy, anti-aircraft fire,
siege, maximum effort. It was my kind of flying and there could be
no better cause – the relief of the Negev.

We flew seven nights a week, with special Rabbinical dispensation to fly on the Sabbath, for nearly two months. The weather,
as expected, was perfect throughout the entire operation.

15 ATC aircrew in front of a C46 at Ekron, November 1948. Gordon Levett wearing tie and waistcoat; Moonitz on extreme left; de Havilland Rapide in background

16 ATC's DC4 Skymaster, as used in the Balak and Dustbowl operations and El Al's first flights

17 Maurice Mann, another English ex-RAF pilot, of 101 Fighter Squadron in front of his Messerschmitt 109, summer 1948

18 Insignia of 101 Fighter Squadron, Israeli Air Force

Whenever possible I flew the DC4, which had supplanted my affection for the C46. The DC4, well-named the Skymaster, looked magnificent at night, parked and floodlit in the desert. She made a dramatic nightscape, a *son et lumière* of men and machine. I would sit on the sand at the entrance to the operations tent at Ruhama with a mug of coffee and a cigarette and watch as soldiers hurriedly unloaded the aircraft. She looked huge and graceful, sleek and shining except for oil and sand-dust streaks sweeping from her four engines. I felt a warm satisfaction that I had brought her here to this desert and would soon take her back into the air where she belonged. A machine yes, an inanimate thing yes, but I felt anthropomorphic about her. At the touch of my fingers she would become alive again, her heart would throb, she would fly, climb and soar in her own amphitheatre in the sky and take me to the stars. And when we were done she would bring me back to the crust of the earth. Unquestionably she. Not he, or it.

For those eight weeks of Dustbowl we became nocturnal. It was as well we were young. We got back to our beds after up to three return flights at about seven o'clock in the morning. We slept during the day, but the grunts and snores of men sharing bedrooms and the traffic and the full summer heat made our sleep fitful. Most of us gave up after an hour or two and went down to the beach to doze.

On one occasion I left the others and found a pleasant restaurant-bar on the beach, with outdoor tables and showers. Although my face was tanned my body was still European white, contrasting with the bronzed figures around me. I ordered a light lunch in English and was reading an English book. I asked the waiter to delay my lunch while I had a quick dip in the sea. After the swim I went into the crowded communal showers. There was a hush as I removed my bathing suit and got under the shower. When I removed the soap from my eyes I saw that everybody was looking at my genitals. I brazened it out, got dressed and returned to the table.

When I got up to leave two policemen stopped me at the exit and asked for my papers. Their English was rudimentary. I pointed out that nobody in Israel had papers. Passport then. I tried to explain that my passport was somewhere in Czechoslovakia. They escorted me to the police station just off Allenby Street where after two hours of nonsense I got angry – it would soon be time for the crew pick-up truck to Ekron – and started banging the table. Like most Englishmen abroad I was indignant that they did not speak English. 'Mahal,' I shouted. 'Me Mahal pilot.' I flapped my arms like a bird. I eventually persuaded them to telephone Hayman Shamir at air force headquarters. When he arrived to vouch for me it was the first time I heard him laugh. He said the police advised me to get a passport, or get circumcised, preferably both.

A few Israeli junior pilots who had completed a basic flying course at an Italian flying school on the outskirts of Rome joined us as co-pilots. They were salad green, but the air force was looking to the future. One of those cadets was Morty Fein. Nearly twenty years later, renamed Mordecai Hod, he was Commander-in-Chief of the Israeli Air Force in the Six-Day War of 1967, a war which opened with one of the most brilliant campaigns in aviation history with the destruction by the IAF of 300 enemy aircraft on the first day and a total of 452 over the six days.

Most of the cadets were *Sabras*, a nickname derived from a local prickly fruit for those born in Israel. Most *Sabras* of that generation were born and bred in a kibbutz, a communal way of life where self-motivation and co-operation ruled. Usually if one asked a *Sabra* to do something it would be done. Order him to do so and it would not.

There was some friction between the *Sabras* and the Americans. It was not antagonism, more like the competitive spirit between a home team and a visiting team.

Arguments had begun regarding the dichotomy of Jews now that Israel was reborn as a nation. A new dimension, a mix of nationalism, patriotism and loyalty, had been added to the perennial argument of whether a Jew was a member of a race, a religion, or both. Many Israelis, particularly the *Sabras*, argued that since midnight of 14 May 1948, it was anachronistic, schizophrenic and a contradiction in terms for a Jew to call himself an American Jew, an English Jew, a Russian Jew, *et al*. One does not call someone a French Englishman. Before that midnight there was no choice, for the British would not let Jews enter the Promised Land. But the British had now gone. God's promise to Abraham, Isaac and Jacob had been fulfilled. The gates of the Promised Land are now open to all Jews and your exile is now self-imposed. There is no longer any need to be the eternal wandering Jew, carrying anti-Semitism around in your suitcase. There is no need at Passover, in the Diaspora, to yearn for Israel and to drink the annual toast: 'Next year in Jerusalem', for you can go now. You can catch an aeroplane or a boat to the Promised Land, become an Israeli and unpack your suitcase for the last time. If you do not, you are a humbug Jew and a potential traitor to one side or the other of your dual loyalties if your mother-country were to declare war on Israel.

There were other seeds of dissension. The Israelis in ATC, as elsewhere in the services, were getting, like me, nominal pay. It did not occur to us that we should get more, but many of the Americans in ATC were getting 600 dollars a month or more, a goodly sum in those days, plus living expenses. Some Israelis resented this, I think unreasonably. Most of the Americans were married, with a home and a family to maintain back in the States. If their skills were needed by Israel those bills had to be paid.

The out-and-out mercenaries in the air force, some half a dozen or so, were Gentiles, mostly fighter pilots. They were getting enormous sums. One American fighter pilot was getting 2,000 dollars a month and a 500-dollar bonus for every enemy aircraft he shot down. They did their job well, but I did not care for them. At the toss of a shekel they would have been on the other side.

A further cause of friction was the premature interest shown by some of the senior American members of ATC in a future Israeli national airline. ATC's aircraft, aircrew and groundcrew could obviously form the nucleus of such an airline in due and proper course. But it was unseemly to be holding private meetings and jockeying for position in this potential airline when the war was by no means won, or lost.

The short flights of Dustbowl were a welcome change from the long hauls of Balak. For most pilots, taking-off and landing is the grist of flying, but aeroplanes, like motor cars, do not thrive on the wear and tear of short journeys, particularly on a diet of desert dust. They prefer the constant cruise and the occasional refreshing showers of a long haul. But our aeroplanes stood up well. We knew them all by now and had our favourites. Apparently identical aircraft can perform and behave remarkably differently. One of the C46s, number RX 133, was the runt of ATC's aircraft litter. It always had something wrong with it – vibration, mag-drop, a squeaky brake, soggy George, one wing low, 10 mph slower than its siblings – niggling things not serious enough to ground it.

We averaged two return flights a night. Loading and unloading took the time. When flying troops only, we could manage three return flights a night. We watched the eastern sky anxiously in the early hours of the morning. In the Middle East there is little twilight and night and day arrive with little preamble. So too did the Spitfires of the Egyptian dawn patrol to strafe and bomb. It was imperative that we got the aircraft away from Ruhama before first light. There were some tense moments when aircraft developed last-minute snags.

Pussy and I were taxi-ing RX133 to the take-off position at Ruhama about twenty minutes before dawn, with about thirty weary Israeli troops in the back, when the cockpit and instrument lights flickered and went out. We hurriedly checked fuses but could not find the fault. I asked Pussy to see whether the troops had any torches or candles between them. He hesitated a moment before realizing I was serious. I watched him over my shoulder as he went gesticulating along the rows of troops sitting on the floor of the cabin. After several discussions in Hebrew, one torch and two candles materialised. The torch battery was flat. I finished taxi-ing to the take-off position in the dark. There was a puny sliver of moon. I completed the usual cross-talk with Pussy for the take-off cockpit check and then added in the same formal tone of voice: 'Light candle, please.'

'You're joking,' said Pussy.

'It will be dawn in ten minutes,' I said. 'Light candle, please.'

He lighted the candle with his Zippo lighter, held it over the instrument panel and started laughing. He was still laughing help-lessly when we reached a thousand feet. So was I. I told Pussy that it was part of RAF training. He went one better and explained to the troops in the back who had seen what was going on that it was normal procedure to fly C46s at night by candlelight.

ATC completed Operation Dustbowl by mid-October. In those eight weeks we completed over 400 return flights at night, airlifting 4,000 tons of food supplies for the besieged kibbutzim, over 10,000 troops to and from Ruhama and war material for the forthcoming campaign.

The scene was set for the most crucial battle of the war – Operation Yoav – to break through the Egyptian siege of the Negev from

178

within and without and drive the Egyptians out of the northern Negev. But a pretext was needed to break the United Nations truce and restart the war without upsetting world opinion. As agreed by the terms of the truce the Israelis sent a food convoy to a besieged kibbutz in the Negev. The Egyptians fell into the trap and fired on the convoy. With the truce broken the delighted Israelis withdrew the convoy. The war was on again.

It was to be a different war. This time the Israelis had more than just a few rifles and courage to fight with. They now had experience, a few tanks, armoured cars, half-tracks, artillery and mortars and the support of an air force of over one hundred aircraft.

Yoav started on the evening of 15 October, with all-out attacks on the Egyptian front by the air force. These attacks continued throughout the campaign, resulting in total Israeli air superiority.

ATC found a niche in the renewed war. In addition to continuing the airlift to Ruhama, and a new strip at Urim, we became night bombers using the C46s. Our targets were, ostensibly, the Egyptian Army headquarters and army base at Gaza and the railway marshalling yards at Khan Yunis and Rafah. But, in effect, by bombing at night without bomb-sights or bomb-racks, it was crude area bombing.

So far in this war I had not directly killed or maimed. I now had to decide whether I could or should. Conscience is not a problem for a serviceman fighting for his country. He does as he is told and consciences are held in abeyance for the duration of any war. But I was fighting for an alien cause. I could obey or disobey any order I wished without penalty for I had not pledged or signed an oath of loyalty. I had to make up my own mind about bombing. Some of my bombs would inevitably drop on civilian men, women and children, just like the Egyptian bombs on Tel Aviv. But Arab could kill Jew and Jew could kill Arab, legitimately and morally, because they were enemies at war. The Arabs, however, were not my enemies, nor I theirs. I wanted the Israelis to win for their war was a just war, a war of survival. But I did not want to help Israel to victory by indiscriminate bombing.

One man's conscience is a tiny thing in war. A trivial thing, a tiresome thing, to everybody but him. Even so it would be easy for me to say no. I knew that Remez or Shamir would excuse me from bombing operations if I wanted to wear my conscience on my sleeve, Remez with understanding, Shamir with weary disdain, for Israel now had enough pilots to carry my conscience easily.

The crisis of conscience ended in a fudged compromise. I persuaded myself that if I tried to avoid civilian targets it would be all right, but I was still uncertain when I took off from Ekron at night on my first bombing sortie. The target was Gaza. The bombs were loaded on wooden racks in the cabin of the C46 and lashed with rope. The cargo doors were removed to make it easier for the two soldiers to chuck out the bombs by hand at my shouted signal. They wore rope harness attached to the aircraft to stop them following the bombs out. Cyril Cohen, an English Jew from St. John's Wood, was my co-pilot.

Few of us in ATC knew much about bombing or anti-aircraft fire. The B17 crews on their daylight bombing sorties had reported fairly heavy, radar-controlled anti-aircraft fire along the Gaza Strip. I decided that 12,000 feet was the best height and climbed in wide circles over Ekron. It was a brilliant Mediterranean night with a full moon clearly illuminating land, sea and sky. Gaza was on the horizon, ten minutes away. Distances were short in that war. I remembered to un-synchronise the engines.

When the searchlights suddenly popped up and started searching for us I was surprised to discover that I was frightened. As the searchlights crept closer in the enemy sky I felt desperately vulnerable in this fragile aluminium eggshell of an aircraft. We had no parachutes. It was a long fall from 12,000 feet. If we were hit it would take about three minutes before we smashed into the ground. I was beginning to wonder why I had been so desperately anxious to get into action in the Second World War. The noise and buffeting caused by the absence of cargo doors was like the roll of drums. I lined up on blacked-out but clearly visible Gaza and started the bombing run. The soldiers in the back were manhandling the bombs closer to the cargo door exit when the four searchlights caught us and the anti-aircraft fire started. The searchlight beams transfixed and blinded us no matter how much I weaved. Eyeless over Gaza, I thought. The patterns of death were beautiful as the shells burst and blossomed into magnificent clusters of colour, blue, yellow and red edged with black smoke. I could hear the crack of the closer shells and there was faint turbulence when we flew through dead bursts. We could have read a book in the cockpit by

the searchlights. I thought it would be a damned silly place and way
to die and was desperately tempted to shout 'Bombs away!' and
clear off. But the witness of a crew brings courage. I circled but I
could not see anything resembling a military target. I slammed the
throttles open wide, dived and turned towards the peaceful sea.

'What was that for?' asked Cyril reasonably.

'Couldn't find a target,' I replied. 'We'll go in low from the sea.'

I let down low over the sea, pointed the nose at the base of the
searchlight beams that were thrashing wildly about the sky in search
of us and roared over Gaza at roof-top height. We must have
surprised them for there was no anti-aircraft fire, but I still could not
identify a military target. Cyril and the crew were getting edgy, as
well they might. None of them had flown with me before, none
was privy to my conscience and there was indecision in the cockpit.

'We'll go in at two thousand feet from the north-east and hit the
railway line. Tell the chaps to get all the bombs ready. We'll do one
continuous bombing run down the line until all bombs have gone.'

Cyril did not say a word. I respected him for it. Two thousand
feet was the best height for identifying targets, but being within the
range of most calibres, the worst for anti-aircraft fire. We went in.
The railway line, glinting sharply in the moonlight, was easy to
identify from that height.

'Bombs away,' I shouted. The searchlights caught us again and
pinned us against the sky like a moth as we followed the railway
line. Anti-aircraft fire rose lazily to meet us. It was different flack.
Light and medium stuff mixed with lots of tracer. We were going
flat out but it took an unconscionable time to throw the bombs out.
We were approaching Khan Yunis before I heard the shout 'Bombs
gone' from the rear. I turned and dived for the sea. I never did find
out whether we hit the railway line or how many we killed that
night.

I did several more bombing missions over Gaza, Khan Yunis, El
Arish, Rafah and Damascus.

On 20 October the road to the Negev was opened and the besieged
kibbutzim and villages were relieved. The Egyptians in the Negev
were eventually pushed back seventy miles. The Israelis captured
Beersheba, capital of the Negev, extending the land of Israel from
Dan to Beersheba as it was in King Solomon's time. Substantial
gains were made south of Jerusalem. On the coastal strip the

Egyptian finger pointing menacingly at Tel Aviv only seventeen miles away was pushed back fifteen miles towards Gaza. At Faluja, 4,000 Egyptian troops, including a certain Captain Gamal Abdel Nasser, were surrounded. The besiegers besieged. Later a British Arab Legion officer named Lockhart, familiar with the terrain, was secretly infiltrated into the Faluja pocket to discuss his plan for a withdrawal. His plan was submitted to Supreme Headquarters in Cairo who replied: 'Expel the English drunkard Lockhart. His plan will be a disaster. Fight to the last man.' They refused to surrender despite heavy artillery and air attacks and held out gallantly until the end of the war.

Israel's tiny navy sank the destroyer *Emir Farouk*, the flagship of the Egyptian Navy, and ended the blockade of Israeli waters. A cease-fire was agreed by both sides on 22 October.

Operation Yoav had lasted seven days. The first of Israel's swift, incisive, surprise campaigns so characteristic of later wars.

Chapter 25

I RARELY THOUGHT of England, my England, that year. It was, apparently, a halcyon summer in England, with London as host to the 1948 Olympics and Compton and Edrich on the rampage. The *Palestine Post*, the only English-language newspaper in Israel, sometimes printed the latest cricket scores, but England was very remote. I did not miss it. I had little to love England for. I had no home there and had loosened my roots by joining an alien cause. I was more at home walking along Ben Yehuda Street in Tel Aviv than King's Road in Chelsea. I revelled in that sense of freedom, that lifting of the spirit that comes from Mediterranean warmth, light and beauty. I seldom recalled that I was not Jewish. I was as bronzed as everyone else and wore the same khaki slacks, open-necked shirt and sandals. My name could be mistaken for Jewish. That I did not look like the stereotype Jew did not matter. Few did. Israel was a tiny nation and I was beginning to be known and recognised. Shopkeepers and strangers said 'Shalom' warmly to me. I am a remote man, but in Israel I had many friends. It was good to be part of the miracle of 1948.

I met Yael about this time. Yael is not her name. She was my age, single and the sort of woman that always gets a second glance. It was comic to see the look of agonised longing as men appraised her. She was tall and high-waisted, her shapely legs went up a long way from the ground, her bosom was French Empire. She had corn-silk hair, with wide-set eyes that reflected the colour of the Mediterranean. Her nose was a tiny button, her complexion was pale and flawless – she kept out of the sun – and her lips were heart-breaking. She looked Scandinavian but she was a *Sabra*. Her native tongue was Hebrew but she spoke English fluently, with an attractive accent. Curiously, for a *Sabra*, she had a soft spot for Englishmen and English manners. She was rebuked frequently during the Mandate for fraternising with the enemy, the British. She was in the Air Force and had contrived a job as liaison officer between the IAF and ATC. She wore khaki uniform, but the cut and swing of her skirt, with an unauthorised slit at the back, the elegant silk shirt and the expensive suede flat shoes were not Air Force issue. She was probably the only bourgeoise *Sabra* in Israel. There was a slight air of Lady Bountiful about her. She had a very upper-class English way of sweeping into shops and patronising the assistants. I usually waited outside. I was well aware when I started to court her that I would have to watch out, otherwise I would become her poodle. We became lovers on a night when the *khamsin* blew, a hot, dry, desert wind from Africa. I was surprised to discover she was a different person horizontally. Yielding, submissive and utterly feminine. She called me Gideon, Hebrew for Gordon.

As with Jennifer years before, privacy was a problem. Yael's home was in the north, where her parents were wealthy citrus farmers. Meanwhile she rented a bed-sitting room in a pleasant block of flats in Tel Aviv. Male predators were not welcome by the landlady after dark. Yael's room was on the ground floor at the back, so on my nocturnal visits I climbed in and out of the window. We greased the window with cooking oil to stop it squeaking. Occasionally we overslept and I beat a retreat through the window while Yael was distracting the landlady in the kitchen with a 'Good morning, how are you?' conversation. It is exhausting making love silently. We put our heads under the pillows whenever we got the giggles.

In the circumstances of Israel, a foreign war, an alien cause, it was fitting that I should find a local girl to love but our relationship was stormy. Although she was a *Sabra* she was almost detached from her Judaic roots. Despite the transcendental nature of what was going on around her she seemed impervious to being Jewish. As far as she was concerned being an Israeli was more important than being a Jew. She rarely, if ever, expressed a specific Jewish thought or reaction and never went to synagogue. I once shouted at her in exasperation that I was more bloody Jewish than she was. Her stance was not intellectual, merely instinctive. She was a good illustration of the Jewish race versus religion argument. She did not believe in Judaism, therefore she was not a Jew. She was born and lived in Israel, therefore she was an Israeli. *Ergo*, one can be an Israeli without being a Jew but, conversely, one cannot be a true Jew without being an Israeli. Finally, as far as she was concerned, a Jew is a person who regards himself as a Jew.

With the success of the campaign in the south against the Egyptians, followed by the cease-fire, the Israelis were now hoping that somebody would be foolish enough to start something and break the truce in the north. Kaukji and what was left of his irregulars duly obliged, giving the Israelis the opportunity of launching Operation Hiram. It was astonishing how the Arab Goliath permitted the Israel David to pick off its member-nations one by one. Not once during the year-long War of Independence, except for the first few days of the initial invasion, was there a co-ordinated, simultaneous attack on all five fronts by all the seven Arab nations involved. It is, of course, misconceived to expect the Arabs to be united. They are as disparate as Europeans. The Saudi Arab is as different from the Lebanese Arab as is the Italian from the Dutchman, and the Egyptians are not Arabs anyway. Nevertheless, one would have expected that with a common language, a common religion and a common aim – the destruction of Israel – the Arabs would have united for the purposes of war and co-ordinated their strategy. Had they done so then they would have won the war. If they did so today they would probably annihilate Israel within a month. If America let them.

Operation Hiram, with strategic support from the Air Force, was a brilliant success. Within nine days the Israelis captured the whole of Galilee and the north up to the old British Mandate borders of Lebanon and Syria. It was the last major campaign of the war on the northern front.

The successes of Operations Yoav and Hiram led to Israel's victory and survival. There were many more graves to be dug on both sides before the end of the War of Independence but Arab confidence and morale had suffered grievously. To their astonishment they were on the defensive and paying a heavy price for their chronic disunity.

Chapter 26

ATC's AIRLINE LOBBY persuaded the government that now was the time to launch Israel's national airline, both for practical purposes but also to show the flag, Israel's new flag.

Our good and faithful DC4 Skymaster was tarted up, seats and a galley installed and the new airline's name: *Israeli National Aviation Company* (later changed to El Al) emblazoned along the sides of the fuselage. She also proudly wore Israel's first newly granted international registration number: 4X ACA. She looked like mutton dressed as lamb.

INAC's first airline flight, to Geneva, in September 1948, in effect El Al's inaugural flight, with ATC's chief pilot, Sam Lewis, as captain, was a great success, with flashlight bulbs popping and world-wide publicity. The flight was seen as a gesture of defiance to the Arabs and an appeal for recognition by the rest of the world of Israel's right to live.

There was much jockeying to be the crew of the next flight, to Paris. Apart from the pioneering aspect of the flight itself, a night in the flesh-pots of Paris would be welcome after the austerity of war-time Israel. To my surprise, for I was not part of the airline lobby, I was selected as co-captain with Moonitz. We had a crew of five. Navigator, wireless operator, flight engineer and two stewards. A local tailor made up our pale blue uniforms. Moonitz and I wore four rich gold braid stripes, gold embroidered wings and gold trimmings on our peaked hats. We looked like banana republic admirals.

To avoid enemy fighters we took off from Ekron late at night, with several VIP passengers, including Cabinet ministers and generals, aboard. The weather was perfect, the moon huge. The cabin windows were blacked out and our navigation lights were off. I was in the left-hand seat. Moonitz and I had agreed that I would captain outbound and he would captain inbound. We were good friends. As we climbed westwards into the night I remembered the envious glances of those left behind, including Yael, as we taxied out. Israel was still besieged, isolated and claustrophobic.

That was a special flight in my memory. I will try to recall what was so special about it. After all, 40 tons of precision engineering and 35 souls hurtling through the night, two miles high, at 230 miles an hour, heading for Le Bourget, is no longer remarkable.

I find the early hours of the morning the most bewitching time of flying and so it was on this flight. The passengers asleep, the cabin staff and the rest of the crew dozing, their heads nodding and snapping back guiltily. There was a quietness throughout the aeroplane. The four engines hummed a lullaby, the air had the night's smoothness, the radios were quiet, the instruments glowed steadily and reassuringly and the world below was asleep. Only the moon and stars witnessed with me the magic of night flight.

By now my flying skills were at their peak. There was little that could happen in flight where I would make the wrong decision or do the wrong thing. The unnatural nature of man in flight had become as natural to me as breathing and sitting at the controls that beautiful night over the Mediterranean I sensually revelled in my solitary art. This obedient aeroplane was an extension of myself, its wings were mine and we were one, an affinity of man and machine.

For most pilots of my vintage, the DC4 Skymaster was queen of the skies at that time. Only one other aircraft, the Lockheed Constellation, was comparable. They both pioneered the sleek cigar-shape and nose-wheel configuration that contrasted so vividly with their clumsy-looking, tail-wheel, arse-dragging predecessors. The nose-wheelers looked eager for flight as they moved off down the runway. The tail-draggers huffed and puffed to get their tails into the air before they looked as if they might fly.

Much as I loved this aeroplane, this apotheosis of contemporary aircraft design, I did not trust it. Like all aircraft this beautiful machine, honed and built to tolerances of less than a thousandth of an inch, powered by fuel from the bowels of the earth and with a million moving parts reined feather-light to my finger-tips, was a stupid thing, with suicidal tendencies. In an instant, at a whim, it would hurl itself against a mountain peak, dive to the bottom of the sea, crash to the ground, enter a wing-snapping thunderstorm. Thus it was that Moonitz and I mattered. The pilot will always matter, but then he mattered more.

Flying has become an automated science. Flight planning decisions are made by the operations-room computer and are carried out in

187

flight by the aircraft computers, with the crews monitoring a binary, high-flown world of certainty. The passengers are safe, the pilots bored except when taking off or landing. But in those far-off days, in war and peace, we flew in glorious uncertainty, guided and guarded by a cynical distrust of man, machine and weather. We were rarely lost, but half the time we did not know where we were. Our compass, which had changed little since Columbus, might tell us where we were heading, but not always where we were going. The new-fangled radio-compass could give us a navigation fix if there were two or more ground transmitting stations within reach, but it had limited range, was vulnerable to electrical interference and was useless on long ocean flights. Dead reckoning told us where we ought to be, but rarely were.

We made crucial in-flight decisions on most long-distance flights. We frightened ourselves or were frightened regularly. Occasionally we were within the parameters of drama or disaster. Often, after landing, we blew out our cheeks and said 'Phew'. The camaraderie of pilots was born of the knowledge that the safe arrival at our destination was due not to science, but an art created by a combination of skill, judgement, instinct and, sometimes, luck. Whenever we bumped into old flying friends at the crossroads of the world the first topic was who had bought it. We knew that the deceased would not mind that we were as much interested in how they died as in their death, for a lesson might be learned.

I had been thirsty for some time before I remembered that I was now an airline captain with stewards and a galley aboard. I gave Moonitz a nudge and woke the rest of the crew. There was work to be done. We all ordered coffee. It came in cups and saucers. After years of drinking thermos-flask coffee from paper cups it was hot, fresh and deliciously decadent. The navigator rubbed sleep from his eyes and gave me a minor adjustment of course to steer, the obligatory alteration that navigators always request after a nap. The wireless operator reported our position to Athens control, reported all's well back to Ekron and got a weather report from Rome. There was a major cold front in our path. It seemed odd to be legitimate, to be reporting our position and flying openly in an Israeli aircraft. It was still dark and my turn for the crew bunk. Moonitz took over while I went for a nap.

I glanced through the cabin door at our passengers. They were all asleep, collars loosened, ties and hair awry, mouths slack. Senior figures though they were, they looked vulnerable and I felt paternal towards them.

The navigator was shaking my shoulder with a firmness that denoted urgency. Moonitz wanted me. It was daylight. My senses checked everything as I sat up. Engines sounded all right; there were no sinister noises; the slipstream sounded right; we were flying symmetrically and straight and level. What, I wondered as I went up to the cockpit, was wrong?

Moonitz pointed dead ahead. We both looked in awe. About ten miles ahead of us was the expected cold front. But this was no ordinary cold front. The two opposing masses of warm and cold air had whipped themselves into a frenzy and there, stretched across our path, was the result: a rare, classic, fully developed line-squall. The frontal cloud was a solid, almost vertical curtain reaching from sea level to a towering height and stretching from port to starboard as far as we could see. At its base was a rolling, boiling, frothy cloud that whipped the sea into untidy, angry waves. Amidst the front we could see the ominous anvil tops of several cumulo-nimbus thunderheads. Early horizontal sunlight bathed the scene in an eerie, orange-turquoise glow. We were witnessing a meteorological freak. It should not happen here, it should not happen at this time of the year, it should not happen at this time of the day.

Moonitz and I went through the pilot's catechism:

'Can't get over it,' said Moonitz. I nodded. We were not pressurised. We might manage flying over the front at 20,000 feet or more without oxygen, but our passengers would not.

'Can't go under it, it's on the deck,' I said.

'Can't go round it, it stretches too far,' said Moonitz.

'Can't turn back, it's too late,' I said. We would have to go through it.

I pressed the button for one of the stewards. The turbulence had started and he looked unwell and anxious already. He was a restaurant waiter and had not flown before. I explained we were heading for very rough air and that he was to collect the dishes, batten down the galley, fasten passenger seat-belts and get sick-bags ready. 'Nothing to worry about,' I added.

'Ha,' said Moonitz. The flight-engineer sat on the jump-seat between Moonitz and me, we might need his hand on the throttles,

189

as we adjusted the controls for battle. Mixture auto-rich, cowl-flaps closed, main tanks on, climbing rpm, throttle back to 140 mph, check de-icers, carburettor heat on, cockpit lights on, seat-belts tight. Finally I switched George off and took control. George was a boy and there was a man's job ahead.

For a few moments after we entered the frontal cloud the turbulence was moderate, but without warning the full ferocity of the line-squall hit us. We became the plaything of giants as violent air-currents tossed us up and down like a 40-ton shuttlecock. I shouted to the engineer to handle the throttles and to Moonitz to help me with the controls. Even with the strength of two men we were still at the elements' mercy. The theory of flight had collapsed. With the nose pointing upwards we were descending at thousands of feet a minute, with the nose pointing downwards we were rocketing upwards, with left bank we were turning right, with right bank we were turning left, with throttles wide open we were near stalling speed, with throttles nearly closed we were exceeding structural safety speed. Several times violent gusts threw us beyond a vertical bank. It was a maelstrom of violence and a bedlam of noise. The engines protesting, the airframe groaning, the wind-screen wipers frenzied, rain lashing us like a kettle-drum and hail firing at us as though determined to pierce our thin aluminium shell. Films of ice appeared and disappeared like ghosts. We blundered through from one cumulo-nimbus to another. Lightning flashed and St. Elmo's corposant fire did a *danse macabre* along the wings. We were near to losing control or shedding a wing. It did not help that we had scarcely seen a cloud in Israel for months, much less flown in one. We both wore poker faces, more afraid of showing fear than fear itself. Our knuckles on the controls were white. We knew that fate was hunting. Moonitz suggested quarter flap. It made little difference. As a last resort I put the undercarriage down. The uproar worsened as the slipstream thrust through the open undercarriage bays. I read somewhere that the earth's atmos-phere produces more energy in one day than man has in all history. I could believe it that morning. We tried to climb out of it regardless of the oxygen problem, but every hundred feet the gallant DC4 gained the elements took away.

Suddenly, as though the giants wearied of us, we were spat out the other side of the line-squall into urbane, clear blue sky. It was over.

We talked about it. Between us we had flown the world, in all seasons, but none of us had experienced anything like that before. I went back to the passengers. The cabin was a shambles but nobody was hurt. I assured the passengers it was all over but their faith in me had gone. They looked at me accusingly as passengers do when the going has been rough. The navigator said it had lasted only fifteen minutes. That could not have been true unless time had stopped.

We were flying up the Rhône Valley, nuzzled by the white-tipped Alps to starboard and the Massif Central to port, when we were greeted with the usual European weather, this time a warm front. The first spots of rain blemished the windscreens and unbroken cloud slanted down to the northern horizon as we requested a weather report from Le Bourget. We were not surprised when they informed us that their weather, actual and forecast, was heavy rain, low ceiling and poor visibility. As we entered cloud I thought my stipend of £6 a month was being well earned on this flight.

We studied the instrument landing charts for Le Bourget. Neither Moonitz or I had landed there before. I would have to carry out a blind radio-range instrument landing, something I had not done for three years. Moonitz had not carried out an instrument landing since his crash at Ekron five months before. It was the blind leading the blind. Not the most therapeutic of rehabilitations for Moonitz.

Blind-flying instrument landings are never easy even for the experienced airline pilot in current practice. It is the epitome of a pilot's skill. More so in those primitive days without VOR or DME or GCA or ILS. The final approach is a blind three-dimensional juggle of height, speed, attitude, distance, heading and stop-watch timing, while searching for the threshold of the runway. Every aerodrome is different, every sky is different, every circumstance is different when doing an instrument landing. It can never be routine. It is a part of flying which is treated with respect by all pilots, for more people are killed on instrument landing approaches than at any other time in flight.

The radio-range instrument landing system was deceptively simple. A radio beam in his headphones guides the pilot to the threshold of the runway. On one side of the beam the letter A is transmitted continuously in morse code. On the other side the letter

N. Down the centre of the beam the As and Ns blend into a steady note indicating that the aircraft is on the correct flight path. The steady note was narrow and elusive, with cross-winds blowing the aircraft off-beam. Along the beam were spaced two markers, outer and inner, which bleeped and also flashed a light in the cockpit when the aircraft passed directly overhead. The aircraft had to be at the prescribed height when passing over the markers. Finally, there was the cone-of-silence, a few seconds of blissful silence confirming that the approach was good and that the runway should appear through the gloom at any moment.

The control tower informed us that the ceiling was down to 500 feet and visibility half a mile in heavy rain. As we started the let-down procedure I mentioned to Moonitz that I was a bit rusty and asked him to monitor my approach. He was pleased to be distracted from his thoughts. With the landing chart on his lap he led me from behind as I bracketed the beam. Steer this, he said. Steer that, too low, too high, speed 115, 120, 115, left, left, steady, too low, more throttle, right, steady, steady, steady. I kept my eyes on the instruments and one ear on the beam. Moonitz, hunched and intent, looked through the windscreen at a wet, grey, swirling nothing. The strong cross-wind drifted us out of the beam until I got the angle of correction right. We passed the outer marker at the correct height but were too high when we passed the inner-marker. Down, down, down, said Moonitz. I was chuffed when we hit the cone of silence at the correct height. Between us Moonitz and I made one good airline pilot. But the runway did not appear. Gusts of heavy rain thrashed us and pushed us off the beam. I edged back and let down lower. Moonitz called out our height and airspeed as we edged lower still. I did not envy him.

'Three hundred feet,' he shouted. It was a foolhardy height, below safe limits. I had my hands ready on the throttles to over-shoot and try again when suddenly the murk lifted, the cloud broke and twin rows of brilliant runway lights beckoned us to safety.

In 1948, tarmacs were dramatic. Croydon and Le Bourget, where Lindbergh and many other aviation pioneers had landed after historic flights, perhaps more than most. Civil international flying had not yet become routine. War-bred airliners emblazoned with stirring, not yet commonplace names, fired the imagination as they taxied to and fro with the roar and blast of propellers. Converted bombers flew as airliners and freighters. Dwarfed, but still proud, war-surplus Dakotas bustled everywhere carrying the hopes of new operators. There was an electric tension in the passengers' lounge born of excitement, drama, adventure, travel and a bravado that concealed the fear of flying. Most of the aircrews wore medal ribbons. It was a small, exciting world, a pioneering world still. I was glad to be part of it.

I sank into my bath in the L'Etoile Hotel in Paris, with a very large whisky and soda, a cigarette and yesterday's *Times*. I was tired but it was a pleasant tiredness. It had been a demanding flight and we had managed it well.

We had not packed mufti and went out for dinner and our night on the town wearing uniform. We were tanned and looked good. We left it to the taxi driver to choose a restaurant, not kosher, we added. He made a good choice and we were given a great reception. The war in Israel was front-page news. The food was good, the wine on the house. Despite an aviation tradition that pilots never get plastered in uniform – it frightens would-be air travellers – I did. We were fêted wherever we went. As usual, my Jewish comrades drank circumspectly. We finished up in Pigalle, then the only Mecca of those seeking the topless or more, and found a basement night-club where again we were fêted. Everyone in Paris seemed pro-Israel. It had taken two thousand years for the Jews to become popular. But I had an uncomfortable feeling that the plaudits were reflecting the view of the French that we were giving the 'Wogs' a good bashing. There were few, if any, in Israel who thought of the Arabs or the war in those terms.

We left for Israel the following afternoon in order to arrive after dark. We had new VIPs aboard including Henry Morgenthau and Elliott Roosevelt. I had a hangover and it was pleasant to sit in the right-hand seat and let Moonitz do the worrying. But there was little to worry about on the return flight for wisps of high cirrus signed a truce in the sky. The Janus sky had turned the other face. A serene face, blue and gold by day and silvered moon by night. I felt I was heading home.

Chapter 27

I T WAS NOVEMBER 1948, and I decided it was about time I became a fighter pilot. It was my last chance to fulfil an ambition denied in the Second World War.

Israel's only fighter squadron at that time was 101 Squadron, based at Qastina in the south. Its original Messerschmitt 109 fighter aircraft brought in by ATC, were slowly being replaced by the intermittent arrival of 40 ex-RAF Spitfire IX fighters from Czechoslovakia and three P51 Mustangs.

The delivery of those Spitfires by several formation ferry-flights from Czechoslovakia to Israel, via Yugoslavia, between September and December 1948, against the United Nations arms embargo, and using relatively inexperienced pilots, was a minor aviation epic.

A secret refuelling base was arranged at Podgorica, in Yugoslavia. The flight from Podgorica to Israel was 1,300 miles. The normal maximum range of a Spitfire was about 450 miles. The Spitfires were stripped of everything not vital to flight including radio, armament and oxygen, and extra fuel tanks were fitted under the belly and in the fuselage. It was estimated that the Spitfires would have about twenty minutes' fuel left when they arrived in Israel.

The Spitfires were led and shepherded by ATC's C46s and the DC4 Skymaster. Israeli naval ships were anchored along the route and a Dakota aircraft, loaded with air-sea rescue equipment, stood by at Haifa.

I did not envy the pilots strapped into the Spitfire's cramped cockpit for seven hours, mostly over the sea, with a single engine. Fortunately the Spitfire was equipped with a rubber pee-tube.

During this operation, which was completed in winter weather, three Spitfires crashed, killing two pilots. A further five Spitfires force-landed in Greece or Rhodes and were impounded. Little was won cheaply or easily by Israel in that war, but the arrival of the Spitfires consolidated Israel's air superiority in the Middle East.

I had a tussle with Hayman Shamir to get transferred to 101 Squadron, but there was little for ATC to do during the cease-fire and he reluctantly agreed. He knew that I had flown Spitfires and

Hurricanes in the RAF and assumed that I had done so in combat. He warned me that he might soon have to transfer me back to ATC, but clammed up with a grin when I asked why. He liked being arcane.

That evening I packed my possessions into a rucksack and went to the Galei Yam Bar facing the beach in Tel Aviv, the fighter pilots' favourite watering hole. I knew most of the pilots. There were several of them, including Syd Cohen the commanding officer, sitting at tables drinking thin, local beer. They all wore vivid red baseball hats. There was no bar to lean on. It seems only the British like to drink standing up. Yael joined me later. There were the usual agonised groans of frustration when she walked in. At midnight we stole a large American station wagon and drove the twenty-odd miles to Qastina, dropping Yael off at her bed-sitter on the way. For several months the operation of Israel's sole fighter squadron depended upon stolen cars. We learned how to rip out ignition wires and by-pass the ignition key. The police collected our booty regularly from the aerodrome. It became known as Syd's used car lot.

The pilots of 101 Sqadron were as mixed as their motives. Jews, Gentiles, mercenaries and idealists. *Sabras*, Israelis, Americans, Canadians, South Africans and English. Ex-RAF, RCAF, SAAF and USAAF. Several had Second World War kills and medals to their credit. Jewish names – Cohen, Auergarten, Lenart, Weizman, Lichtman, Senior, Alon, Mann – contrasted with Gentile names – Doyle, McElroy, Goodlyn, Peake, Wilson, Sinclair. It was probably the best fighter squadron in the world at the time. Over 40 years and four wars later it probably still is.

The ground crews were all Jewish. Their job would not pay enough to attract mercenaries. All ground crews in all air forces are the same; scruffy, black-nailed, unsung. One of them at 101 Squadron did a Levett and became a pilot. In 1973, at the twenty-fifth anniversary celebrations of the State of Israel, that ex-erk, by then General Binyamin Peled, Commander-in-Chief of the Israeli Air Force and one of the masterminds of the Entebbe raid, shook my hand and grinned recognition as he presented me with a gong for services rendered to Israel in 1948/49.

It was an extraordinary sight to see the three premier fighter aircraft of the Second World War, the British Spitfire, the American

P51 Mustang and the German Messerschmitt 109 lined up neatly together on the tarmac, all painted with the insignia of the Israeli Air Force, the Star of David. It was even even more extraordinary to fly into battle with the three different types together in formation. It was an odd, ironic quirk of history, and a fitting reparation for the Jews, that the Luftwaffe's notorious Messerschmitt 109 should now be fighting for Israel. Most of the experienced pilots at 101 Squadron flew all three fighters in action. We climbed out of one and into the other as serviceability and operations required. It was a unique experience to fly a Spitfire, a Mustang and a Messerschmitt in combat on the same day.

The Czech-built Messerschmitt 109 (more correctly known as the Avia SC-199) was not popular with the pilots. It was, surprisingly, much smaller than the Spitfire or Mustang. With its splayed feet, upside-down engine, paddle-bladed propeller and ugly, bulbous spinner, it looked waspish and business-like. Owing to the lack of the usual Daimler-Benz engine they were fitted with the lower-powered and heavier Junkers Jumo engine used in the Heinkel 111 bomber. This engine and the necessary airframe modifications reduced the performance of the aircraft. Like the Spitfire, its undercarriage retracted outwards and the landing wheels were narrowly close together. It was a tricky aeroplane to handle on the ground, particularly with a cross-wind, and had a tendency with inexperienced pilots to ground-loop on landing and sometimes finish up on its back. Worse, the cockpit hood was hinged on the starboard side and was pulled over the pilot's head to lock on the port side, instead of sliding backwards and forwards like most other fighters. This meant that pilots had to take-off or land with the hood shut, trapping the pilot inside if the aircraft should finish up on its back. The entire squadron spent most of one afternoon releasing an unhurt pilot who was trapped in his upside down Messerschmitt after somersaulting on landing, with the ground soaked in petrol and the petrol tanks dripping relentlessly. I can still hear today his screams begging us to be careful and not cause a spark. Despite all this the Messerschmitt did not deserve the exaggeratedly poor reputation it gained in Israel.

In mock dog-fights we concluded that the Messerschmitt could out-climb, out-dive and out-zoom the Spitfire and Mustang. The Spitfire could out-turn the Messerschmitt, the most important manoeuvre in air combat, and both could out-turn the Mustang. The Mustang was the fastest, the Messerschmitt the slowest, though there was not much in it. The Mustang had the best visibility, important for a fighter aircraft, the Messerschmitt the worst. The Spitfire cockpit fitted like a glove, the Messerschmitt like a strait-jacket, the Mustang like a too comfortable armchair. The Spitfire had two 20 mm cannon and four 0.303 machine guns, the Mustang six 12.7 mm machine guns, and the Messerschmitt two 20 mm cannon and two 7.92 mm machine guns synchronised to fire through the arc of the propeller. There were tales of bullets hitting the propeller, but I think this was more of the anti-Messerschmitt myth. Keeping so many different types of guns firing was an armourer's nightmare. Despite the pros and cons the Spitfire was everyone's first choice.

I had brief familiarisation flights on the three aircraft. The first was on a Spitfire which I had not flown for seven years. The snug, untidy cockpit, the smell of glycol and the long nose were instantly familiar. The Spitfire weighs less than four tons. Knowing that my recent experience was with the 25-ton C46 and the 40-ton Skymaster, most of the pilots turned out to watch my over-controlling antics. I had a red face when I landed. After I had got the Messerschmitt and the Mustang up and down a little less ham-fistedly I was considered ready for action.

Everyone assumed that as I had volunteered for 101 Squadron and was an ex-RAF pilot I knew all about the 'Scramble! Tally-ho! *Achtung* Spitfire!' fighter-pilot stuff. I did not reveal that all I knew about being a fighter pilot was gleaned from *Biggles*. The night before my first patrol I tried to recall the imperatives. Beware an attack from the sun. Height is precious. Close, short bursts. Keep a good look out. Use your rear-view mirror all the time. Wear goggles and gloves in case of fire. Do not follow your victim down. Do not steer the same course or hold the same height for more than a split second. Keep some ammunition left for defence on the way home. If baling out, pull the rip-cord at the last minute. If you crash-land in enemy territory get away from the aircraft as quickly as possible after putting a match to it. Stay with it if in friendly territory.

My first operational sortie with 101 Sqadron was dawn patrol with Syd Cohen, the CO, in Spitfires. I was to be his number two.

The purpose of the flight was to look for or cause trouble in the Khan Yunis–Rafah–Gaza front-line area. In addition to our machine-guns and cannon we had a brace of 250-pound bombs apiece. Being number two meant that I covered Syd's tail while he navigated, reconnoitred and sought out targets in the air or on the ground. 101 Squadron had adopted the Luftwaffe method of hunting in pairs rather than the large, unwieldy formations favoured by the RAF in the Second World War and still used by the Egyptians. Whatever method was adopted everyone split up when battle began.

Syd and I had breakfast together in the communal mess. It was the usual Israeli breakfast: cold, hard-boiled egg and a green salad festooned with olives and cottage cheese. No bacon, of course, but the bread was leavened. I had long since given up trying to get a drinkable cup of tea in Israel and now drank black coffee. I did not eat much. All I could think of was that at last I was a fighter pilot.

It was still dark. Syd and I were the only people in the mess apart from the cook. We were wearing casual mufti, without wings or badges of rank. We did not look like fighter pilots breakfasting before dawn patrol. I could hear our two Merlins being tested distantly in the darkness. Dawn Patrol! I felt a bit like David Niven or Errol Flynn. I promised myself I would buy a white silk scarf. Syd was the calm, reassuring Spencer Tracy type. I felt confident that he would not lead me into undue trouble. Nevertheless my ashtray was full by the time we left the table to go to our Spitfires. They were moist with dew.

While we sat strapped in our cockpits waiting for dawn I fiddled with this and that and adjusted the gun-sight until it reflected a ghostly bull's-eye outline on the windscreen. The brass gun-button on the control column was worn smooth by pilots' thumbs.

The radio crackled in my headphones. 'Let's go,' said Syd.

It was a brilliant dawn. Sharp, clear and cool. Shadows were long as we climbed with the sun towards the Gaza Strip. Syd soon sighted an Egyptian train heading south-westerly from Rafah on the same railway line I had night-bombed with the C46. Either I had missed, or they had repaired the line very quickly. Moderate anti-aircraft fire weaved pink, black and white filigree patterns around us as we circled the train and prepared to attack. Syd went in first and dive-bombed twice. His first bomb missed completely, his

second was a near miss. It was my turn. Both my bombs missed by
a mile. We had shifted a lot of sand. We then strafed the locomotive
several times. I was astonished at the clatter and the recoil effect on
the Spitfire as the guns fired. I was so absorbed by the puffs of sand
as my bullets hit the desert that I nearly flew into the train. It spurted
steam and stopped. Passengers were jumping out and scrambling
underneath. Mothers were handing down children and babies from
the windows. After our sixth or seventh pass we circled, looking
down at our handiwork. The locomotive was badly damaged. By
unspoken agreement neither Syd or I had attacked the passenger
coaches. Our meek flight hit the headlines. According to the press
we had destroyed a vital ammunition train and caused heavy losses
among Egyptian troops on the train. Truth is indeed the first
casualty of war.

My next operation was as number two to Jack Doyle, escorting
four Harvard AT6 aircraft on a bombing raid on the besieged, still
defiant Egyptians, including Nasser, at Faluja. Doyle was an ex-
RCAF fighter pilot. His mount was a Spitfire, mine a Messerschmitt.
We had different radio frequencies and could not communicate in
the air. We were an odd sight as we flew in loose formation to
Faluja; Harvard trainers masquerading as bombers, escorted by a
Spitfire and a Messerschmitt.

To the east of Faluja we saw eight Egyptian fighters. Four of
them were Spitfire XVIs. I could not resist the temptation of
shouting '*Achtung* Spitfire' into the microphone. The other four
were Italian Fiat G55s, a rare but first-rate Second World War
fighter.

As Doyle and I climbed into the sun I remembered a rumour that
ex-Luftwaffe aces had joined the Egyptian Air Force. It would be a
bizarre fate for an Englishman in a Messerschmitt to be shot down
by an ex-Luftwaffe pilot flying a Spitfire. A dog-fight at last! I was
excited but not afraid. Most pilots in combat feel it is the other chap
who will die. To think otherwise would be a self-fulfilling
prophecy. The Harvards dropped their bombs hurriedly on Faluja
and returned to base. They were no match for the fighters. The
enemy had not yet seen us. By now we were in a perfect attacking
position, about 4,000 feet above them and between them and the
sun – bright, blinding sun even though it was winter. The Mediterranean to the west insouciantly reflected the deep blue sky. I noticed

a ship's long white wake. It was a beautiful day for an appointment in Samarra. Doyle grinned at me and pointed downwards with his index finger, his thumb cocking an imaginary gun. I nodded and followed him down. He attacked a Fiat before they saw us. I locked on to a Spitfire and fired. Bits flew off the Spitfire and the white trail of glycol told me his Merlin engine was probably mortally wounded. I was about to finish him off when I saw another Spitfire coming up on my starboard side and broke off the attack. I turned steeply trying to shake him off, but he was still there. Looking back over my shoulder I watched, hypnotised, the tiny, pretty, orange lights twinkling at me from the leading edge of the enemy Spitfire's wing before I realised I was staring eternity in the face. I was looking down the barrels of machine guns and cannon that were trying to kill me. I realised I was being a bloody fool trying to out-turn a Spitfire in a Messerschmitt. I rammed the control column harshly forward and dived in as violent a manoeuvre as I had ever flown. Dust and dead flies flew up from the cockpit floor and my head banged against the roof of the cockpit canopy, but despite the heavy negative gravity forces imposed by the manoeuvre the fuel-injected engine continued to run sweetly. I knew the Spitfire's Merlin engine would not if he tried to follow. It was not fuel-injected. The engine would hiccup and miss for a second or two, time to save my life. I dived beyond the vertical to make sure. He disappeared. I did not need to look at the airspeed indicator to know I was nearing 450 mph when I pulled out of the dive and zoomed back into a gaggle of Spitfires. But I could not fire. Doyle had a unique advantage in this mêlée. He could fire at any Spitfire. I had to make sure I was not firing at him. The Egyptians had a similar problem. I saw a lone Fiat G55 below me heading home towards the Egyptian Air Force base at El Arish and I used my superior height to catch him up. I did not know the strengths and weaknesses of the Fiat, but it did not matter for his evasive manoeuvres were elementary. I fired a short burst from his starboard quarter. He flew on, straight and level, at my mercy. Perhaps he was injured. I did not like the role of killing a sitting duck and considered lowering the undercarriage and waggling the wings at him in the accepted signal demanding his surrender, but it was too dangerous. It would slow me down and there might be other enemy aircraft lurking about. I fired again and again. Black smoke trailed from his engine as he flew in a steep, descending arc towards the sea. I did not follow him down and turned back to Faluja. But the sky had suddenly become quiet and empty. It was over. After I landed the armourer was peeved that I had a little ammunition left. I explained why. He pursed his lips.

At de-briefing Doyle and I each claimed one Fiat G55 destroyed and one Spitfire probably destroyed. That evening Cairo radio admitted the loss of three aircraft, confirming three-quarters of our claims, and untruthfully claimed that they had shot down five of ours.

I could not get to sleep that night. In the quiet, early hours of the morning I sat up, switched on the bedside light, lighted a cigarette and reflected on the previous day's events. The day I had killed a man, probably two. I wondered about them. Were they young, old, married, fathers? Being Egyptians, they probably had moustaches, brown eyes and warm, courteous personalities, with a lively sense of humour. One, I knew, was lying at the bottom of the Mediterranean in his aircraft, like Saint-Exupéry.

I did not feel elated at my first experience of gladiatorial man-to-man combat. I remembered only that there had been little nobility or dignity in that dog-fight circus. The cause I was fighting for was not in my mind during the action. What had motivated me was the swashbuckling, vulgar thrill of being a fighter pilot, and the simplistic morality of military combat.

I got up and browsed through my small collection of books. It took me a long time to find what I wanted. When I did I nodded. It was in a letter written by Saint-Exupéry to André Gide after he had been in combat: 'I now know why Plato places courage on the lowest rung of the virtues. Never again shall I be able to admire a man who is only brave.'

Chapter 28

I N THE TWENTY-ODD missions I flew in 101 Squadron I was well aware that in the circumstances of that war it was inevitable that the Israeli Air Force and the Royal Air Force would clash. Treaties signed between Britain and three of Israel's enemies, Iraq, Jordan and Egypt, called for close relations and mutual military assistance if needed. There was also the reluctance of Britain to accept that its power and influence in the Middle East, as elsewhere, were in decline. Finally, there was British pique and resentment that one of the major causes of that decline in the Middle East was being kicked out of Palestine by parvenu Israel. Britain still refused to recognise Israel, still called its citizens Jews, rather than Israelis. Jewish people know that when they are referred to as 'the Jews' in clipped tones by Gentiles it is usually meant as a pejorative adjective.

Three RAF fighter squadrons, No. 208, equipped with Spitfire XVIIIs, No. 213 and No. 6 equipped with Hawker Tempests, and No. 13 Squadron, a photographic reconnaissance squadron equipped with Mosquito aircraft, were based in the Suez Canal Zone, then administered by the British. It was fifteen minutes in a Tempest to the Israeli–Egyptian front lines where there was a war going on. RAF aircraft were also based in Jordan and Iraq. Operation Horev, the last major battle of the war, from 21 December 1948, to 7 January 1949, to push the Egyptians back to where they had started at the old Palestinian–Egyptain border, was in full swing. The scene was again set for muddle, mischief and tragedy.

Just before noon on 7 January 1949, two pilots of 101 Squadron, Slick Goodlin, an American, and John McElroy, a Canadian, took off from Qastina in their Spitfire IXs for an offensive patrol over the El Arish–El Auja–Rafah front-line area. Earlier that morning Doyle had shot down an Egyptian Spitfire in the same area. It was a dull, cloudy day. McElroy was ex-RCAF and had won the Distinguished Flying Cross and Bar for shooting down fifteen German aircraft and several probables in the Second World War. Goodlin, a distinguished pilot, had done his bit for Britain by joining the RCAF as a pilot long before Pearl Harbor. Later, after a spell in the American Navy, he became a test pilot with the Bell Aircraft Company, testing Second World War fighters and, after the war, senior test pilot of the Bell XS-1 rocket aircraft, the first aircraft to exceed the speed of sound. When, after months of testing, the Bell XS-1 was ready for the historic flight, Goodlin resigned over a contract dispute with Bell, thus sadly missing the opportunity of breaking through the sound barrier for the first time and engraving his name in aviation history. Chuck Yaegar, an American Air Force pilot, did it instead. Both McElroy and Goodlin had already shot down several Egyptian aircraft.

At the same time as McElroy and Goodlin took off from Qastina, four RAF Spitfires of 208 Squadron took off from their base at Fayid, in the Suez Canal Zone, for a reconnaissance of much the same front-line area where McElroy and Goodlin were seeking trouble. The Spitfires were flown by Flying Officer Cooper,* the leader, Flying Officer McElhaw, Pilot II Sayers and Pilot II Close. Their Spitfires had red spinners, the same as 101 Squadron.

Looking down on the front line, McElroy and Goodlin saw columns of smoke rising over a thousand feet from an Israeli armoured column that had been attacked from the air. Circling above the column were several Spitfires. McElroy and Goodlin attacked the Spitfires. McElroy shot down two, Goodlin shot down one, the fourth was shot down by ground fire. The 101 Squadron pilots returned triumphantly to Qastina and victory rolls over the aerodrome. After they had landed Goodlin walked over to McElroy and said 'I think they might have been Royal Air Force Spits.' McElroy laughed, 'You're crazy,' he said.

Goodlin was right. The Royal Air Force had lost four Spitfires. Cooper baled out, was picked up uninjured by Bedouin tribesmen and started his return journey back to Fayid by camel. McElhaw baled out, was uninjured and taken prisoner by Israeli troops. Close also baled out and was taken prisoner by Israeli troops, suffering from mild concussion and a hair-line fracture of the jaw when his head hit the tail of his Spitfire as he baled out. There were a lot of

*Later Air Commodore Cooper, aviation correspondent of the *Daily Telegraph*. He was also involved in the clash between the RAF and the Egyptian Air Force, described in Chapter 20, during which he shot down two Egyptian Spitfires. The boot was then firmly on the other foot.

parachutes mushrooming in the sky that day. Sayers's aircraft crashed vertically into the desert and he was killed.

After the four Spitfires had become overdue the RAF decided to carry out a reconnaisance of the same area to find out the fate of their missing aircraft and at three o'clock that same afternoon a formidable gaggle of four RAF Spitfires and fifteen Tempests of Nos. 6, 208 and 213 Squadrons took off from the Suez Canal Zone in search of their comrades.

At the same time the Israeli Air Force was put on full alert. Four Spitfires of 101 Squadron, led by Ezer Weizman – nephew of Israel's first President, and later himself to become President of Israel – took off on patrol and spotted the nineteen aircraft, which they assumed to be hostile, over the front line area near Rafah. They attacked and in the ensuing dog-fight one RAF Tempest of 213 Squadron was shot down by Bud Schroeder, an American. The pilot of the Tempest, Pilot Officer Tattersfield, was killed. Several other Tempests were damaged. Some of the RAF aircraft returned fire but, unbelievably, the guns of 213 Squadron's Tempests were not cocked and all 101 Squadron's aircraft returned undamaged to base.

I had spent the day off with Yael and returned to 101 Squadron at Qastina that night unaware of the day's events. The squadron was bristling with tension and excitement. Was Israel on the brink of war with Britain?

Long before dawn all available aircraft and pilots were at instant readiness. We sat in our cockpits in the dark awaiting the RAF's next move. Years later I learned from discussions with Pilot Officer Heald of 213 Squadron, based at Deversoir, who was injured and his Tempest damaged in the dog-fight, that the RAF spent that night, humiliated and angry at its loss of five aircraft, planning to destroy the Israeli Air Force the next day.

I had spent a restless night. I was still not sure as I sat in the Spitfire's cockpit waiting for dawn, what I would do if the Royal Air Force attacked and we were scrambled. Could I fire at an RAF aeroplane? I remembered E.M. Forster's apophthegm that if he ever had to choose between cause and country he hoped he would have the guts to choose the cause. I do not know for I was not put to the test. At the last minute wisdom prevailed and the British government forbade retributive action by the RAF.

19 The remains of ATC's runt C46, RX133, after Pussy Tolchinsky's crash during Operation Uvda at Avraham in the Negev, February 1948

20 An IAF B17 Flying Fortress on a bombing run over Egypt, summer 1948 – probably the same B17 involved in the Algerian fiasco ten years later

21   An RAF Spitfire of 208 Squadron at Ramat David, 1949

22   Spitfires of the Israeli Air Force 101 Fighter Squadron

A monumental political stink was created by the two incidents and the loss of the five RAF aircraft. In the war of words afterwards there were untruths on both sides. There was no direct communication. Israel still did not exist in British eyes. This was not the first time the Israeli Air Force and the Royal Air Force had clashed. On 20 November 1948, an RAF high-flying photo-reconnaissance Mosquito aircraft was shot down at 25,000 feet by Wayne Peake of 101 Squadron, flying a P51 Mustang. The Mosquito crashed into the sea, south of Tel Aviv, killing the crew of two.

Contemporary army reports stating that the RAF Spitfires shot down had been attacking and strafing the Israeli armoured column were incorrect. Not that it mattered. That the RAF was there, over the front lines of war, flying the same type of aircraft as the Egyptians, sufficed that they should be attacked. In air combat one does not have time to differentiate and identify, particularly when all sides are flying similar aircraft. If it is not one of yours over a combat zone it is one of theirs. If any nation is foolish enough to poke its nose into a war between two sovereign nations it will almost certainly get it bloodied.

In fact the Israeli column had been attacked by *Egyptian* Spitfires a few minutes earlier. Five RAF Tempest aircraft of No. 213 Squadron had circled and watched the attack before returning to base. The four doomed Spitfires of No. 208 Squadron then arrived on the scene and circled. It is not surprising in the confusion that McElroy and Goodlin assumed they were Egyptian aircraft responsible for the carnage on the ground.

After much research in dusty files at Kew there is no doubt in my mind that, no matter how perfidious Albion was in that war, the Royal Air Force did not attack Israeli troops on the ground. In the two incidents on 7 January, several RAF aircraft jettisoned their wing drop-tanks to increase speed and manoeuvrability. It is probable that these bomb-shaped tanks were mistaken for bombs by observers on the ground.

A comparable untruth was given official countenance by a signal from RAF Headquarters, Middle East, to the Air Ministry in London confirming that, according to Bedouin tribesmen, Flying Officer Cooper was fired upon by 'Jewish' aircraft as he was descending in his parachute.

The British government claimed that the incidents occurred

solely on the Egyptian side of the border. If true, so what? In fact it was not true. No pilot can be certain of his position within a mile or two, certainly not in combat over desert. Tattersfield's Tempest crashed on the Israeli side of the border. Close admitted to me the next day when I visited him in hospital that he had crossed the border. From my experience I would wager no-one knew where the hell they were within two or three miles. The British accused the Israelis of removing the wreckage of two of the crashed RAF Spitfires to their side of the border to mislead world opinion. They did move them. For priceless spare parts. The border was a bogus issue. Neither the Egyptians nor the Israelis respected the border. Both sides crossed it umpteen times. That's what wars are for.

Unknown to the Israelis, the RAF had been carrying out photo-reconnaissance flights over Israel and the front lines for several months. Some fifty such flights took place. Before the incidents on 7 January, the RAF had already completed two reconnaissance flights over the same area that morning, using five aircraft. The British government admitted that several of those photo-reconnaissance flights were accompanied by Egyptian aircraft. It also admitted that on certain occasions, reconnaisance photographs were shown to the Egyptians. Perfidious Albion indeed.

The RAF was, of course, doing as it was told, though I doubt that it was told to fly into a dangerous combat zone with guns at half-cock. That was their own foolishness. The British government's view of events leading up to 7 January, and its admission of blatant involvement on Egypt's side, is best revealed by quoting two memoranda written at the time by Bevin, the Foreign Secretary.

The first, written to the Minister of Defence, was dated 10 December 1948, after the RAF Mosquito had been shot down: '*The Jews*★ are technically in the wrong but we cannot expect that world opinion will wholly blame them for shooting down an aircraft which was making a photographic reconnaissance of their airfields. . .'.

The second, written to the Prime Minister, Attlee, was dated 28 December 1948: 'If there is further evidence of our carrying out these flights over Palestine, we shall be criticized for performing warlike acts . . . . I consider, however, that the political risk

★My italics. By now everybody else was calling them Israelis.

involved should not be allowed to over-ride the operational advantage of continuing the flights . . .'.

I attended a top-level operations meeting to discuss the possibility of using the RAF captured pilots Close and McElhaw as hostages for the release of Jews, still being held, unbelievably, as illegal immigrants behind barbed wire in British Cyprus seven months after the end of the British Mandate. I was asked as an Englishman how Britain would respond. Violently, I said, but deviously, by supplying enough arms and support to Jordan and Egypt to ensure that Israel lost the war. I did not add that in that event I would probably end my days in the Tower of London. After heated arguments the idea, though morally sound, was dropped.

Chapter 29

THE INCIDENTS OF 7 January coincided with the successful
completion of the major Israeli offensive in the south, Operation
Horev. The Egyptians were pushed back to where they had started
eight months before, the old Palestine–Egyptian frontier, apart
from the Gaza Strip. For them it had been much ado about nothing.
Egypt admitted defeat by agreeing to enter into immediate negotiations for an armistice agreement and a cease-fire was agreed by both
sides.

Suddenly the entire southern front became eerily quiet. The
Egyptian Air Force and the RAF had gone to ground and doves of
peace were beginning to fly. Israel was in a state of euphoric relief. If
Egypt, their major foe, who had sworn to drive the Jews into the
sea, was now suing for an armistice, the other Arab states could not
but soon follow. There were many odds and ends to be tied up,
many kinks in the borders to be straightened out, a few more deaths
to die but, unbelievably, victory and peace were imminent, though
wars seem to end more leisurely than they begin.

The besieged Egyptians at Faluja, including Captain Gamal
Abdel Nasser, were released and returned to Egypt under UN
auspices.

A week or two later I was called to Hayman Shamir's office. I had
not seen him for weeks. He had put on weight and substance and
wore an ill-fitting, air-force blue battledress uniform with new
badges of rank. Ranks were slowly being introduced, starting at the
top. Hayman was now General Shamir. It suited him.

After brief preliminaries about each other's health, he asked
whether I would be prepared to leave 101 Squadron to set up and
command a new air force transport squadron on RAF lines from
what was left of ATC and its C46s. Emphasis was to be placed on
training new, indigenous aircrew. It was to be called 106 Squadron,
based at Ekron. I would be its commanding officer with the rank of
Lieutenant-Colonel. I smiled at that. I was still English enough to
feel that foreign ranks were not pukka. My pay would go up to 16
Israeli pounds (then par with sterling) a month, all found.

The Israeli Air Force was beginning to grow up. Now that the critical days were presumed over, the IAF wanted to train its own people, *Sabras* and immigrants, and not critically depend again upon volunteers and mercenaries from abroad. Elementary and advanced flying training schools had already been established in Israel.

ATC had already begun to wither. It had not done much these last few weeks apart from bombing raids. Some of its aircrew and ground staff had gone back home to the USA. Others had joined the new state airline, El Al. A few resented the air force's attempts to introduce a modicum of discipline and authority. It was time to put an end to ATC's air force within an air force. Those that were left were invited to join me at 106 Squadron or go home. The same thing was happening throughout the fabric of Israel's entire society, government, military and civil. It was an inevitable but sad moment. I felt a pang at the passing of a unique anarchy.

Hayman had timed his request right. Perhaps I was getting old – I would soon be twenty-eight – but I did not want to kill anybody any more.

'You've concluded I'm not a British spy then?'

'It doesn't follow,' he grinned.

With some misgivings, for I was not sure that Israelis and Mahal Jews would like to be bossed about by an English Gentile, I accepted the job.

It was not long before the rag, tag and bobtail of ex-ATC aircrew, volunteers from other air force units and new sprog pilots from the training schools settled down, with new recently introduced uniforms and badges of rank, as 106 Squadron in old RAF huts at Ekron. I appointed Henry Woolf, an English Jew and ex-Fleet Air Arm pilot, as squadron adjutant. He turned out to be an Aladdin. He rubbed his lamp, and petrol bowsers, a Jeep, filing cabinets, paper clips and drawing pins appeared like magic. My major contribution on the ground was to organise a bar and canteen on NAAFI lines. I arrived at my office one day to find a plaque screwed to the door. It was in Hebrew. Apparently it read Sgan Aluf★ Gideon Levavi, Commanding Officer. I wish I had taken it with me when it was time to leave.

★Lieutenant-Colonel

Discipline was accepted. Everyone knew it was time to prepare for the next war. I was surprised to find that I could command silence when I walked into squadron meetings. But, in Israel, nobody calls anybody Sir.

Hayman had said there was urgency in our training programme. Characteristically he did not explain why. We flew night and day and soon turned out our first batch of new Israeli captains. Most of them had been co-pilots with ATC. Many later became captains with El Al. I was particularly pleased when Pussy Tolchinsky made the captain's left-hand seat.

The reason for the urgency was revealed at a meeting at HQ early in March. The cease-fire had held on all fronts and the armistice with Egypt was signed on 24 February 1949. Armistice negotiations were continuing, albeit slowly, with the other Arab states. But, despite the cease-fire, there was still some unfinished business.

The area stretching nearly 120 miles in the form of an inverted triangle from Beersheba to the Gulf of Aqaba, leading to the Red Sea, had been allocated to Israel in the United Nations partition plan. It was an empty, Old Testament desert wilderness, but it had, for Israel, two jewels in its thorny crown. Buffer land for defence strategy, and the potential for a deep-sea port and trade gateway to Africa and the Far East on the Gulf of Aqaba.

The area had been ignored by both sides during the war, but Jordan had recently infiltrated here and there, had installed isolated Arab Legion posts and now made claim to it in the armistice negotiations on the grounds that possession is nine-tenths of the law.

Until now Israel had been too busy fighting for its life. It now had a breather to fight for its future. But fight it could not. One shot and the war could flare again and Israel needed peace more than the Arabs. It would have to be occupation by stealth. Code name Operation Uvda.

Two brigades were to advance secretly from Beersheba. One along the Jordanian frontier, the other through the unexplored Negev desert and mountains to the west. If they met any opposition they were to withdraw. The two brigades were to be supplied and reinforced by air by 106 Squadron. Success, military and political, was dependent upon not a shot being fired.

We were confined to Ekron as troops and supplies arrived. There was a good feeling among 106 Squadron. When we held squadron briefings I thought we looked in fine fettle. Men look good in uniform. That and the touches of discipline had dispelled our wild brigand look.

A site on a flat plateau, covered with natural gravel, about thirty miles north of the Gulf, close to King Solomon's mines, was chosen for our landing strip. We christened it Avraham. On 5 March 1949 an advanced spearhead of army and air force personnel set off overland for Avraham. They sent a signal back to Headquarters that it was all clear. The two brigades could start their two-pronged advance and the airlift could start.

Late that same afternoon I led the first flight of two C46s on the one-hour flight from Ekron to Avraham. We were loaded with thirty fully equipped troops, two Negev desert army scouts to help find Avraham, arms and equipment, provisions and a huge galvanised iron tank full of fresh water. We had recently introduced proper weight and balance procedures when loading the C46s, but I suspected more stuff had been loaded when my back was turned. Slick Goodlin, who had joined 106 Squadron from 101 Squadron, was co-pilot. Our suspicions were confirmed half-way down the runway. Only after we had rammed on full emergency power and dropped a touch of flap did the C46 lurch unwillingly into the air. We had to maintain that power to climb to our cruising height of 5000 feet and then had to maintain climbing power for cruising. We were indicating about 130 mph, normal was 175 mph. We were grossly overloaded. The other C46 floundered at our wing tip, the crew waving us on furiously. We had to maintain radio silence. Three Spitfires from 101 Squadron climbed up to escort us to Avraham. They had to circle to stay with us. I had time to admire once again that beautiful aeroplane as they banked in silhouette against the sky. Our old comrades, Syd, Ezer and Jack, grinned and urged us on from their cockpits. We responded with Gallic shrugs and upturned palms. I decided not to turn back. If we pressed on at this power we would burn a lot of fuel and lighten our load for landing. I hoped the strip at Avraham was smooth.

To find Avraham I had the best navigator in the squadron and the two army scouts but with a captain's sixth sense I soon realised they could not find it. The anxious way they scanned the terrain and then their maps told me they could not relate the two. I could not blame them as I looked down on that wilderness. It was an awesome desolation of gaunt mountains, deep, dry wadis and desert. There was not a tree, shrub, or sign of man. I thought of Moses and his children of Israel wandering in that hostile, pitiless wilderness for 40 years over 4,000 years before, with manna from heaven sometimes their only food.

Our maps were useless. The Spitfires waggled their wings and were gone, for they were getting short of fuel. I was humiliated at the thought of returning to Ekron. Final responsibility for the shambles would rest with me. It would soon be dusk and we would not be able to try again that day.

I had already turned back with the other C46 when Slick saw coloured flares shooting into the sky to the east. The advance party had heard us.

The landing strip was perfect. We landed easily and smoothly at high speed because of the load. I had some explaining to do to the captain of the other C46 after he landed.

The troops cheered. It was our fresh water, tea bags and fresh milk they wanted more than anything else. The first thing I did on returning to Ekron in darkness was to arrange for the immediate installation of a radio navigation beacon at Avraham and to suggest to headquarters that army scouts should stay on the ground.

We continued the airlift with only one further major incident. It involved, seemingly inevitably, our old friend RX133 and Pussy. He was taking off from Avraham on a return flight to Ekron when his port engine failed shortly after becoming airborne. Probably because he was overloaded with thirteen people and five tons of land-mines he could not control RX133 on one engine and crashed into the desert, fortunately on soft sand dunes. Shortly after impact the aircraft caught fire and the land-mines started to explode. Astonishingly nobody was seriously hurt, but RX133's days were over. Her remains still lie half-buried in the sands of the Negev desert, the only remaining relic of Avraham.

On 10 March, the two brigades reached Eilat on the Gulf of Aqaba within two hours of each other and hoisted an improvised Israeli flag to reclaim the sovereignty of the once thriving trading port the Israelis had lost to the Syrians 2,720 years before. Now it was a tiny ghost village with a few roofless adobe huts and an abandoned, once British, border-police station.

Operation Uvda was a total success. The whole of the 120-mile triangle from Beersheba to Eilat was occupied, doubling the size of Israel, without a shot being fired. Jordan gave up any claim to the area and it became an integral part of Israel. It was a good campaign to end the war with.

A few days later I borrowed an army Jeep in Eilat and drove alone a few miles into the desert. I parked and immobilised the Jeep and climbed high into the hills overlooking the gulf. I was bruised, hot and exhausted by the time I got to the top but it was worth it. I looked down on the cross-roads where four countries met: Egypt, Saudi Arabia, Jordan and Israel, bisected by the Gulf of Aqaba. The beautiful wilderness and mountains of the Sinai desert shimmered in the glare and heat. The Gulf stretched south without a ripple towards the Red Sea. Not a solitary boat marred its glassy surface. I sat there for a long time in the silence of centuries, unbroken even by bird-song, looking down on the landscape of the Old Testament. A landscape familiar to Abraham, to Moses and the Exodus, to King David, to King Solomon and the Queen of Sheba, to the Syrians, the Persians, the Romans, the Crusaders, the Turks, the Arab Revolt led by Lawrence and now, a fitting climax, the return of the nation that was there first, Israel.

Lebanon signed an armistice on 23 March 1949. Jordan signed on 3 April. Syria, always the most intransigent of Israel's foes, signed on 20 July, the official date of the end of the War of Independence. The small forces of Yemen and Saudi Arabia went home. They did not bother to sign an armistice, neither did Iraq.

The war was over. It was not, of course. It was merely adjourned *sine die*.

We had a wild party at Ekron. I doused Yael, Hayman Shamir and the American chargé d'affaires with a fire extinguisher from my vantage point up in the rafters. The chargé d'affaires returned fire. Yael's provocative nipples showed through her dress for the rest of the evening.

I took a few days' leave and spent it with Yael at a small *pension* on the edge of the Sea of Galilee. We could hear the water gently lapping at night. I had wanted to stay at a kibbutz in the Negev desert, but she would have none of it. I let her wear the trousers sometimes. She also insisted that I wear uniform. It meant there were no questions asked when we checked in as Lieutenant-Colonel and Mrs Cohen.

I waited until we were satiated with rest, love-making and the day and night beauty of Galilee. We were drifting in a dinghy where Jesus had allegedly walked when I told her I was going home. She looked puzzled.

'You mean Ekron?'

'No. My home. England.'

'Gideon,' she pleaded, 'surely your home is here now?'

In my heart I nodded. In my mind I shook my head despite the many options open to me in Israel. I had been arguing with myself and Yael since the war ended. I had been asked to stay on by friends in the air force, the defence ministry, El Al and the man in the street. Hayman had offered me a permanent career in the air force. El Al offered me the opportunity of acquiring Israeli flying licences and a captaincy. I could become a kibbutznik. Yael's parents were prepared to offer me a job on their citrus farms if I formally became a Jew and married their daughter. They had no sons.

I had sought counsel from Israeli friends. From Pussy, Syd, Hayman, Aharon, Ezer. From bartenders and café proprietors. I was a founding father of Israel. I had given more than a year of my life – it might have been all – to Israel's struggle for birth and survival. Israel was right for me. I was known and respected. In England I was nothing. When I walked the sun-drenched streets of Tel Aviv or Jerusalem, when I plucked an orange, when I looked down on that tiny country from the air, I felt an affinity, a kinship, a belonging. The small things were right too. Being abroad, driving on the right, waking up to the Middle East sun, sea and sky. The open-necked shirt and sandals, the healthy tan, the pioneering and the lack of stultifying tradition. The al fresco café evenings, the equality of underdogs who were no longer underdogs, the ready smiles, the Israeli *joie de vivre* and wry humour. And the beauty and love of Yael. No, I did not want to return to the cold, grey skies of northern Europe. I badly wanted to stay on. I had qualified as an Israeli as much as anybody and could become one merely by declaring an oath of allegiance and having a minor, though at my age uncomfortable, operation.

One did not have to be a Jew to be an Israeli but few were not. Israel is a secular nation but Judaism permeates its culture and mores far more than do the religions of other western nations, and to be an Israeli and not a Jew would be an uneasy role to play. I felt that if I did stay on I could only do so as a Jew. But Judaism was a religion which appealed to me even less than my own rejected Protestantism, though I find the Old Testament a better yarn, better told, than the New.

Above all other considerations I realised that if I stayed on it might be seen as a reward. It was reward enough that I had been there at the right time, that unique moment in history when at last a permanent shield was built by the Jewish people against anti-Semitism. It was reward enough that I had participated in perhaps the greatest humanitarian cause in all history. That I had helped establish a tiny nation on the globe which all Jews everywhere from now until the end of time will consider their ultimate sanctuary against persecution. As a Gentile my contribution in moral terms was significant. I did not want to sully that significance by accepting tribute. I wanted no anti-Semite to be able to say: 'This man helped Israel's cause in order to build a career.'

Much as I argued with myself, with Yael and friends, much as I wanted to stay, I had to go.

One of my last flights for Israel in that war was appropriate. It was a fly-past by the entire air force over Tel Aviv, Haifa and Jerusalem on the first anniversary of the State of Israel, 15 May 1949. To the uninitiated on the ground it was probably impressive, but in the air we grinned as we looked at each other. It was the craziest air force in aviation history.

First was a formation of light, slow aircraft, Piper Cubs, Austers and a Rapide. Next came a formation of Harvards, a Bonanza, a Norsemen, a Lodestar. The third formation consisted of C46s, B17s, Dakotas and a Beaufighter. Finally, there was a large formation of Spitfires, Mustangs and a solitary Messerschmitt 109. They were a patched-up, battered-looking lot, but like old soldiers they all had stories to tell.

Flying them in the name of Israel were crews from America, Canada, England, France, Belgium, South Africa, Austria, Holland, Hungary, Sweden, India, Russia, Newfoundland, Norway, Poland, Czechoslovakia, and Israelis. I was in the middle, leading a flight of five C46s, all that was left of the ten that started their saga 18 months before. As we criss-crossed Israel showing the flag we were all profoundly moved. I doubt that there were many dry eyes on the ground as the citizens of one-year-old Israel looked up and saw their air force signing in the sky the end of Jewish persecution.

PART III

FERRY PILOT

Chapter 30

M Y SECOND POST-WAR rehabilitation was no easier than the first. I returned to England homeless and without a penny, trying not to look back on Yael and Spitfires and golden beaches. I was held at Heathrow airport when I landed and driven to Scotland Yard in a black Wolseley police car and interviewed by Special Branch. They were particularly interested in the events of 7 January when the RAF and IAF clashed and whether I had been involved. The interview became an interrogation until I demanded to be charged or released. I was released and did not hear another word.

I got a private pilot's licence and did occasional ferry-flights to Europe and America and the Far East but, without professional licences, I could not find a permanent flying job. Several dismal years passed during which I was, between ferry-flights, a floor-walker at Woolworths, a factory floor sweeper, a removal van driver, a horse and cart driver for a brewery, a life insurance sales-man, a textile representative in the Far East and a driving instructor. I also tried to write. I stared at the blank foolscap and it stared back. When I did manage to write something it was a mere bouquet of words with no content. I had a minor talent at shuffling words about but I had little to say. I felt like putting an advertisement in the *New Statesman*: Chap who can write but has nothing to say, wishes to meet someone with something to say who can't write. I had not realised that if one has nothing to say, one has nothing to write.

In 1953, I suddenly found myself a married man with a six-year-old stepson. Marriage, parenthood and a mortgage were mantles that fitted uneasily on my shoulders. I did not love Alice but I was more fond of her than any other person I had met before; a reason-able basis for a mature marriage. Peradventure she was Jewish. We lived in a civilised flat in St. John's Wood, a legacy from Alice's previous marriage. Grahame, my stepson, and I were very polite to each other.

I was now working as a sales executive for Powers Samas, manufacturers of punched-card accounting machines. I doubt there was ever a squarer peg in a rounder hole. It was my job to call on prestigious companies, examine their existing methods of accounting, stock-control, pay-roll, etc. and plan, sell and supervise the installation of new, highly complex accounting machines. More often than not it brought chaos. I wore the trappings of board-level selling. Savile Row pin-stripe suit, heavily striped Harvey and Hudson shirt, subdued knitted tie, Locke bowler, impeccably rolled umbrella and a Parker 51 pen. Trouble was I did not know a debit from a credit.

Suddenly half my allotted span had gone. I was thirty-five and my moods fluctuated between angst and ennui. I sometimes woke with a start in the middle of the night in dread of the future. I began to dislike shaving intensely for it forced me to look at myself. The razor found my face more complicated. Hairline on the retreat, but hair now sprouting furiously from nostrils, ears and eyebrows, three teeth missing at the back, new moles and warts on my body and a deafening smoker's cough. I tried several times to give up smoking 40–50 cigarettes a day but it was an unequal struggle against the tobacco barons. They had succeeded in making the whole scenario of smoking much too seductive. Then, one could slot a man by the cigarettes he smoked. The working class smoked Weights or Woodbines or rolled their own. The bourgeois smoked Players, Gold Flake or Senior Service. The swells smoked Churchman's No. 1, Balkan Sobranie or oval-shaped Passing Cloud. The epicene smoked de Rezske or Du Maurier through elongated holders. I smoked Craven A, a classless cigarette. I gave up giving up and comforted myself that as I was able to pass the Private Pilots' licence medical my heart, lungs and eyes seemed as good as new.

In mid-January 1955, I was sitting at my desk in High Holborn, trying to sort out the shambles of a system I had installed at the Canadian National Railways office in London. It was a bleak morning. Wind and rain thrashed the windows outside, condensation ran rivulets inside. Lights were on everywhere. I was brooding on the tortuous path and wrong turnings that had led me to where I was now, in a job I detested and at which I was hopeless, sans prospects, sans capital, sans flying, when the telephone rang. A faintly familiar voice asked whether I was Gordon Levett, alias Gideon Levavi. It was Leo Gardner, one of the pilots in Israel's ATC during 1948/49. I had not seen him since. He was speaking from New York in the middle of his night and asked whether I might be interested in helping him to ferry several Spitfires from Israel to Burma. Might I be interested ?! I resigned immediately, was given permission to leave my job without notice, and got gloriously drunk with my office colleagues in our local office pub. They looked at me with surprise and envy. I had been the office duffer and they had not known I could fly. Spitfires at that.

Leo arrived by El Al from New York the following day and stayed at our flat. He had changed little in six years. He was the sort of pilot who looked as though he had walked out of an Ernest Gann novel. Five years older than me, medium height and stocky – the Spitfire would be a tight fit – he was a good pilot with umpteen thousand hours to his credit, mostly civilian transport flying. There were not many corners of the globe he had not visited. His brown eyes were crinkled from peering at endless horizons. The lines of his face curved upwards reflecting his smiling, easy-going personality. He always wore a black leather zip jacket, with a pilot's pocket calculator protruding from the top pocket. We spent the evening talking about Spitfires – he had not flown one before – and reminiscing about 1948/49. Seven ex-ATC pilots had died in air crashes since then. He then filled in the background to the Spitfire operation.

Israel, now aged seven, was steadily building relations with the rest of the world, apart from Arab countries. To further this cause in the Third World, particularly in Africa and Asia, Israel was offering its formidable technological, scientific and agricultural skills in return for political, diplomatic and commercial relations. This form of civilised bribery was necessary to counter the formidable world-wide opposition of Arab and Muslim countries against any recognition of Israel's right to exist.

As part of this plan Israel, having recently re-equipped with jet fighters, had sold thirty ex-Israeli Air Force Spitfires to the Burmese. Burmese pilots and ground staff were being trained in Israel. Bedek, the Israeli aircraft manufacturing and overhauling company, had completely rebuilt the Spitfires. In effect, the Burmese were getting new, zero-hour aeroplanes. A far cry from 1948.

What had not changed were the Arab view that they were still at war with Israel, and the continuing Arab blockade of Israel, including the Suez Canal and the Red Sea. Additionally, the Arab League economic boycott campaign to stop neutral countries trading with Israel was having an effect, including landing rights. Most countries rejected the Arabs' demand. Many, including what was once Great Britain, did not. Consequently, delivering the Spitfires the 6,000 miles to Burma was a problem. Shipping them through the Mediterranean and around the Cape would have been a lengthy, expensive business and the Spitfires were needed urgently.

Israel decided to fly the aircraft, with Burmese markings, covertly to Cyprus, keeping their origins secret. From there a British ferry company, Field Air Services, would ferry them openly and legally, with suitable paper-work, across Arabia to Burma, using RAF bases at Habbaniya, Bahrein and Sharjah for refuelling. Six Spitfires were delivered successfully using this route before, inevitably, the Israeli origins of the aircraft leaked out and hit the headlines. The Arabs clamped down on this leak in their blockade and applied pressure. True to form the British government withdrew permission for the Spitfires to land and refuel at the RAF bases.

The Israelis decided to take over delivery of the remaining twenty-four Spitfires themselves, using a tortuous route via Turkey and Iran, avoiding Arab territory. Secrecy was still essential to avoid Arab League boycott pressure on Turkey, Iran, Pakistan and India to withdraw landing rights, and possible interception by Arab fighter aircraft.

Leo and I reported to the Israeli embassy, then in Manchester Square. The blue and white flag waved a welcome in the wintry scene. Hayman Shamir greeted us. It was like old times. Shamir was now a director of Bedek and had come from Israel to supervise the Burmese operation. After telling me that he had finally concluded that I was not a British spy he said that he had bumped into Yael the day before in Knightsbridge as she climbed out of her Rolls, wearing mink and pearls and looking gorgeous. She had married an English millionaire merchant banker and now lived in London. I always felt that would be her destiny. At least she had married a Jew. She asked after me.

Hayman later introduced us to two pilots, both English, who were to join us as ferry pilots. One was Sonny Banting, a 57-year-old veteran. The other was Jackie Moggridge, a woman. We were to ferry the Spitfires from Israel to Burma, four at a time in open formation, with Leo leading.

I tried hard not to be impressed that Jackie was a pilot and a good one, but Sonny was determined to treat her with his elaborate Edwardian courtesy, despite her complete emancipation as a woman in a man's world. Sonny's laboured gallantry – the 'let me, no let me, after you, no after you', even in the middle of the desert or at 15,000 feet – became tiresome at times. Jackie was married, my age, a good age for a woman, attractive rather than pretty, with a stunning, full-prowed figure. She had flown with the Air Transport Auxiliary during the Second World War and with the RAFVR after the war. She had successfully delivered two Spitfires from Cyprus to Burma with the previous set-up but she did not let this potential one-upmanship affect her appealing anxiety to please. She was a practising Catholic and invariably wore a crucifix necklace dangling down her impressive *décolletage,* a dichotomy which aroused my lust and guilt simultaneously. I wondered sometimes during the next few months whether her naivety and ingenuousness were not disingenuous. We were an unlikely-looking quartet to be flying Spitfires half-way round the world. It was a curious quirk of fortune that I should be involved in a secret operation linking Israel and Burma, two countries writ large in my life.

We flew to Israel in an El Al Constellation. There was another reunion in the cockpit. I had instructed the El Al captain on C46s in 106 squadron, in 1949. He let me fly the aeroplane. Jackie asked me whether I had been to Israel before and I told her a bit of my background. She flushed, for she assumed from my story that I was Jewish and she had previously made some mildly anti-Semitic remarks. Nothing serious, there was no malice in her, but the usual gratuitous remarks that Jewish people have to put up with. An air hostess served a kosher meal with smiling charm.

'Nice girl,' remarked Jackie.

'Yes, she's Jewish,' I said. 'A Jewish girl serving Jewish food in a Jewish plane flown by Jews to Jewland. You're in a tough spot.' She nodded and smiled an apology.

Chapter 31

AFTER A QUICK check in a Harvard with an Israeli Air Force instructor I climbed into a Spitfire for the first time in six years. It was like the prick of a needle to an addict. My angst and ennui had vanished. The Spitfires looked magnificent. They had been rebuilt with loving care by Bedek down to the last coat of camouflage paint on the top surfaces, the sky-blue under-belly and the exotic looking triangular Burmese Air Force markings. They were sold to the Burmese for £8,000 each, including spares, armaments and radios. I could have bought half a dozen. Today they would be worth, in that condition, £500,000 each.

To avoid Arab territory our route was a tortuous six thousand miles via Lydda, Diyabakir, Kermanshah, Abadan, Sharjah, Karachi, Jodhpur, Kanpur, Calcutta, Rangoon. It was back to seat-of-the-pants flying, wearing leather helmet and goggles, primitive oxygen masks and my old white silk Biggles scarf. We would be flying off the beaten track beyond the interminable yak-yak-yak of flying controllers, over deserts and mountains, landing at remote aerodromes, without navigational aids and relying solely on dead reckoning and map-reading. I doubt there was a pilot alive who would not have changed places with us given the chance. We flew back in more mundane fashion by BOAC. I did six ferry flights. It took seven months.

All the ferry flights had their moments but it was the fourth which I remember most.

It was first light when the four of us took off from Lydda, formed up into open formation and climbed westerly across the coast of Israel for the turning point forty miles out over the Mediterranean that would keep us well clear of Lebanon and Syria – still at war with Israel.

As the coast disappeared and we were alone with the sea and the sky I felt the unease that attacks all pilots when flying single-engine aircraft over long sea crossings. I checked and rechecked the instruments, refusing to accept their assurance of all's well. The engine lost its smooth, untroubled beat and the Spitfire became a host of individual parts. Cables that could fray, bearings that could parch and seize, filters that could clog. A million nuts and bolts that could work loose and bring catastrophe. Perhaps even the theory of flight would collapse, leaving me hurtling into the sea 12,000 feet below. Simultaneously with the appearance of the Turkish coast the engine cleared and throbbed sweetly.

An hour later we landed at the Turkish Air Force base at Diyarbakir. Owing to a magneto problem on Leo's Spit we stayed overnight as guests of the air force. Over dinner in the officers' mess the commanding officer, resplendent with rows of medal ribbons, regaled us with his flying exploits against Lawrence and the Arab revolt during the First World War.

The following morning we took off for Kermanshah and climbed to 20,000 feet as we headed easterly over the gaunt, barren mountains where Noah's Ark anchored. Within an hour the weather challenged us. Clouds merged and sloped down towards the horizon ahead and the first spots of rain appeared on our windscreens. As discussed in our pre-flight planning we manoeuvred into vee formation with Sonny tucked in underneath. We had just about settled down when we entered cloud. I was a bit concerned about Jackie for I doubted that she had much experience of flying tight formation in cloud but she held her station well. Fortunately it was a warm front and there was little turbulence. Unspoken in all our minds as we pressed on at 20,000 feet, gulping oxygen from our uncomfortable masks, was what would the weather be like at Kermanshah, surrounded by mountains. They had no blind-landing facilities.

About thirty minutes before our estimated time of arrival Leo called Kermanshah over the R/T to get the weather and a QDM course to steer to the aerodrome. There was no reply. He tried again and again and again until our ETA elapsed. There was no reply but the crackle of airwaves. We circled helplessly in cloud, tension building up. I was glad I was not leading. Leo ordered Jackie to try, hoping the unusual sound of a woman's voice might wake them up down there. She repeated the call several times but there was nothing but silence, damnable, mocking silence. Leo tried switching frequences. Silence. The situation was serious. It would be bad enough with one aeroplane, but with four it was almost impossible to resolve without baling out.

'It's useless,' said Leo, over the R/T. 'They must be on a different frequency. What do we do now? We can't turn back, we haven't enough gas.'

'Turn south towards the plains. We can let down there,' suggested Sonny.

'But that's Iraq,' protested Leo.

'Who the hell cares.' I said. 'This is an emergency.'

We turned south and flew deeply into the forbidden territory of another country at war with Israel, away from the mountains, before beginning our descent. We were down to 2,000 feet before we broke out of cloud and found ourselves over featureless desert.

'Anybody know where we are ?' asked Leo optimistically after we had circled a few times.

'Ha.'

'Ha.'

'Ha.'

'You're a great help,' answered Leo acidly. 'Get your maps out. Watch out for Iraqi fighters.' We were not armed, of course.

We edged out into open formation and got out our maps. Our conflicting and irascible observations confirmed that we were completely lost.

'OK,' decided Leo. 'We'll fly due east until we hit the railway or run out of gas.' The Iranian State railway ran due north and south. It was a good move, the railway would pinpoint our position, *if* we were west of it.

We flew steadily eastwards. The heat was so intense at that low height we had our cockpit hoods open. The desert slipped by. The parched rivers and wadis were impossible to identify. Our fuel gauges told us our season ticket for flight was fast expiring. Bad airmanship had got us into this mess. We should have turned back when the weather challenged us to a duel.

When we were down to our last few gallons of fuel we discussed baling out or crash-landing. None of us fancied baling out and we all voted to belly-land on the flat desert.

'We've had it,' announced Leo a few minutes later. 'We'll have to crash-land. One at a time. I'll go in first. After I've stopped, land as close to me as you can. Land with your straps tight and your hood open. Keep your undercarriage *UP*. No heroics. You'll go over on your back if you land with your wheels down.'

We were watching Leo descend in a wide arc towards his shadow

23   The flag of Israel raised at Eilat, 10 March 1949

24   Gordon Levett standing on the clipped wing of his Spitfire at Sharjah, February 1955, during the Spitfire ferry operation from Israel to Burma

25   Jackie Moggridge astride a donkey at Sharjah, March 1955, during one of the Spitfire ferry flights from Israel to Burma. Gordon Levett second from left

on the desert when we all saw a runway. The R/T burst into a shriek as we all tried to transmit simultaneously.

'OK, I've seen it,' Leo shouted. I saw his undercarriage coming down as he turned steeply towards the deserted runway. There was a spurt of sand as his wheels touched down.

We followed him in and parked neatly along the runway. All our fuel gauges showed empty. The concrete runway cut starkly through the silent desert. There were no buildings and no sign of anybody. We were all tired, parched and hungry. We reeked of oil, petrol, glycol and sweat. We had no idea where we were. It could be hostile Iraq, with our incarceration and confiscation of the four Spitfires, or Iran.

A neglected tarmac road bordered the runway. We sat on our parachutes by the roadside. After twenty minutes of desert silence a solitary lorry sped by, ignoring us.

'Did you notice the number plate?' asked Leo.

'It was Arabic.'

'That's Iraq.'

'No. It was Persian.'

'That's Iran.'

While we were arguing about our fate a small truck approached and stopped. The driver stepped out onto the sand.

'Is this Iraq?' asked Leo.

'No, Iran,' he replied, perplexed. 'I am the manager of the petrol storage plant at Andemeshk,' he said, pointing to the horizon. He had seen us circling. We checked the maps. Andemeshk was 150 miles from Kermanshah! An aeroplane had not landed there for years. Jackie crossed herself.

Our good fortune continued for he had 100 octane petrol. With the aid of chamois leather filters we refuelled the Spits from five-gallon cans. As we finished the setting sun flirted with the horizon and sent blood-red horizontal beams across the desert. It was too late to take off for Abadan. The manager invited us to stay the night at the oil company's guest house. It was air-conditioned, had a good Indian cook, running hot water and canned beer. Aware of what might have been, we revelled in luxury and a good night's sleep before leaving for Abadan early the following morning.

A cable from Tel Aviv awaiting us at Abadan ordered us not to land at Sharjah to refuel but to use Bandar Abbas, wherever that was, instead. The Arab League boycott sleuths had discovered that we had been using Sharjah to refuel and had put pressure on the local sheikh who promptly cancelled our permission to land there. He had been unaware that the Spitfires originated in Israel.

We checked the facilities charts and discovered Bandar Abbas was on the southern Iranian coast at the eastern end of the Persian Gulf. There was no information on the chart and nobody knew much about it except that it was an abandoned desert strip with no staff, communications, or radio facilities and had not been used since the Second World War. We were assured that petrol and oil had been delivered there especially for us.

As Leo felt poorly with a tummy bug, I led the leg to Bandar Abbas. Navigating was easy for we followed the Iranian coastline. After two and a half hours we tucked into echelon starboard formation and let down into the heat haze. As previously arranged we roared low over the small, sleepy port of Bandar Abbas and circled it several times to signal our arrival to the local Iranian Oil Company manager. The others followed like dutiful ducklings as I then traced the dusty track that straggled fifteen miles across wadis and desert and led to the aerodrome. There were some anxious moments before I found it. It was distinguished only by a torn windsock hanging limply in the still air. There was not a soul or a building in sight. To the north mountains rose steeply to six thousand feet, to the south the Straits of Hormuz shone like polished jade.

Detaching myself from the others I flew low over the strip and selected the best landing path. The surface looked flat and firm and there was ample room for landing and taking off.

'It looks OK,' I said to the others over the R/T. 'I'll land first, towards the south. The rest of you follow me in.'

I used the precautionary landing technique, full flap, high angle of attack, nose up, tail down, dragging it in with lots of throttle, hood open, head switching from side to side to see where I was going. Slamming the throttle shut I touched down with a deliberate thump and appeared to be doing a normal landing run when the earth tilted, the nose banged into the ground and I banged my face on the gun-sight. I was stunned for a few seconds before I realised what had happened. The landing wheels had sunk into a quagmire of mud and the Spit had tipped forward, smashing the four blades of the wooden propeller and burying its nose in the mud with the tail pointing at the sky. I was lucky that the Spitfire did not go over onto its back. I reckoned afterwards that I was doing about 20 knots when she went over.

I grabbed the microphone quickly to tell the others not to land but it was too late, another Spitfire was touching down. I shouted over the R/T to the other two circling above not to land and to stand-by. I watched the Spitfire's landing run. I thought it was going to make it but suddenly the left leg sank into the mud. The Spit ground-looped and did half a cartwheel before dropping back with its left wing resting on the mud. Incredibly, the propeller blades were not damaged. It was Jackie.

Angrily I squelched over to her. She was all right. 'What the bloody hell did you land for?' I shouted at her. 'Couldn't you see there was something wrong?'

'We thought you were hurt and needed help,' she replied, a bit peeved. 'We didn't know the field was like this. We tried to raise you on R/T.' I realised I had been stunned longer than I thought and apologised.

We looked around while deciding what to do next. Our two Spitfires were like birds with broken wings, helpless and undignified. Deep ruts showed our landing paths. Barren rock and desert undulated to the distant mountains. The heat enveloped us, bathing us in sweat. Jackie's nose was shiny, mine was bloody. She dabbed at both with tissues. There was total silence broken only by the occasional creak as the Merlin engines cooled down and Leo and Sonny circling overhead. We were totally alone and cut-off. The not everyday arrival of two Spitfires had caused not the slightest stir. Not even a bird twittered excitedly. It was uncanny and I felt we should talk in whispers. It was as though we had gone through a time and space warp and landed in another world, another century.

I got the maps out, made up my mind and spoke over the R/T to Leo and Sonny circling overhead. They had about forty minutes fuel left.

'You can't land here, it's a quagmire. My prop's smashed. I'll need a complete new prop unit. I don't think the engine is damaged; the mud took most of the shock. I think Jackie's Spit is OK. You'll have to land at Sharjah.'

'What about the sheikh?' asked Leo.

'Bugger the sheikh,' I replied, 'this is an emergency. Sharjah is about 110 miles, course one-nine-five, ETA about twenty-five minutes. I'll get in touch with you there when we get to Bandar Abbas.'

'Snafu,' said Sonny.

'Negative,' I said. 'Fubar.'

'Could have been worse,' said Leo.

'How?'

'You could have got stuck with Sonny down there,' he said, as with a waggle of wings they turned south for Sharjah.

After we had unpacked our hand luggage from the gun panels there was nothing to do but wait, confident that the uproar we had created in the sky over Bandar Abbas had alerted Iranian Oil. Four Spitfires flying low at full throttle in tight formation produces an effective calling card.

I was uneasy at the sort of reception we might get. The Israeli origin of the Spitfires had become the world's worst-kept secret. Iranians are not, of course, Arabs, but they are predominantly Muslim and the hatred of Israel is religious inspired, rather than racial or nationalist. Jackie had not packed a skirt either. I got out the two Very flare pistols just in case. They are not very lethal but they are spectacular.

After a long wait a lorry appeared on the primitive road from Bandar Abbas. The driver did not speak English and gestured us to sit next to him. I was loath to leave the Spits unguarded but I was even more loath to leave Jackie behind alone.

Bandar Abbas was a shambles. Torrential storms and floods had swept away most of the straw and mud-brick dwellings. Only the more substantial buildings still stood. Black Bedouin tents and goats littered the higher ground. There were yapping pariah dogs and skinny, furtive cats everywhere. Native women passed by in strict purdah, balancing clay water jugs on their heads. Their heavily kohled eyes peered at us through the dramatic black leather masks that concealed their faces.

We stopped at the house of Mr Dustmalchi, the local manager of the Iranian Oil Company. It doubled as his office and home. He was friendly.

Over too-sweet tea I explained our problems. It took a long time. He shook his head and explained that the storms and floods had destroyed all communications with the outside world. All lines were down and there were no radio communications. Bandar Abbas was completely cut-off and likely to remain so for several days. There was no way of communicating with Sharjah or Israel. Neither were there any aircraft mechanics, or spares available, or a crane to help lower my Spitfire. He did have petrol, oil and a works engineer, Imran, who might be able to help and who was on his way.

'Can you put us up?'

'Yes, of course. I have a spare bedroom for guests.' Jackie blushed at the singular but kept quiet. It was Hobson's choice. Dustmalchi had assumed we were married

While we were waiting for Imran, Dustmalchi arranged for the army to guard our Spitfires and his wife showed us our room. It was basic but clean, with a basin, fly-screens and mosquito nets. There were two beds.

Imran, the engineer, was tall, swarthy and magnificently hook-nosed. His classic features showed generations of wind, sand and stars. I could imagine him astride a camel, sword in hand. More to the point, he was an able engineer. Jackie agreed to stay behind to unpack and get things organised while we drove out to the strip in his open truck, followed by a lorry loaded with his Indian labourers.

Imran inspected the two Spitfires. He knew nothing about aeroplanes but he had a lot of common sense. With the aid of his labourers we pushed Jackie's aircraft backwards to drier ground. The sun was drying out the ground fast. After explaining to Imran that it was essential that the tail of my Spitfire should not come down with a thump, I watched mystified as he got his men to build a pyramid of mud and sand under the Spitfire right up to the tail. He then got me to slither up the fuselage and tie several ropes around the tail and stay up there to add my spindly weight. The men then slowly shovelled the pyramid away, at the same time pulling down on the ropes, gently lowering the Spitfire to the normal position. It was ingenious.

I anxiously examined the two aircraft. They were both filthy with mud. As far as I could judge by moving the broken stumps of the propeller my engine was all right. There were a few scrapes under the nose cowling but the carburettor and radiator air intakes were undamaged and the oil and glycol levels were normal. Jackie's aircraft was undamaged save for a scrape under the port wing-tip. Imran arranged for his men to give the Spits a wash and polish.

Early the following morning Jackie and I were awakened by the unmistakable mellifluous roar of a Merlin engine low overhead. We jumped out of our beds, ran to the verandah and saw Leo circling Bandar Abbas like an angry wasp, very low, waggling his wings and blipping his engine. I loaded a Very pistol with a red flare and fired it vertically into the sky. Jackie waved a sheet violently. Leo saw us and, circling tightly with his cockpit hood open, pointed vigorously and repeatedly to the north. It was obvious he wanted us to get out to the aerodrome fast to talk to him over the Spitfire's radio. The ant-like file of masked women water-carriers stopped and watched, wondering no doubt what we were going to do next. Jackie suddenly realised that she was revealed to Muslim Bandar Abbas in a fetching, black, diaphanous nightdress. She fled from the lusty grins of the male population.

We borrowed Dustmalchi's Jeep and drove furiously to the aerodrome, with Leo shepherding us from the sky. After switching on the R/T I reported our situation, particularly the lack of communications, which Leo had guessed anyway. I asked about their reception at Sharjah. 'All right, so far,' he said. 'The sheik is in Mecca. A few dollars here and there helped.'

Leo had communicated with Israel, via Tehran. Bedek were flying a new propeller and a mechanic from Israel to Tehran by a Sabena aircraft – fortuitously chartered to fly Jewish immigrants from Iran to Israel – and hoped to charter a Rapide aircraft in Tehran to fly to Bandar Abbas. The Rapide would buzz Bandar Abbas on arrival. Leo or Sunny would fly over the aerodrome on alternate mornings at ten o'clock to give us any news. He asked whether we needed woman's things or anything else. Jackie shook her head. I asked Leo to drop me some dollars and decent cigarettes.

'What about your batteries?' asked Leo anxiously. We needed them for the radio as well as starting the engines.

'Under control. I've arranged for Iranian Oil to recharge them regularly.'

'That's it then,' said Leo. 'Shalom.' He made a low pass and headed back to Sharjah.

Jackie and I lazed the days away suspended in time in a cocoon of highly charged unreality. We went out alone to the Spitfires or swam and sunbathed in the Gulf in the brilliant mornings, siesta-ed with the rest of Bandar Abbas during the 100-degree heat of the afternoon and went for long walks along the beautiful, lonely shores of the Gulf after dinner. We were both aware we were in an enforced, thus innocent, romantically intimate situation. We often held hands as we left our footprints in the sand or sat on the tiny rusting jetty looking out over the Gulf. We were the only Westerners in Bandar Abbas. The past seemed divorced, the present a gossamer thing protected by isolation, the future distant. We were enjoying the tease of our relationship: the will we, won't we. Chemistry and vibes and the romantic imperatives of our exotic exile were at work. We were both old enough to weigh things wisely, to resist the impetuousness of youth, but we were still young enough to want to respond fully to an undoubted mutual attraction. But we did not. It helped that we had little in common apart from flying. Her anodyne was God, mine was beer. Her (dis)ingenuousness maddened me. My iconoclasm upset her. I also suspected that she would not have been able to handle an affair, no matter how ephemeral. By unspoken mutual consent we left it at holding hands and goodnight kisses. She told me months later that before Bandar Abbas she would not have thought gallantry my strong point.

On the sixth day Leo flew over from Sharjah ordering Jackie not to wait for me but to join the others at Sharjah as soon as possible and carry on to Burma. The Spitfires were needed urgently. There was no further news about my propeller.

'That's stupid,' she protested. 'Leo and Sonny can carry on to Burma and you and I continue together when your new prop has been fitted. If you go down on your own nobody will know where you are.'

'True enough,' I said, 'but orders is orders.'

The following day we drove out to the field, accompanied by Imran and his labourers to prepare the strip for Jackie's departure. After we had chosen the take-off path, the labourers scrutinised every inch filling in soft patches with dry shingle and sand. Then we drove the truck monotonously up and down rolling the surface into some semblance of firmness. We then checked the oil and glycol levels of Jackie's Spitfire, added some reserve petrol for the short flight to Sharjah, polished the windscreen and fitted the newly-charged battery.

233

We tied the Spitfires down for the night and walked slowly along the strip on a final inspection. It was a serious moment. I stamped my heel into the surface. We stared at the hole my heel made. I turned to Jackie. 'Try taxi-ing tomorrow. If you can taxi you can take off. Four o'clock. That will give the sun more time to dry it out.'

Turning to Imran, I said 'We will need about fifteen labourers, a fast truck, ropes, axes, fire extinguishers if you have any, buckets of sand and shovels.'

'Right,' said Imran. He was a man of few words.

'Will you call the men? I'd like to explain tomorrow's programme and what we want them to do.' The men gathered in a circle around us.

'The lady pilot is taking off tomorrow,' I began, nodding to Imran to translate. 'The ground is not entirely satisfactory, but it will be many days before it is completely dry or it might rain again and she must leave urgently.'

Imran continued translating. The labourers whispered among themselves, shaking their heads.

'There is,' I continued, 'a very slight possibility that the aeroplane may suddenly stick in the mud and somersault onto its back with the lady pilot trapped inside. If it does it might catch fire.'

After Imran had translated this, with suitably graphic gestures, the men shook their heads violently. We had become good friends.

'If this does happen we will not have much time. Before she starts her take-off we will all get into the truck with axes, ropes, fire extinguishers and buckets of sand. When the lady pilot starts her take-off we will follow her in the truck. If she crashes we must get this side panel open,' I pointed to the emergency release panel, 'with axes if necessary and pull her out. If there is a fire we will use fire extinguishers and sand buckets. If we can't get her out that way then we must lift one wing and release her from underneath. We will need about fifteen men to lift the wing.' I waited until Imran had caught up. 'Just one more thing. If there is a fire, it is possible that the petrol tanks may explode.' There was a mutter of rebellion as the men looked accusingly at me. 'It is the lady pilot's wish that she leaves tomorrow,' I added hurriedly, passing cigarettes around.

'Please detail two men for the axes, two for the fire extinguishers and six for the buckets,' I said to Imran. 'The remainder are to keep clear until I give further instructions. They must not get in each other's way. Everything clear?'

'Perfectly,' said Imran. 'They offer their prayers.'

'I prefer their sinews,' I replied.

'I think I should be the one to decide that,' Jackie interjected. 'Tell them I return their prayers.'

That evening Jackie said goodbye to Dustamalchi and his wife, the chief of police, the army officers, the doctor and his wife, Imran and several other local dignitaries. We all sat on the verandah drinking coffee. It was a sad gathering. Most of them were politically exiled in Bandar Abbas as a punishment by the Shah and envied Jackie's departure. After they left and the Dustmalchis had gone to bed, Jackie and I got up and leaned against the balustrade that overlooked Bandar Abbas. We gazed at the feeble lights and the candlelit black Bedouin tents and listened to the painful ee-orr of mules. A peasant asleep astride his donkey passed by in the moonlight beneath us. He must be heading home, I thought. The unshaded verandah light swung gently in the evening breeze like an incense burner, throwing light and shadow across our faces. The sea glittered with silver, the close sky with stars and the dark mountains to the north isolated Bandar Abbas from the rest of the world. We put our arms around each other and kissed, for it was a rare moment.

The following afternoon we drove out to the airfield followed by a convoy of cars and lorries. Bandar Abbas was taking the day off to see a woman fly a Spitfire.

After checking the surface of the strip with Imran and Jackie, I squeezed Jackie's bags into the gun panels while she gave the Spitfire a final pre-flight check. Everything was ready. Jackie strapped on her parachute and helmet and climbed into the cockpit. I motioned the watching crowd back until they stood in a long, thin line like spectators at a football match. The temperature was in the high nineties.

'All clear?' she shouted.

'All clear,' I answered.

'Contact!' As though nothing had happened the Merlin burst into life. Jackie signalled to me to pull the stones away from the wheels and slowly opened the throttle. I urged her on as she gave more throttle until she lurched uncertainly through the clinging

sand. We followed her in the truck. She taxied slowly to the end of
the field, turned, lined up with the take-off path and switched off to
cool the engine down.

I jumped up on the wing, 'How was it?'

'Not bad. She needed about 1,300 revs to keep moving.'

'As much as that. Do you want to go? It's up to you.'

'Yes. It'll take a week for the surface to get bone dry.'

'How are the temperatures?'

'A bit high. Radiator's 105. I'll wait a few minutes.'

'Do you want to jump out?'

'It isn't worth it. I'll sit here.' She eased off her helmet and
loosened the straps. I shielded her head from the sun with a map.
Imran's truck with the labourers on board was parked nearby,
facing the same way.

'Don't forget, keep your brakes on as long as you can and the
stick back as you open the throttle. As soon as you feel the tail
lighten slam on full emergency throttle, through the gate, and
watch out for the swing. She'll swing like hell to the left at plus
eighteen boost. Use full right rudder bias. If you go over, cut the
switches and petrol. We'll be right with you.'

'Stop fussing,' she said. 'I'll be all right.'

'Keep your carburettor air-filter open; that will give you another
inch of boost,' I said.

'What about the sand?'

'Bugger the sand.' We waited another ten to fifteen minutes.

'She's cool enough now,' she said. I tightened her straps again,
trussing her up like a chicken.

'Hey, that's too tight,' she protested.

'It won't be if you go over on your back.'

She put her helmet on but left the oxygen/radio mask off. She
looked small and vulnerable.

'All set?' I asked.

'All set,' she replied. We looked at each other. We were both sad
that the desert interlude was over. I leaned down into the cockpit
and kissed her with difficulty. Twice. It was funny kissing someone
in a Spitfire. I jumped down and stood on the running board of the
truck. Imran was in the driver's seat.

The Merlin started again easily. With a final wave Jackie opened
the throttle and held the brakes on. More throttle. More. The air-

craft shook with rage at being held back. As the tail lightened, Jackie released the brakes and with a lurch the Spitfire charged into exultant action. There was a snarling roar as Jackie then slammed the throttle fully open to emergency power normally used only in combat. She kicked full right rudder to stop the swing. We were racing with her in the truck . . . 40 . . . 50 . . . 60 . . . 70 mph. The Spitfire stuttered in its headlong dash for airspeed as the wheels scored into damp patches. The long nose was swaying and bobbing, the crowd were waving. I prayed she would not abandon the take-off and cut the throttle. If she did she would go over on her back. It was only the brutal maximum power of the 1660 hp Merlin engine with the stick held back that was keeping the Spit the right way up . . . 75 . . . 80 . . . she was beginning to leave us behind . . . 85 . . . 90 mph. At last she soared violently and steeply into the air. It was a good piece of flying. Imran looked at me as he stopped the truck. 'I think she just made it, yes?' he said. I blew out my cheeks and nodded. He was right.

Chapter 32

WITH JACKIE GONE and no more flying visits from Leo or Sonny – they would by now be on their way to Rangoon – I felt even more isolated and remote. I grew a wispy beard and might have been Robinson Crusoe. The temperature climbed higher each day and I looked as dark-skinned as my hosts. I had become such a familiar figure in this tiny port of exile that nobody bothered any more to give me a second look except young women in purdah who giggled behind their masks whenever they saw me. I never did find out what was so funny.

Without Jackie I soon got bored. Unusually I had not packed any books and there was not an English book to be found in Bandar Abbas. I was also getting surfeited with black olives, goats' milk, goats' cheese, humus, unleavened bread, undrinkable canned beer and unsmokable cigarettes. And I was anxious not to miss the next Spitfire ferry flight from Israel to Burma.

I went out to the aerodrome every day. Once when I went with an army major we discovered that the guard had fallen asleep in the shade under a wing and had accidentally fired his rifle, damaging the port wing-tip and destroying the navigation light. The poor devil was terrified. He stood rigidly to attention while the major went berserk, slapping his face with full force left, right, left, right, until I stepped between them. I hurriedly made light of the damage for I was convinced that the major was about to shoot him.

Two weeks after Jackie's departure I got a garbled message through army communications that the propeller and the Bedek mechanic were on the way from Tehran by taxi, with the propeller strapped to the roof. I looked at my maps and did not believe it. It was a thousand-mile drive, from one end of Iran to the other, by primitive roads, across deserts and mountains towering 10,000 feet high.

A week later I was dozing under the Spitfire's wing when the guard prodded me awake and pointed to the foothills towards the north. There was a dust-trail heading our way. We watched as it curled and hairpinned down the hills towards us. It was a lorry or an armoured car perhaps. It got closer. It was the taxi. A huge, battered Chevrolet with my propeller strapped flat to the roof, with the four blades sticking out each side. With a flourish and a final cloud of dust it braked to a halt close to the Spitfire. Dov, a Bedek senior line-chief and an old friend, got out wearily. He held out his hand. 'Doctor Livingstone, I presume,' he said.

It was high noon, with the Spitfire almost unbearably hot to touch, but we started fitting the new propeller immediately. There were no snags and we were done by late afternoon. Dov then got out his biggest hammer and bashed the port wing-tip into some sort of aerodynamic shape and taped up the in and out bullet-holes. The navigation light did not matter for I did not plan to fly at night. We then gave the Spit a thorough servicing, including checking the oil filters, before and after running up, for traces of metal caused by the shock of the propeller hitting the ground, but the filters were clean.

My last night in Bandar Abbas was pleasant, for Dov was a seasoned traveller and had packed several bottles of good whisky and cartons of cigarettes. I threw another farewell party on Dustmalchi's verandah for our Iranian friends and gave Imran and Dustmalchi a bottle of VAT 69 and a carton of Pall Malls each. Rare gifts. Dov had Jackie's bed for the night.

The whole population turned out once again for the dawn take-off. The strip by now was bone dry. It felt good to be strapping on a parachute and helmet again. It had been almost a month since I had crash-landed. I had decided not to risk landing at Sharjah and being impounded, but to fly the 750 miles direct to Karachi. I waved goodbye to the spectators and to Dov who was facing another thousand-mile drive back to Tehran. I had offered to fly him, sitting on my lap, to Karachi where he could catch BOAC, but he firmly declined.

After taking off I dived low and waggled the wings in salute and thanks and set course for Pakistan. The propeller was rough but tolerable. Engine temperatures and pressures were normal. As usual I reached up and behind the back of my head to pull the cockpit hood closed but I pulled the wrong knob. With a whoosh the hood was gone. I had jettisoned it by mistake. It was about the daftest thing I ever did flying. It was draughty at over 200 mph and map-reading was like trying to read a newspaper in a gale but I was not too bothered. I could probably scrounge a hood from the Pakistan or Indian Air Force.

239

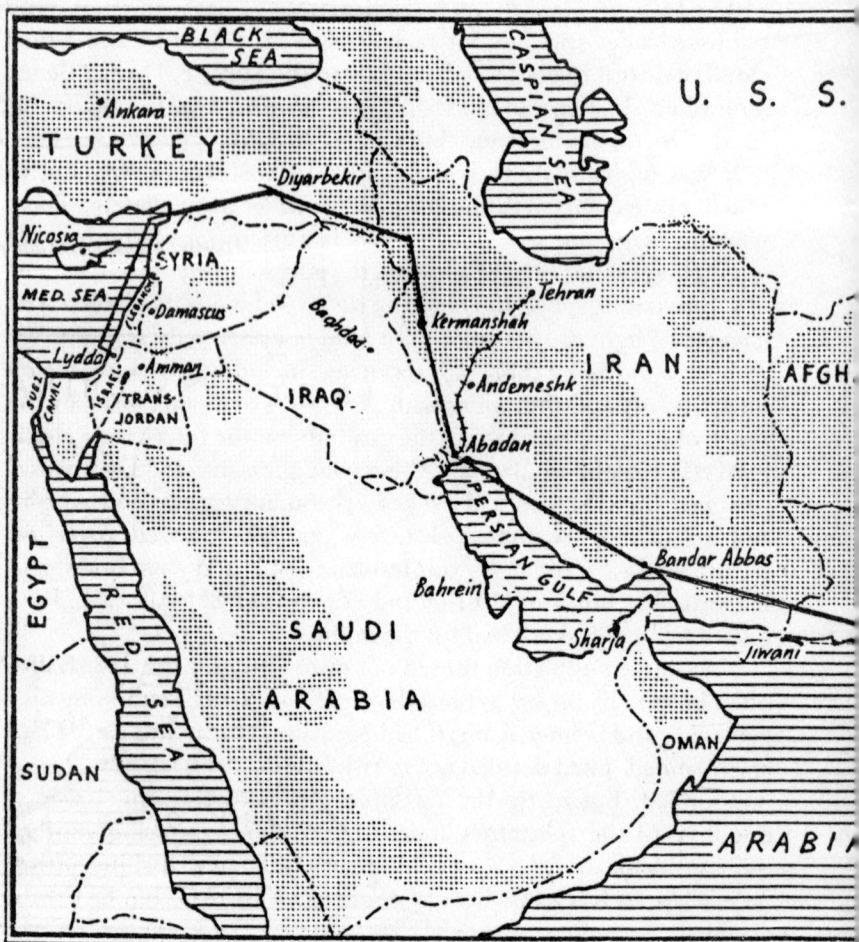

26   Spitfire ferry route from Israel to Burma, 1955

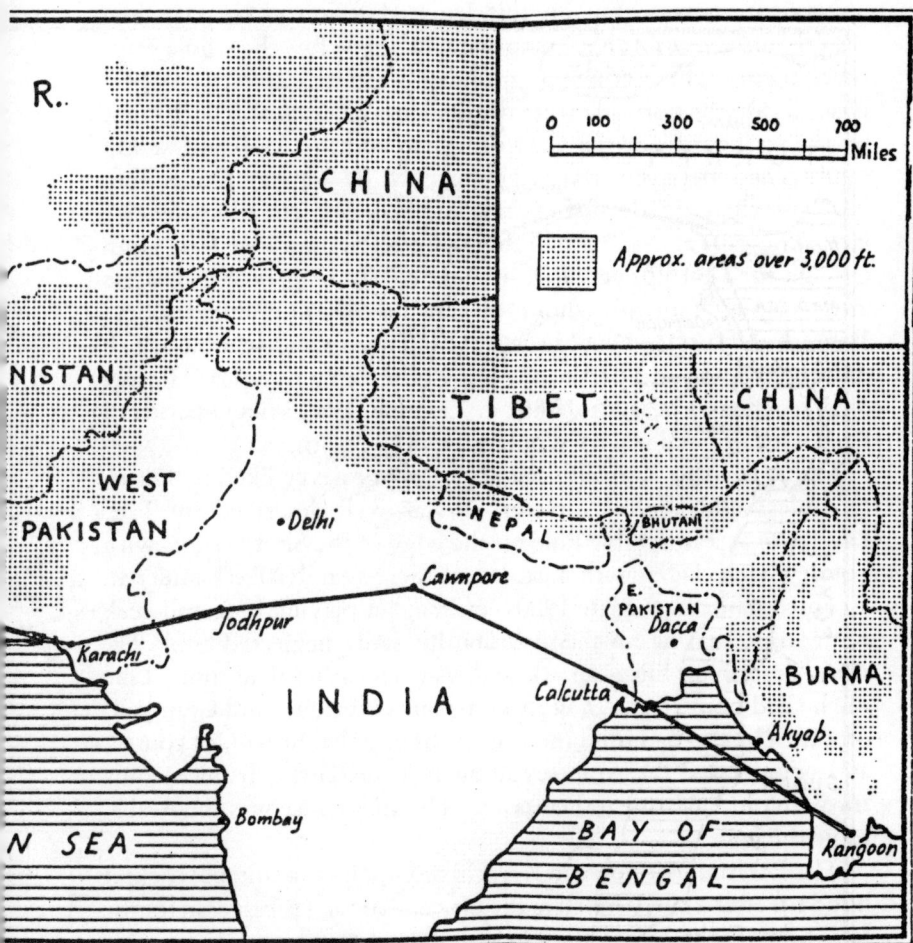

Navigation was easy on this leg as I followed the coastline easterly for about three hours to Karachi. I flew low the whole way, revelling in flight after being grounded for so long. Every prospect pleased. On the port side were the khaki mountains of Baluchistan, on the starboard side the Gulf of Oman and the Arabian Sea and sandwiched between were the pure white sands of unending beaches where gentle surf embroidered the shoreline like delicate lace. The canvas was memorable from a few hundred feet. High enough for a bird's eye view, low enough to be part of it. League after league, hour after hour of sun-blessed, unpolluted glory. Beneath the surface I could see reefs and shoals and schools of fish darting away in panic from the huge bird flying overhead. Rarely did I see man or beast or village in 750 miles and I knew that after I had swiftly passed silence would gratefully return.

I have been to Karachi several times and never liked it. Dirty, charmless and slightly sinister, it was well described by T.E. Lawrence as a miserable hole on the edge of the Sind Desert, with hot dry winds laden with dust. It was there as an RAF erk under an assumed name in the late 1920s, once again playing hide-and-seek with fame, that he finished writing his sadly neglected book *The Mint*, describing life as an erk in days even earlier than mine. Like me he had been an erk at West Drayton, Uxbridge, and Cranwell, of which he too had fond memories. Before that he had, of course, as a colonel, led the Arab revolt against the Turks, from Medina through old Palestine to Damascus. His alien cause was the Arabs, mine the Jews.

The Pakistan Air Force in Karachi did not have a suitable cockpit hood so, after a curry lunch in the officers' mess, I pressed on for the two-hour flight across the Great Indian desert to the Indian Air Force base at Jodhpur. They did not have a hood either so I took off again for another two-hour flight to the IAF base at Kanpur, with a slight diversion to Agra to see the sun setting on the Taj Mahal. It was dark when I landed with some difficulty at Kanpur – I had forgotten that there is virtually no twilight in India. After three flights, 1,600 miles and over seven hours of hurricane force winds in a cramped seat, in one day, my head did not feel my own and my bottom was numb.

I was warmly and courteously welcomed by the Indian Air Force. They scoured their stores and found an old cobwebbed hood which they fitted overnight. They also, without being asked, gave the Spit a wash and polish. In the officers' mess, more RAF than the RAF, I had a delicious curry dinner, drank several pints of Worthington beer from pewter mugs, listened to and told tall flying stories and played several rubbers of bridge before going to bed tired and happy.

The next morning, after the Indians had refused to accept a single rupee, two IAF aircraft escorted me for the first few miles of the leg to the IAF base at Barrackpore, Calcutta. Their five-bladed, Griffon-engined Mark XVIII Spitfires looked magnificent and made my near-obsolete Mark IX look old-fashioned as they flew in close formation on either side. I was sad to see them go after fifty miles or so as they waved and peeled off. Independent India was only eight years old but it was already a far cry from the Raj India I knew in 1945.

The Spitfire, having a liquid-cooled engine, is not a good tropical aeroplane. Engine temperatures were high, pressures low and the cockpit temperature hovered at 125 degrees when, after lunch and refuelling, I took off from Calcutta for the last leg to Rangoon. It was the monsoon period but the weather forecast was good. I decided to fly low again and to follow the Burmese coast to get a good view of Burma. Abandoned aerodromes of the Second World War, their runways cracked by weeds, slipped past the port wing: Chittagong, Cox's Bazaar, Akyab, Sandoway and Bassein, ghostly cenotaphs to the aircrew who did not return from the Burma campaigns.

Despite the weather forecast I kept a suspicious eye on the sky ahead. Skies are bland only to deceive, particularly during the monsoon season when the sky is as untrustworthy and dangerous as a rabid dog. Ominously the giant cumulo-nimbus clouds building up on the horizon were beginning to hold hands and join up. Their peaks, towering high in the sky, were forming into anvil shapes, a sure sign of tumult and trouble. The sky began to look like a mad painter's palette; turquoise, orange and gold, highlighted by sheet-lightning. Sunbeams thrust through the gaps in the clouds like swords. There is nothing subtle about a monsoon. I was in the pilot's classic dilemma. Press on or turn back. There are always seductive reasons for pressing on when one should turn back. Mine was that I wanted to catch the others up in Tel Aviv and not miss the next ferry flight. I pressed on. Nipping between gaps in the clouds I opened the throttle and began the long climb to get above it. At 10,000 feet I turned on the oxygen and instrument lights. Rain leaked through the cockpit hood. 15,000 . . . 20,000 . . . 25,000 . . . 27,000 . . . 28,000 . . . 29,000 feet. The controls were sloppy at this height. Even with the oxygen mask I was gasping for breath. I was as high as Everest but it was hopeless. The clouds leered down at me from Olympian heights and the gaps were closing fast. I was a tiny speck in a titanic sky, a lone salmon battling against Niagara Falls. I was also cold – there is no heater in a Spitfire – and wet. I turned, throttled back and dived, thriftlessly discarding the hard-won altitude in an attempt to squeeze underneath the storm. The clouds forced me to fly so low I was looking up at palm trees. I headed for the sea where no hills lurked and jettisoned the now empty long-range belly tank to give more manoeuvrability. I knew as I skimmed the angry waves that I had passed the point of no return and the monsoon had built up behind me as well. Inevitably the moment came when the gap between cloud and sea closed and against my will I was forced to zoom up into the clouds, into blind-ness, turbulence and vicious rain. It did not help that the Spitfire is ultra-sensitive on the controls and not easy to fly on instruments, particularly in turbulence. The odds were that I was heading for an unmarked grave in the Bay of Bengal with the Spitfire as my shroud. Apart from keeping the Spitfire on an even keel I had no control over my fate. Either the clouds broke and I lived or they did not and I almost certainly died. I switched on the radio and called for help. There was no reply but the crackle of lightning in the head-phones. It was an academic appeal anyway. Only Moses could help; by cutting a swathe through this sea of cloud.

I don't know how long the game of blind man's bluff went on; fifteen to twenty minutes perhaps. There were several false dawns, a lightening of the shadows hinting at sunshine. I did not know where I was except that to avoid mountains I was heading further out into the Bay and I was worried about fuel. There was not much to spare on the Calcutta–Rangoon leg and I had used a lot on the climb and going round in circles. I kept calling on the radio hoping that someone out there could give me a QDM bearing or news of the weather. There must be some blue sky somewhere.

Crises in flying usually end suddenly, with a bang or an anti-climax. It was the latter this time. Nature's mood changed. The rain eased off, the turbulence lessened, the murk lightened and with blinding suddenness I shot out of the cloud into clear blue skies. The fickle old enemy had adjourned to fight another day.

To my relief I could just see the Burmese coast on the port horizon and I set course for Mingaladon aerodrome. It was not long before the giant, gold-plated Shwedagon pagoda, 326 feet high in the centre of Rangoon, glinted a welcome in the sunshine. I beat up the aerodrome, which had changed little since my 194 Squadron days in 1945, and ended the fourth ferry flight with an ego-boosting, flashy, side-slipping approach and landing. After all, nobody knew what a near-fatal ass I had just made of myself over the Bay of Bengal.

After switching off I slumped in the seat, sadly watching the instruments drop slowly to zero. The end of a major flight is always a poignant moment for me. It usually takes me a few seconds longer than the aeroplane to return to earth.

The Burmese supply officer greeted me laconically as though I had just completed a meek little flight from a nearby aerodrome. I responded similarly, feeling rather sorry for him. How could he know that parched deserts, proud mountains, deep waters, the skies battlefields and the conquest of fear bound me closer to the Spitfire than to him, earthbound denizen of a smaller world.

'Where's the belly tank?' he asked.

'At the bottom of the Bay of Bengal.'

I got back to Israel in time to join the others for the next ferry flight which had been delayed by a fatal crash of one of the Spitfires. Because of my absence an Israeli Air Force pilot had been seconded to Bedek to air-test the next batch of four Spitfires, normally my job. While on a test flight the engine seized and broke up. It is believed that scalding oil blinded the pilot when he opened the hood. He tried to bale out but his parachute caught in the tail and dragged him behind the vertically diving Spitfire. He was killed when it crashed on the edge of the aerodrome at Lydda. I visited his grave in respect, for it might have been mine.

Shortly before leaving London for the ferrying operation Jackie had appeared on Richard Dimbleby's 'Down Your Way' BBC radio programme. An enterprising London literary agent, John Johnson, heard the programme and wrote to Jackie suggesting she should write her autobiography. She agreed and after scribbling away for a few weeks between ferry flights she showed me several pages of closely hand-written foolscap. It was dreadful stuff and I told her so as tactfully as I could. She did not speak to me for a week. Letters from John Johnson were following her all over the world. She gave up at about page 40. In a rash moment I suggested that I could try writing the book for her as ghost-writer.

I bought a portable typewriter, reams of lightweight foolscap, a *Thesaurus* and an Oxford pocket dictionary, and took them with me wherever I went in one of the gun-panels of the Spitfire. I also bought Saint-Exupéry's *Night Flight*, the best book ever written about flying and pilots, and Scott Fitzgerald's novel *The Great Gatsby* to re-read, hoping that something of their lyrical style would rub off on me. I found, however, that while I could start a chapter with an exotic pastiche of Exupéry/Fitzgerald, I finished up in my own style, whatever that was. To try to write a book was an impudent, presumptuous thing for me to do. I had no qualities or qualifications other than the wish to write, a dubious motivation. It was agonisingly slow work. I would smoke two or three cigarettes while deciding whether to write bacon and eggs, or eggs and bacon, but after getting over the hump of starting, I managed to maintain a target of writing two finished foolscap pages a day. It helped that writing about Jackie was writing about flying, for flying had dominated her life as much as it had mine.

We airmailed batches of sweat-stained manuscript under Jackie's name to John Johnson in London. His response to each batch was encouraging. I needed the encouragement, for I was already discovering the intellectual loneliness, the flagellating anxieties and the craving for praise that is a writer's lot. Whatever the outcome, it was a happy circumstance to climb out of a Spitfire and sit at a typewriter under the sun.

After completing the ferry flights Jackie and I returned to England together to finish writing the book.

I made the usual first-book mistakes. It was over-written, riddled with coagulated sentences and purple passages. I had yet to learn that good writing is true, not clever. Here and there in the book was a tiny glimmer of talent but it was lost in the dross. Jackie was no help; she did not know a synonym from an antonym and was rigid with the truth. I argued, using Samuel Johnson's edict, that one who tells a good story seldom tells the truth, the whole truth and nothing but the truth. It was confusing writing in someone else's first person, a woman at that, and writing about myself in the third person through her eyes. I finished up mildly schizophrenic and androgynous.

The book was published in 1957 by Michael Joseph, under the uninspiring title *Woman Pilot* by Jackie Moggridge. Reviews in *The Times, Telegraph, Times Literary Supplement* and the posh Sundays were moderately kind. Later, a paperback version was published by Pan. Both versions sold reasonably well. Sadly my name did not, of course, appear on the title page. *Woman's Own* offered an enormous sum, £1,500, for serialisation rights but they cancelled at the last moment. I don't know why. There was talk of a film to be produced by the Rank Organisation but that also came to nothing. After a few months the book sank without trace. I did not appreciate at the time how fortunate I was to get my first attempt at a book published, both in hardback and paperback, by distinguished publishers, particularly on a subject of such narrow interest. By the time the literary agent had taken 15 per cent and Jackie 50 per cent of the royalties there was not much left for eighteen months' work.

Chapter 33

IN AUGUST 1957, I had just read a curt letter from my bank manager when the telephone rang. It was Lord Calthorpe who at that time dabbled in buying and selling aircraft. He had sold a de Havilland Rapide to Air Madagascar, a subsidiary of Air France operating in Madagascar, and asked if I would like to ferry it out there for a fee of £100, plus expenses. I cashed his cheque before admitting that I would have done the flight for nothing.

The Rapide was an old-fashioned twin-engined wood and fabric biplane of the 1930s era. Not having flown one before, I borrowed some Pilot's Notes. They did not make impressive reading. It had a cruising speed of 130 mph, an endurance of 4½ hours and a maximum range of 585 miles. I concluded that three-hour legs of about 400 miles should be the basis for flight-planning. I also decided that this would not be a press-on flight, for the Rapide had no navigation or radio equipment whatsoever on board, apart from VHF R/T. It would be dead reckoning, map reading and a wet finger in the wind every inch of the 7,000 odd miles to Madagascar on the bottom half of the globe, without an automatic pilot.

I got advice from the London Aero Club, off Park Lane, on what route to take. It turned out that I was to follow the path blazed by the old pre-war record-breaking flights, though I would not be getting any headlines.

I laid out the maps on the floor at home – they stretched from the living room through the hall into the kitchen and back again – and started drawing tracks. The route was fairly direct. There were no unfriendly territories to avoid, for although the sun was setting on the British Empire the Union Jack still flew over most of the route and one was still called Sir or Sahib or Bwana after one landed.

The itinerary, stretching from 50 degrees north across the Equator to 20 degrees south, was: Portsmouth–Southampton (to clear Customs)–Beauvais–Le Bourget–Lyon–Nice–Ajaccio–Elmas –Tunis–Djerba–Tripoli–Benghazi–Marble Arch–El Adem–Marsa Matruh–Cairo–Luxor–Wadi Halfa–Atbara–Khartoum–Kosti– Malakal–Juba–Soroti–Kisumu–Nairobi–Mombasa–Dar es Salaam

–Mtwara–Mozambique–Maintirano and, finally, Tananarive. Several of the African maps had large blank areas marked *unsurveyed*. Just reading that itinerary set the adrenalin flowing.

Lord Calthorpe drove me down early to Portsmouth on the day of departure, 1 September 1957. He sorted out the paperwork while I checked myself out on the Rapide. I love flying too much to dislike any aeroplane but I was not too enamoured at first acquaintance with G-AKNE. Admittedly there was a strong, gusty wind when I taxied out over the grass for a couple of circuits and bumps but the Rapide wanted to weathercock badly and the brakes were spongy. I was a bit rusty. I had not flown for five months and that was in a rather different aeroplane, a Spitfire XVIII. The wing loading must have been very low for the slightest turbulence bounced the Rapide up and down like a yo-yo. With a total of only 400 hp from the two de Havilland Gipsy Queen III engines and fixed propellers it felt underpowered. It must have been a very sluggish aeroplane when carrying its full load of pilot and eight passengers.

I tried a three-point landing and then a wheel landing. The tail lifted when braking firmly and I decided that I would use the precautionary three-point landing technique – dragging it in nose high, with lots of throttle – when landing on the primitive strips I had been warned about in Africa. With the cockpit well forward of the leading edge and generous greenhouse windows, visibility was excellent. It was surprisingly noisy and I decided to wear my old RAF leather helmet and goggles. I always wore epaulette stripes and pin-on wings when ferrying abroad. It helped when dealing with bureaucrats.

I knew the Rapide and I were going to have a long, intimate relationship, as the flight plan was for three weeks, so I decided to give her a name. Aeroplanes are like cats – they respond better when you speak to them by name and stroke them. I thought the Rapide old-fashioned and prim rather than racy, so I christened her Gertrude.

Waving goodbye to the wistful figure of Lord Calthorpe – he had hoped to do the ferry flight himself but couldn't get away – I took off for the short hop to Southampton to clear Customs. I started off badly by putting red on black on the compass and found myself heading on the reciprocal course south-east instead of north-west. I did a swift 180 degrees and flew back over the aerodrome heading in the right direction hoping his Lordship wasn't watching my antics. Gertrude had had the first laugh.

I managed the Portsmouth–Southampton–Beauvais–Le Bourget legs on the first day and, after dodging the four-engined blast of Constellations and Skymasters, parked for the night. I made haste for my favourite Paris hotel, L'Etoile, and a reunion with my favourite chambermaid, Fifi. To my delight they were both available. It had been a long day.

I woke Fifi and then Gertrude early the next day hoping to make Lyon–Nice–Ajaccio in one day. Gertrude seemed happy cruising about 130 mph at 2,000 feet. Whenever I have the choice I fly low rather than high despite the loss of range and speed. I fly to enjoy it, not to get from A to B.

I was sorely tempted to stay overnight at Nice where I had plug trouble but I changed some plugs and pushed on. The sun was just setting over the Mediterranean as I landed at unchanged and still unspoiled Ajaccio. Memories flooded in while I waited on the verandah for a taxi, drinking Corsican white wine, with the Tricolour flapping gently in the balmy warmth.

I knew the weather would be good from now on and if I kept the sun on my left in the mornings, over my head at noon and on my right in the afternoons I would be heading in the right direction. Even Gertrude seemed frisky and to share my mood as we flew the next day from Corsica to Sardinia and then, shaking the dust of Europe from our heels, headed across the Mediterranean to a new continent – Africa. Curiously, despite having flown over most of the world, I had scarcely touched Africa.

After refuelling at Tunis I took off again and arrived at Djerba with the sunset. It was an astonishing place. Badly hit during the war it was a lonely ghost town. The Shell representative at the landing-strip was an Arab youth with a donkey cart, two barrels of fuel and a hand pump. It was dark by the time we had finished refuelling, using my chamois leather as a filter. He gave me a lift astride his donkey. There was one hotel, lit by candles with half the roof missing and no plumbing that worked.

There followed two days of blissful low flying from Djerba to Marsa Matruh, following the north African coast for 1,200 miles, along the shimmering edge of the Sahara desert. The only reminders of man's passing were the sad hulks of burned-out tanks and trucks

27 Spitfires of the 101 Fighter Squadron escorting a B17 Flying Fortress. The 'shadow' at the top is the B17's tail (photograph courtesy of the Jean-Jacques Petit collection)

28 Gordon Levett in front of his Beechcraft C18 Expediter at Idlewild, New York, December 1957, shortly before taking off for the Arctic ferry flight to Israel

29 'Gertrude', the de Havilland Dragon Rapide Gordon Levett ferried 7000 miles to Madagascar, formerly flew with Jersey Airlines (photograph courtesy of *Aeroplane Monthly*)

30 A fully restored Messerschmitt 109 at the Israeli Air Force Museum at Hazerim (photograph courtesy of Peter Arnold)

scattered here and there, relics of the desert campaigns of the Second World War.

I night-stopped at Marble Arch, a deserted wartime airstrip in the middle of the North African desert, with weeds a foot high breaking through the tarmac runway. Before landing I circled the nearby marble arch that Mussolini had built pre-war as the gateway to Tripolitania. It was an eerie folly sticking up out of empty desert, a gateway to nowhere in fact as well as in history.

Again, the Shell representative was an Arab youth with a donkey cart. God knows where he came from or where he went, for I could see nothing but sand dunes reaching to all horizons. I followed Saint-Exupéry's example and slept under the stars that seemed so close overhead. I drank the last of the Thermos coffee and made a pillow of sand under the wing. As I lay there on the edge of the Sahara smoking a cigarette with only the stars as my witness the night silence of the desert was profound. I could have been the only man on earth. I was alone but not lonely. I woke up in the middle of the night stiff and cold and climbed aboard Gertrude to wait for dawn.

At dawn I kept my fingers crossed as I pressed the starter buttons. There wasn't a soul in sight. Number one engine started all right. Number two did not. I kept number one going at fairly high rpm to keep it cool while I climbed out and sucked out excess petrol from number two by giving the propeller a few backward turns by hand. It still would not start. I got out my tool-box and changed the plugs. Number one by now had created a sandstorm. I prayed as I pressed the starter button again. My bones would probably be there now if it had not started, but it did so with a bang and puffs of black smoke. People tell me that it is nonsense but if you put engines upside-down in aeroplanes I am not surprised that plugs get fouled up.

An English pilot I met at Tunis had expressed surprise that I was passing through Egypt. The bitterness of the 1956 Sinai Campaign when Israel captured and occupied the whole of the Sinai peninsula, while France and Britain, in collusion with Israel, attempted to capture the Suez Canal, still rankled. I would be the first British-registered aircraft to pass through Egypt since that campaign. With my history I was a bit apprehensive when I landed on Egyptian soil, particularly Cairo, but they could not have been nicer as I landed at various aerodromes, taxi-ing past the wreckage of aircraft and hangars destroyed by British, French and Israeli Air Forces.

At Cairo I met the river Nile that was to lead me for the next 2,000 miles through Africa. I cut corners here and there but it guided me safely through the deserts of southern Egypt, the heat-baked wastes of the Sudan, the richer pastures of Uganda and the Equator at Lake Victoria.

The sectors Wadi Halfa–Atbara–Khartoum across the desert were some 500 miles across the most barren, inhospitable, desolate wasteland I have seen anywhere on earth. The sun had bleached the landscape a dusty off-white. The horizon danced in the heat. As I looked down and saw the lonely railway that straggled across it I marvelled that men could have built a railway there under that merciless sun with the primitive tools and medicines of the nineteenth century. How many unsung Hampdens, I wondered, were buried in unmarked graves along the track.

Between Wadi Halfa and Atbara I did an unauthorised short-cut across the Nubian desert for 250 miles rather than follow the huge loop of the Nile. It took two long hours across the hottest place on earth. It was a foolhardy thing to do, out of reach and out of touch. The outside air temperature at 3,000 feet was 105 degrees Fahrenheit, with heavy turbulence. The cockpit was like a greenhouse and I made a sunhat out of a map. It was a relief when the Nile eventually nuzzled up from the starboard side. Just the gleam of water in that harsh landscape made me feel cooler.

Between Atbara and Khartoum I discovered that I had picked up a stomach bug somewhere, probably Cairo. Alone and without an automatic pilot it was a problem. For the next two or three legs while the runs were at their worst I developed a system of trimming nose down and then rushing back to the Elsan-type loo in the tail thus bringing the nose up level while I did the necessary. I frequently had to interrupt what I was doing, particularly in turbulence, which seemed to be a feature of flying in Africa, to rush forward and re-adjust the trim. I did not bother with trousers. It was Gertrude's second laugh on me.

By now Gertrude, being a wood and fabric aeroplane, had shrunk in the heat and the flying controls were loose. At Khartoum I got out the tool-box again, crawled underneath the fuselage, undid the lacing that held the canvas skin together – she looked mortally wounded with her entrails hanging out – and tightened up a few turnbuckles.

I stayed the night in Khartoum where the Nile splits into two, the White Nile heading south, still to be my guide, and the Blue Nile sauntering off south-easterly to Ethiopia. They looked the same colour to me. Khartoum was an exotic mixture of poverty and riches. Luxurious river houseboats, lights blazing and grand colonial houses with water-sprinkled gardens mixed up with shanty-town. It reminded me of towns on the Mississippi. The bug had laid me low. I visited a local quack, who gave me some enormous black pills, and went to bed early under a fan and a silken mosquito net.

Gertrude and I had now done 33.45 hours flying together since leaving Portsmouth, well over half-way. Feeling much better but still not 100 per cent, I spent the next morning giving Gertrude an inspection and a wash and brush up. As a precaution I changed number two's plugs again and bought two dozen more for reserves. I paid particular attention to the tyres and the oil and petrol filters but found nothing ominous. Despite her age Gertrude was in good shape. I was beginning to develop an affection for her, though I doubted that I would ever rush out and buy a Rapide.

At noon the sun was pitiless but I felt better and decided to push on to Kosti and Malakal. They were both easy legs with the Nile almost dead on track the whole way. The cement pills worked. Kosti, in the middle of nowhere, seemed a small but thriving community, but on what I could not fathom. Perhaps being on the crossroads of a railway, roads and the Nile helped. Malakal, where several tributaries joined the Nile, was once an important flying base where Empire-class flying-boats on the UK to Cape Town route landed on the Nile for refuelling and a leisurely night-stop. Air travel was more civilised then.

I spent the night at Malakal's only hotel to discover that there are more flies per room there than anywhere else in the world, including Calcutta. Fly-blown, I was not sorry to leave at dawn for Juba.

From Juba onwards the topography, flora and fauna began to change. The ground level rose steadily pushing me higher with each mile. Trees, shrubs and crops flourished, wild game frolicked and lakes glistened. The restful green landscape was balm to the eyes after days of desert glare.

Between Juba and Soroti, near the Equator in Uganda, I said a sad farewell to the faithful Nile as it turned south-west towards its source, Lake Albert, and turned south-east. Without the Nile pointing the way I now had to pay more attention to map reading. I tried getting QDM navigation fixes on the R/T but nobody out there heard me until I got within twenty miles of Nairobi. Between Soroti and Kisumu I crossed the Equator into the southern hemisphere. Navigating was hard work, particularly now that the safety-height between Kisumu and Nairobi was an astonishing 12,000 feet, unless one flew through valleys. I was surprised at the altitude of this part of the country for I had not associated great heights with Africa. Gertrude was wheezing at that height. Me too. The bug had debilitated me more than I thought.

I detoured some fifty miles on the leg from Nairobi to Mombasa on the east coast of Africa, to see Mount Kilimanjaro. I circled it several times at 10,000 feet. It rose majestically, an almost perfect cone against a cobalt-blue sky, to a snow-capped 19,340 feet. Around its waist wisps of broken strato-cumulus softened its lines. I have always been glad that I am a pilot but never more so than that moment when, flying by my own hand and alone, I looked up at the snows of Kilimanjaro.

It was downhill all the way from Nairobi to Mombasa, with a road and railway to guide me. I put the maps to one side, flew low and chased wild game; elephants, lions, cheetahs, wildebeests as ugly as their aircraft namesake, and giraffes, their heads level with my undercarriage. Gertrude, like me glad to be back at near sea level, was in good form, though I had to keep a sharp look-out for bird-strikes.

After days of being land-locked it was a relief to see the Indian Ocean on the horizon. Mombasa is Kenya's major port and its seaside playground. The curved bay was lined with classic palm trees and the sea had that unique Indian Ocean colour which I had noticed in Burma and Malaya, neither green nor blue, but a luminescent mix of opal and jade flecked with the whitest of white surf. I stayed the night in the Travellers' Club facing the beach, where jet-black waiters, splendid in scarlet uniforms topped with a tarboosh, served Tom Collins chota pegs or Worthington in pewter mugs. I had the best dinner since leaving Paris; sadly the meat was soft-eyed gazelle. After several games of snooker I went happily to bed with the surf murmuring a lullaby that soothed after Gertrude's vibrating buzz. The next morning as I was shaving I noticed that the water swirled anti-clockwise out of the wash basin.

The legs Mombasa–Dar es Salaam–Mtwara–Mozambique were what one would expect with an exotic roll-call like that. A thousand miles of exquisite east African coastline so beautiful it put even the north African coast to shade. I flew low the whole way. I must have covered half of that 7,000-mile flight under 500 feet. I knew it would add considerably to his Lordship's fuel bill but an opportunity like that occurs only once in a lifetime.

The weather was perfect, apart from turbulence, as I followed the coast southwards. The sun so penetrating, the sea so translucent I could see the coral reefs and schools of fish beneath the surface. The land was a riot of colour; white, empty beaches, compacted rain forests, gentle hills lush with wild flowers and small, deserted islands strung along the coast. I was sorry when it was time to climb and land at Mozambique, my last stop in Africa.

The penultimate leg from Mozambique to Maintirano on the west coast of Madagascar caused me some concern. It was about 350 miles over water across the Mozambique Channel, just under three hours' flying. I could not miss Madagascar for it is a massive island, some 1,000 miles long and 350 miles wide, second only to Greenland in size, but the east coast looked a bit featureless for deciding whether to turn port or starboard if I did not hit Maintirano on the nose. In fact I did just that with the help of Juan de Nova, a lonely, uninhabited island the size of a football pitch, jutting out of the Indian Ocean a hundred miles from Maintirano.

The last lap, Maintirano–Tananarive, about 240 miles, was also a bit difficult, with a barren, mountainous landscape, no railway and few roads on the west side of Tananarive to help pin-point my position. I had little idea where I was when, about thirty minutes before ETA, I started calling up Tananarive on the R/T for QDM navigation fixes. Either their English or my French wasn't good enough, or they did not know what QDMs were, for my requests went unheeded. The closer I got to where I hoped Tananarive might be the more rugged became the terrain. With safety-height at 6,000 feet I was getting a bit uneasy. It would have been unkind of fate if I cocked-up on the last leg and gave Gertrude the last as well as the first laugh. I added a more urgent note to my calls for QDMs but still no response. It turned out that I had been given the wrong frequency.

I came across a road straggling north and south which I guessed from the map led to and from Tananarive, but which way was which? Should I turn port or starboard? I circled several times trying to work out the direction of the wind before deciding to turn right and follow the road for fifteen minutes followed by, if unsuccessful, the reverse direction for thirty minutes. I had ample fuel. Turning right first was a lucky choice, for Tananarive's runway soon beckoned.

I touched down with Gertrude for the last time with sadness. It had been a memorable flight. Thirty-two legs, eleven countries, 61 flying hours. Gertrude had been steadfast, with scarcely a snag in three weeks' rugged flying. The French were delighted with her for she had been bought sight unseen. I patted her nose affectionately as I left her on the tarmac being prepared for her new life, a far cry from the cold, grey skies of Europe. I wonder what happened to her.

When I got back to the UK – via an Air France DC6 – and a pleased Lord Calthorpe, I found I had lost a stone. A stone well spent.

Chapter 34

IT WAS DECEMBER 1957 when Leo telephoned again from New York. He had recently been appointed chief pilot of Arkia, the newly established Israeli domestic airline.

Arkia had bought two second-hand Beechcraft Expediter C-18s to augment their small fleet. The Beechcraft, after overhaul and refit, were ready to be ferried together from Idlewild, New York, to Israel, using the northern Arctic route via Greenland and Iceland. He was flying one, would I fly the other?

Within two days I was in New York, via a BOAC Stratocruiser, staying at the Henry Hudson hotel on West 57th Street. At that time it was home-from-home for the world's transient pilots. Sit in the foyer and someone you knew would be sure to walk in. Its other claim to fame was static electricity. Touching a lift button was like touching a live wire. Most of us pressed the button with our elbows. The hotel was named after the early seventeenth-century explorer who discovered the eponymous Hudson Bay when in search of a north-east passage to China and was the first to reach the most northern point of Greenland. He came to a tragic end when his disaffected crew mutinied on his fourth exploration of northern Greenland and cast him, his young son and some sick members of the crew adrift in a small boat. Unlike Captain Bligh of the *Bounty* and his crew, they all perished. I hoped it was not an omen, for we would soon be setting course, mid-winter, for Greenland.

We spent the next few days preparing the aircraft at Idlewild. The Beechcraft was a nippy, twin-engine, twin-tail aeroplane, responsive and sensitive to the controls and, with a maximum weight of only 8,000 pounds, amply powered with Pratt and Whitney R-985 450 hp engines. I had flown and liked it in the RAF in the Second World War but remembered it had a mind of its own when landing in strong cross-winds. It had a service ceiling of 20,000 feet, a maximum speed of 215 mph, cruised at 150 mph, with a still air range of five hours, some 750 miles. A long-range ferry tank was fitted in the cabin to increase the range to seven hours, some 1,050 miles. The complicated cross-feed fuel arrangements in the cabin to ensure flow to either or both engines from the ferry tank looked like a plumber's nightmare. The aircraft normally carried a crew of two and eight passengers. On this flight Leo and I would have to do without crew. Fortunately it had a full automatic pilot. We had one passenger each, both innocents of flight. Leo's passenger was his seven-months' pregnant wife, Miriam; mine was Danny, an Israeli civil servant. Both had sublime faith in their pilots. It was just as well, for the only radio and navigation equipment we carried was basic VHF R/T, an ADF radio compass and a wet finger. We had no de-icing equipment.

As the cockpit heating was almost useless and we expected outside air temperatures over the Greenland ice-cap of –50° C, we fitted ourselves out with Arctic clothing at a war surplus discount store. With mush-mush snow-boots, gauntlets, winter woollies, anoraks, scarves, parkas, hand warmers and snow glasses, we looked like Michelin advertisements, particularly Miriam. We borrowed two emergency Arctic packs from the US Air Force, including hand powered transmitters for homing by rescue aircraft. Leo and I agreed not to bother with emergency ditching equipment; there would be no point in prolonging that particular agony.

Finally we got out our maps and charts and decided our route. After some argument we settled on: Idlewild–Sept Iles–Knob Lake –Frobisher Bay– Sondrestrom (north of the Arctic Circle)–Keflavik –Prestwick –London Heathrow–Lyon–Rome–Athens–Lydda. The Idlewild to Prestwick sectors was the route pioneered in the Second World War to ferry short-range aircraft across the Atlantic from the USA to the UK. Much of the territory in and around Greenland was still unexplored. Old flying lags though we were, it was an itinerary to set the adrenalin flowing, particularly in winter. We would fly in loose formation, with Leo leading.

Range and fuel would not be a problem, but on the Arctic sectors there were no alternative aerodromes should the weather be bad except returning to the point-of-departure. It was turn back before reaching that dramatic sounding moment, point-of-no-return, or press on, committed. As our dead-reckoning would be primitive we agreed to knock off twenty minutes from each estimated p.o.n.r. We did some homework on the formula in the Henry Hudson; it was safer there. What we achieved with all this palaver I don't know for, with short-range R/T our only communication, we would not

256

be getting any in-flight weather reports about our destination until it was too late to turn back.

Leo and I scribbled down and sellotaped the mnemonic *Variation west, compass best* to the instrument panels. With variation 37 degrees west in the Arctic it would be disastrous if we applied it to our compass heading the wrong way round.

Our mid-morning departure from Idlewild on 12 December, on the first leg to Sept Iles where we spent the night, was uneventful. The weather was friendly, no snags with the aircraft and all of us enjoying the winter brilliance of the Canadian scenery, with the great St. Lawrence river pointing the way. I was content, as I always am when the compass is pointing to distant places.

After five hours we let down at dusk and landed in close formation. The blast of biting wind and the snow landscape when we opened the doors was a foretaste of what was to come.

After refuelling we checked our fuel consumption. It was a little more than expected, manufacturer's figures are always optimistic, but not worrying. We had ample reserves.

I wanted to make the next two legs, Sept Iles–Knob Lake–Frobisher, in one day. Leo, ever the wise pilot, disagreed. At this time of the year there was less than four hours' daylight at Frobisher and this would mean landing there in the dark if we attempted the two legs in one day. The Arctic, added Leo firmly, is not the place for night flying if it can be avoided.

The leg Sept Isle–Knob Lake was only about 300 miles, so we got up late, had a leisurely Canadian breakfast of flapjacks and maple syrup, donned all our Michelin gear and took off late morning. It was an easy flight, weather again perfect and a single track railway line to follow all the way. It was a lonely line threading its way through the vast, uninhabited, snow-covered landscape. I saw only one train, heading in the opposite direction, furiously puffing white smoke into the cloudless sky. The outside temperature gauge was dropping steadily and the lines of longitude on our maps were beginning to converge rapidly.

Knob Lake had once been an important refuelling base on the Second World War ferry run but was now in ghostly decline, living on its memories, rather like Shannon. The sides of the runway were piled high with snow from the snow ploughs. It was like landing in a ditch. Most of the wooden huts and barracks, once agog with the drama and excitement of young men flying to war, were empty. The skeleton staff there were glad to see us and have something to do.

The next leg to Frobisher Bay – over-flying the emergency strip at Fort Chimo for peace of mind – was some 620 miles, about four hours. We planned a dawn take-off, not too much hardship because dawn did not arrive until 1000 hours local time, to ensure our arrival at Frobisher in daylight. The weather report was good except there might be snow showers, some heavy, around Frobisher Bay.

It was on this sector that we crossed the tree line and flew back into the Ice Age. Once we had passed over Fort Chimo – with a lonely tower there wishing us a good flight – and headed out over water for the 300 miles crossing of the Hudson Strait to Baffin Land, we were on our own. Nobody could help us if things went wrong. Pratt and Whitney separated us from frozen eternity. We had left continental Canada and tamed nature behind us and were now flying over the North West Territories. Though the sun was low the light was brilliant. The atmosphere was so intensely clear one knew there wasn't a speck of man-made dust for a thousand miles. The Hudson Strait, leading to Hudson Bay, twice the size of France, was a deep, cobalt-blue setting against which icebergs glinted. Some were tiny and looked like small sailing dinghies, others were huge cathedrals of ice. The water was so clear we could see their massive depths below the water line. The sky seemed vast. It was a scene of such transcendental, unimpaired beauty I felt we were interlopers.

An hour from Frobisher my automatic pilot became unserviceable and would not hold bank or height. I switched it off and, more from laziness than anything else, took the precaution of teaching Danny the rudiments of straight and level flight.

Frobisher's NDB beacon was comfortingly strong and the radio compass needle scarcely quivered as it pointed the way. Less sanguine, the sun was slipping down fast to its meeting with the horizon and at these latitudes there is little twilight. The outside air temperature was –30° C. It was not much warmer inside. I had let Leo get well ahead in case of problems letting down at Frobisher. In those days it was either VFR, or an NDB instrument landing, not my favourite method of returning to earth.

There was a neat cluster of snow showers just where we didn't want them; slap-bang over Frobisher. And they were beginning to join up and fill the sky. It was getting dark enough to put the instrument and navigation lights on. I was forced to let down and fly under the showers, even though flying low at dusk through fine white snow against a snow-white landscape is not the healthiest of pastimes, particularly with low hills near the aerodrome. Over the R/T I heard Leo landing and clearing the runway. 'Hurry up, Leviticus,' he said over the R/T. 'It's getting dark down here.'

Fortunately, Frobisher had brilliant Strobe lights both on the approach and along the runway and they shone through the murk like lighthouses. With several steep turns, gyros toppling, violent side-slipping and a Spitfire approach we got down just before Arctic night descended. 'That', said Danny, 'was interesting.'

We spent a comfortable night in overheated barracks redolent of the Second World War. Outside it was pitch black, with temperatures down to −45° C when the wind gusted. During the evening Leo and I were informed that our permission to land at Sondrestrom had been withdrawn. No reason was given. Sondrestrom is a USAF Strategic Air Command base, almost certainly nuclear, and they do not give reasons for anything, particularly then, at the height of the Cold War. We heard later that a Douglas Globemaster had crashed there, blocking the only runway. Without spares they had been unable to repair my automatic pilot.

We scratched our heads and got out the charts. Bluie-West-One, another USAF base on the south-western tip of Greenland, was the only alternative route but it was a further 200 miles, making a total of 725 miles, about four and a half hours' flying time, with only three hours of daylight. It was either night flight or back to New York. Had we known Sondrestrom was unavailable we would have routed via Goose Bay and Bluie-West-One. We had an encouraging briefing with the weatherman. The high pressure area was still holding and the weather should be good and winds favourable for the next two days at least but, he added, there is always a chance of low cloud along the southern Greenland coast.

There was no choice. We had to take off in the middle of the night the next morning, 0900 hours, in order to get to Bluie-West-One before dark. Daylight and half-light would be between 1200 and 1500 hours. We were well aware that after four and a half hours flying over the icy and desolate waters of the Davis Straits, out of communication, there would be no alternative aerodrome should Bluie-West-One be socked in. Though it would be difficult to miss Greenland, the largest island in the world, we were aiming for its southern tip between aptly named Cape Desolation and Cape Farewell, so we planned a deliberate mistake to hit the coast of Greenland about twenty-five miles north of track.

We arranged for hot air cowls to be placed around the engines overnight to ensure an easy start in the morning and went to bed early, Leo and I subdued, our passengers insouciant – a classic case of ignorance being bliss. It was a comforting thought that there was a USAF converted B17 Flying Fortress, loaded with air-sea rescue equipment, including a lifeboat slung under the belly, and bristling with radar and radio antennae, on permanent stand-by at Bluie-West-One. Its purpose was to aid crashed aircraft, or seek and find aircraft lost or in distress and guide them to BW1, down to the threshold of the runway if necessary.

We took-off in total darkness at 0900 hours. There was some low broken scud about but we soon topped it. Leo kept his landing lights on until I caught up and we climbed up to 9,000 feet together. The further north we got the closer I kept to Leo; it was comforting to see his grin, though there was little we could do for each other if anything went wrong.

The stars were brilliant and touches of aurora borealis flickered eerily in the northern sky like an ominous preamble to star wars. The temperature in the cockpit reminded me of Baron Munchhausen's comment that it was so cold one's words froze and had to be thawed out later over a log fire to hear the conversation. Our breaths were thick clouds. The heaters were useless. Miriam had four hot-water bottles.

Although the dawn was feeble it was a relief when at last the eastern sky lightened. The sun kept low on the horizon and shed no warmth. It was difficult to believe that this was the same sun that kept the world warm elsewhere. Our timing was good, for almost at the same time the west coast of Greenland glinted on the horizon. Nowhere in the world is like Greenland. It is unique, still in the grip of the ice age. A great continent of ice 2,500 miles long, 1,200 miles wide and up to 10,500 feet thick, some of it still unsurveyed. If the ice-cap were to melt, the sea level throughout the world would rise by twenty-one feet. The ice-cap is separated from the sea by mountainous land along the coast, like the rim of a giant pie crust, through which glaciers have cut deep valleys and fjords. The ice-cap is not smooth, for blizzards of new snow form undulating drifts and dunes much like the sands of the Sahara. Nothing grows or lives there, or would want to. One felt it was the true Arctic, the Ultima Thule, as it was called by the ancient Greeks, who believed it was the end of the world, where darkness and nameless terror lurked.

The NDB at Bluie-West-One was needfully powerful and homed us in without a flicker on our radio compasses. But, the control tower informed us, there was low cloud over the base. As our radio compasses swung 180 degrees informing us we were over BW1, we looked down on unbroken stratus. It was obviously a thin early morning layer with tops about 1,500 feet and ceiling around 700 feet. It might budge, it might sit there all day. Leo and I immediately put plan A into action. Plan B was to land wheels-up on the ice-cap.

We turned westerly out to sea to let down. The only thing we could hit there was icebergs. Leo let down first and reported ceiling about 750 feet, good visibility and no icebergs. I gave Leo about ten minutes to head back to the coast before letting down myself. Danny was getting fidgety. To keep him occupied I told him to remember the *Titanic* and look out for icebergs. It was about 500 feet when we broke through under the cloud.

Now began the tricky part. There are several look-alike fjords on this part of the coast, only one of which, the sixty-mile long Tunugdliarfik Fjord, leads to Bluie-West-One. An NDB beacon at Simitac on the southwest coast helps location but it is easy to take the wrong fjord. But in this desolate part of the world pilots have an old friend. Halfway up Tunugdliarfik Fjord lies the wreck of an old Second World War freighter. If one was flying up a narrow twisting fjord under low cloud and did not come across the freighter about thirty miles from the coast, then one was up the wrong fjord without a paddle, for there was barely room to do an about-turn.

We were lucky. Visibility was good under the cloud base, there were no snow showers and we had chosen the right fjord, for the rusting hulk of the freighter turned up about ten minutes after we entered the fjord. Danny and I thought it was a beautiful thing to behold. Leo too had chosen the right fjord, for I could hear him requesting landing instructions from the control tower.

Bluie-West-One was at the end of the fjord, boxed in on three sides by snow covered foothills. It had a single runway, made up of hinged PSP steel planking, that sloped upwards towards the glacier at the far end of the runway which led to the ice-cap. Regardless of wind one landed uphill and took off downhill. Once one was committed on the landing approach it was unhealthy to go around again unless one was flying in clear weather.

As we negotiated the last bend in the fjord it was a relief to see Bluie-West-One in the clear under the cloud base. The circular base looked like a giant skating rink, with the runway an inviting black ribbon cutting across the middle. By the time we had landed and taxied to the ramp, tied down the aircraft against blizzards and unpacked our sponge-bags, it was dark.

That night brought the onset of violent snow blizzards and we were grounded at Bluie-West-One for six days including, appropriately enough, Christmas Day. I wished I still believed in Santa Claus. We were made very welcome by the US Air Force. Being American, the base, although winding down, was well equipped, warm and comfortable inside. The canteen food was unbelievably fresh and good, including lashings of ice cream and airlifted strawberries. Up-to-date movies were shown twice nightly. The American servicemen eyed Miriam appreciatively. Although normally there were no women on the base, the well-stocked PX store, much to Miriam's relief, had women's things. I bought a Hamilton gold watch at a quarter of the normal price. The Americans know how to look after their servicemen. One shudders to think what Bluie-West-One would have been like had it been a British base.

We sat around waiting for the weather to change. The blizzards, with the wind-chill factor, brought the temperature down to an instant frostbite −55° C. One could lean against the wind. Visibility was nil and ropes were tied between major buildings to guide the way. In conditions like this there was a red alert on the base which meant, *inter alia*, that it was a court-martial offence to walk alone outside. The incredibly dry snow stung the face and forced its way everywhere like desert sand in a Sirocco. With darkness at noon, our body clocks got confused and, emulating the Eskimos on the base, we went to bed when we were tired or sleepy and not necessarily at normal bedtime. Miriam began to wonder whether her child might be born in Greenland.

On the morning of the fifth day the blizzards stopped. It was a relief when the shrieking and sighing of the wind died out. The rest of the short day, with token sunshine, was spent clearing the snow. Snow ploughs drove monotonously up and down the runway, men dug out aircraft and paths and we swept the snow from the two Beechcraft with soft brooms. After thawing out the engines with hot air shrouds we gave them a good inspection and a run-up. By the time we had finished the two-hour day was gone and it was dark again.

Bluie-West-One to Keflavik was 775 miles, some five hours, a long leg without an automatic pilot working. At this time of the year there was no way of avoiding night on this sector. Having checked that the weather would be reasonable, qualified by the warning that meteorology is not an exact science, particularly in this part of the world, we planned a first-light take-off the following morning.

After take-off Leo and I climbed westerly down the fjord before turning back onto course. Safety height over the southern ice-cap was 11,000 feet. Disappointingly, visibility was poor as we spent an hour crossing the ice-cap. There was no horizon and nothing to distinguish between the off-white murk of earth and sky except when looking directly downwards. Looking down on that landscape I wondered what millennia-old secrets lay entombed for eternity in those icy depths, two miles thick. This was a landscape that had nothing to do and wanted nothing to do with man. It was aloof, glacial, pitiless. To challenge it was to challenge death. I was not sorry when we crossed the coast and headed out over the Denmark Strait.

The compass was sluggish, the needle-point pulled steeply downwards by the nearby Magnetic Pole. I promised myself that one day I would stand on top of the world at the North Pole and enjoy the uncanny experience of knowing that everywhere I looked, except up, and the first step I took in any direction would be due south.

As we headed easterly, with Danny handling the controls quite well, the night seemed to be rushing headlong towards us and we were soon engulfed in darkness. There was no moon and the stars were in hiding behind high cloud. It was like being cocooned in black velvet. Leo's silhouette had disappeared to be replaced by the distant blinking of his navigation lights. Time and distance passed slowly. Murphy's Law states categorically that when flying north of the 60th parallel at night, in winter, a mile is longer than a mile and a minute is longer than a minute.

Then three things happened in quick succession.

Being a non-smoker Danny smelt it first. After a few deep sniffs I agreed. There was a smell of petrol, rapidly getting worse. Leaving a doubtful Danny at the controls I went back to the cabin and discovered petrol about two inches deep sloshing about the cabin floor. The main spar prevented it from getting into the cockpit. I rushed back to the cockpit, switched off everything electrical that we could do without and opened the side windows. With wind-chill, the temperature must have been around –60° C. But I was glad to be colder than I had ever been before for it would make the petrol fumes less volatile. By torchlight I discovered one of the fuel hose connections to the temporary cross-feed under the ferry tank had worked loose. Using my tool box I tightened it up and stopped the leak. I went back to the cockpit with soaking, frozen feet and hands and sent Danny back to get clean socks and slippers from my luggage and find some rags for mopping up. There were no rags so we used our spare shirts and underwear, squeezing the petrol into plastic sacks from the temporary Elsan-type loo. Any moment we were expecting the spark that would blow us to eternity. We dare not throw anything out of the windows for fear of an exhaust ember so we packed the half-filled sacks, which we had doubled-up for strength, into our emptied suitcases.

Despite the fact that we were flying a Molotov cocktail and the fumes were sickening I shut the cockpit windows. Freezing to death was worse than burning to death and took longer. Danny had just about finished mopping up when the second thing happened. The starboard engine started to cough and backfire. 'Jesus, now what?' shouted Danny from the back. It was a good question to ask 300 miles and two hours from the nearest land. Engine temperatures and pressures between the symptoms seemed normal. I doubted that it could be carburettor icing at this temperature but I tried carburettor heating anyway without success. Giving control to Danny I went back into the cabin and tried various fuel cross-feed settings but without results. Back in the cabin I tried the fuel booster pumps, again without effect. Giving up, I feathered the starboard engine. It was a relief when the propeller blades knife-edged into the airflow and stopped and the backfiring ceased. After trimming and sorting out throttle and pitch settings on the good engine and closing down the dead engine, I had time for reflection.

With a light load the Beechcraft flew quite nicely on one engine, though the good engine had to be set to climbing power and rpm, and we had ample fuel. With my pulse rate back to normal I decided that, without sparks, we were not stretcher cases yet, merely walking wounded.

And then the third thing happened, about half-way between Greenland and Iceland. I doubt there is a lonelier place on earth on a winter's night.

Just as Danny climbed back into his co-pilot's seat after another wiping up session in the back, the aileron control went haywire and we went into a steep turn to the left. It took a lot of strength to force the ailerons back into the normal straight-and-level position. The moment I released the control column the aileron swung to the left again and we were back doing involuntary steep turns. At least we were turning into the good engine. I got Danny to help me to force the controls back to the normal position and then, for the first and only time in my life, called Mayday – the internationally accepted SOS – on our stand-by radio frequency. Why Mayday, I wondered. Mayday is usually associated with joy, not despair. (I discovered later that it comes, of course, from the French *M'aider*, that is, Help.) Unsurprisingly, only Leo answered. After I had told him what was happening – hearing his voice was absurdly comforting – we both switched to 121.5. the international Mayday emergency frequency. Danny asked if it was serious. I replied, with a ghastly smile, that if it was what I feared, structural failure, he should prepare to meet his Maker.

I repeated the Mayday call on 121.5. thinking, as my voice echoed over the lonely ether, how utterly futile it was. Even the rescue B17 at Bluie-West-One would be of no use. It would take them, flat out, two hours to reach the area and if they did manage to find our wreckage we would by then be two human icebergs.

To my astonishment there was an immediate reply, five-by-five. It was an American voice, clear, relaxed and cool.

I described our problems. 'Jeeze,' he said after I had finished. I then asked him who he was. 'Restricted,' he replied. After I had asked him whether he was sea or airborne he replied that was restricted too. I then suggested giving him a position report. He replied that he probably knew better than I did where we were. It was a very odd conversation for an emergency in the middle of the night in the middle of nowhere. I concluded he was airborne, probably part of the permanent USAF Strategic Air Command early warning patrol.

A more authoritative voice then came on the air. By this time my arms were aching and I was in a bad temper and frightened. The conversation became irascible, but I had to agree there wasn't a damn thing he could do for us. He would inform Bluie-West-One and Keflavik what was happening, keep tracking us on radar and listen out on 121.5. 'Good luck,' he added to his over-and-out.

It was then that I looked down at the base of the control console where the automatic pilot on-off control was located close to the floor. It was half on, kicked by Danny as he climbed into his cramped seat. The relief as I turned it off and the controls went back to normal was countered by how foolish I felt when I had to explain to the Americans what had happened.

After embarrassed apologies to the Americans and Leo, I asked the mystery voice if they would tell me where I was, or was that restricted too. After pointing out that it wasn't where I was that mattered to the enemy (I assume he meant the Russians), but who, what and where they were, they gave me a navigation fix. Despite the distractions of the last hour we were still on course. I then asked him to inform BW1 and Keflavik that we had changed our status from Mayday to Pan (mild emergency). After all, we were still not out of the wood. We were still flying on only one engine and we could still blow up.

Suspecting there was water or sediment in the petrol I decided to throw the Beechcraft about a bit to shake up the fuel system. With the long-range fuel tank in the cabin I could not fly upside down but, blind-flying on instruments, we climbed and dived and stall-turned and imposed as much negative G as I dared. Danny had to use a sick bag. I then unfeathered the starboard engine and started it up. After an initial bout of similar symptoms it settled down with only minor hiccups every few minutes. I took the precaution of shaking up the aircraft every fifty miles or so. I was desperate for a cigarette and asked Danny what he thought. Madness, he said, so I refrained from lighting up.

'Is everything all right now?' asked Danny, his colour returning, his faith in me restored.

'Yes,' I said, 'as much as it ever is in flying.' He sat back. 'You chaps earn your money,' he said.

It was still dark, but the high stratus cloud had broken up and the stars now out of hiding twinkled a friendly truce. Flying had become serene again. Keflavik's NDB beacon rang clear in my earphones and the radio compass needle pointed dead ahead. Very soon the lights of Iceland sparkled brightly on the horizon.

After landing at Keflavik we snatched a few hours sleep while mechanics sorted out the starboard engine problem; it was water and sediment in the ferry-tank. We then spent the rest of the day ripping out the carpets, cleaning up and defuming the Beechcraft with the aid of hot air ducts. The next day we took off for Prestwick. This was the longest leg of the ferry flight, 875 miles, about six hours, with an hour's fuel reserve. As we flew into warmer latitudes and a more convincing sun, our extremities began to thaw out and daylight lingered longer. There was no smell of petrol and under Danny's disapproving gaze I lighted a cigarette.

It was midnight when we landed at Prestwick, but Leo wanted to press on, so after refuelling and some haggis, we took off for London Heathrow where small and non-scheduled aircraft were still welcome in those golden days of flying. It was instrument flying all the way down the spine of England and low cloud, rain and poor visibility at Heathrow, but Leo and I asked for radar approach and a GCA radar-controlled let-down and landing, and it was a piece of cake.

I always enjoyed landing at Heathrow after a spell abroad. The cool, clear, confident voices of flying control, the feeling that one was in good hands, the courteous customs and immigration staff, English manners, orderly queues and driving without horns blaring. And the feeling that one was at the heart of aviation, old and new, as one taxied past the beautiful Lockheed Constellation, the handsome Boeing Stratocruiser, the magnificent DC7 Seven Seas, the hideous, arse-dragging Avro York, the unabashed Dakota and then a surge of British pride as one saw the de Havilland Comet, the Vickers Viscount and the Bristol Britannia, three brilliant British aircraft showing the new pure jet and turbo-prop way to the world, albeit briefly.

The remainder of the ferry flight: Lyon–Rome–Athens–Lydda, was uneventful and we landed at Lydda to a fulsome welcome. Our flight across the Arctic had made the newspapers. They remembered to call me the *Shabbes Goy*. I spent a few days on the beaches at Eilat, then small and unspoiled, thoroughly thawing out, followed by a few proving flights on desert strips for Arkia with the Beechcraft. They proved to be very successful in the years ahead on the domestic network.

Having turned down the offer of airline training and a captaincy with Arkia, I collected my fee of £100 and expenses and returned to London on the flight deck of an El Al Britannia flown by an old friend. Miriam was successfully delivered of a healthy daughter six weeks later.

Chapter 35

IT WAS 1958, time to review my situation. I was approaching forty, life's late summer, a dangerous age not to be settled down. The only long-term security available to pilots is to be an airline captain with four gold braid stripes and years of seniority, and that I would never be. I was too old and *passé*. If I did get a commercial pilot's licence and managed to get a job with a dodgy airline it could only be as a co-pilot and I had no intention of spending the next twenty years sitting in the right-hand co-pilot's seat after twenty years of being top dog. Sadly I had to turn down an offer to join the Burmese Air Force. Alice was not the type to wear a *longyi*, smoke cheroots and go native.

Now that aviation was on the threshold of jumbo jets and computerised science, rather than art and the seat of one's pants, the days of the tramp pilot were drawing to a close and my flying days were numbered. It was time to close the hangar doors and walk whistling into the sunset.

With the confidence of having had *Woman Pilot* published, I converted our spare bedroom into a study, Alice went out to work as a secretary and I started writing a novel.

After six months and 200 pages the novel was going badly. Worse than that, it was rubbish. I could describe setting and action quite well but the characters and their motivation were wooden and cliché-ridden. I could not flesh them out or bring them to life. I burned the manuscript. Alice was shocked when she came home and found the ashes in the grate.

In the next few days two things happened. After a series of interviews I was offered an unbelievably good job as a sales executive with Associated Television in London and, once again, I got a telephone call from Leo Gardner. He had an uncanny knack of contacting me at the right moment. This time Leo was telephoning from Tel Aviv. Would I join him on a flight from Israel to somewhere in South America, the details of which he could not discuss on the telephone? I could not possibly say no to the former or refuse the latter. I telephoned the sales director of ATV who had offered me the job and begged a moratorium. I fibbed and said that I had committed myself to this flight before applying for the job at ATV. I promised it would be my flying swansong. Fortunately he was ex-RAF aircrew and he gave me a month. I was in Tel Aviv the next day, via El Al.

Leo met me at Lydda, re-named Lod airport, and we drove straight to the Ministry of Defence to see Colonel Shapiro, an old friend and our contact for several covert flights in the past.

Shapiro remembered my cup of tea. 'Tea for the Shabbes Goy,' he shouted to his secretary. He enjoyed having a maverick English Gentile mixed up in his conspiracies. Leo drank black coffee. When the tea arrived it was in a glass, with a slice of lemon and no milk. The British had failed to establish in Israel their three verities of empire; tea with milk, driving on the left and cricket. Perhaps the thirty-year mandate had not been long enough.

Shapiro gave us our orders. They were simple and top secret. Using an Israeli Air Force B17 Flying Fortress bomber we were to fly arms urgently 7,500 miles to Santo Domingo in the Dominican Republic.

The Flying Fortress was being prepared away from prying eyes at an air force base in the Negev. When Leo and I arrived for a test flight the air force markings were being removed. The aircraft looked weary and scruffy. The engine cowlings were battered – always a sign of an aircraft's age – and the camouflage paint was peeling off, but we patted it affectionately, for it was an old friend. In 1948, Leo had helped smuggle it and two other Fortresses out of America in defiance of the American Neutrality Act (for which, years later, he was fined $10,000) and fly them secretly to Israel, via Czechoslovakia, despite the United Nations arms embargo. I had escorted it several times on bombing sorties when I was in 101 Squadron. It looked more suitable for a museum than a flight half-way around the world, but its age did add a certain charm. Mechanics were also removing the machine guns bristling from the turrets in an attempt to make it look more pacific. It was a waste of time. The Flying Fortress could never look other than what it was; a big, fat, ugly, aggressive man-o'-war. It had no markings.

After an uneventful test flight Leo checked me out. I had not flown a four-engined aircraft for nearly ten years but it was good to have a fistful of throttles again. After one take-off, circuit and landing we considered I could fly a B17. Life was simpler then. I was surprised how easily the Fortress handled. It proceeded through the air in an avuncular fashion, rather like a large Avro Anson, landed at the ridiculously low speed of 75 mph and flew happily on two engines.

We checked the route planned by the Ministry. As always when flying to or from Israel the route was devious. It is not healthy to cut corners when flying an Israeli aircraft in the Middle East. The shortest route is usually out of the question. Israel was still surrounded, except to the west, by hostile Arab countries which would not hesitate to press the button and ask questions afterwards if one should stray over their territory.

The route was Israel–Brindisi–Algiers–Casablanca–Dakar–Natal–Belem–Caracas–Santa Domingo. The Dakar–Natal leg, 2,800 miles across the South Atlantic, was a bit worrying. We would not have much fuel left even with the north-easterly Trade Winds on our side. We discussed installing a long-range ferry tank in the fuselage, but time was short and we had a light load which should give us the edge. Leo pointed out that we could both swim and the water would be warm at that time of year.

We returned to our hotel in Tel Aviv to pack and have a quiet evening in readiness for a midnight take-off. Meanwhile the bazookas, machine-guns, mortars, grenades, small arms and ammunition were being loaded. The manifest documents described our cargo as spare parts.

We took off at midnight, 24 February 1958. Our R/T clearance with Lod control tower was bogus. In case anyone with hostile intent was listening in or picking us up on radar, we purported to be a TWA Constellation bound for Athens. I was flying the aeroplane, from the left-hand seat, with Leo doing the navigating, R/T chat and general chores. He preferred it that way.

After climbing west into the Mediterranean night, we levelled off at a comfortable 8,000 feet, settled down to cruise settings and set course for the long seven and a half hour flight to Brindisi, where we would refuel. As the oxygen equipment was primitive and the masks uncomfortable, we had decided not to exploit the B17's high-altitude turbo efficiency, except on the Dakar–Natal leg. The instruments glowing hypnotically in the dim cockpit lighting signalled all's well despite the fact that the four Wright Cyclone engines were nearly twenty years old. It was a typical Mediterranean night with a brilliant moon shafting beams through the scattered cumulus clouds and turning the four propellers into silvered discs. It was the sort of night that makes one glad to be a pilot.

Brindisi turned up promptly just before dawn. We had planned it that way. At that hour officialdom's defences are partly down. The night shift would be bored and tired, the day shift not yet arrived. Although measures had been taken to ensure that our documents and what we were up to would not be too thoroughly investigated by the Italian airport authorities we felt uneasy. We circled the airfield, approached and landed and taxied to the parking tarmac with impeccable rectitude, hoping to avoid drawing attention to ourselves, but there were several ground staff lined up on the tarmac watching us intently as we parked and switched off. We hoped that their interest was aroused merely by the fact that we were flying a Flying Fortress, a rare bird in those days.

We refused breakfast. I organised packed lunches and Thermos coffee and completed the bogus flight clearance formalities while Leo arranged the refuelling. It seemed to me I was surrounded by knowing looks, winks and nudges as I filled in the forms. The weather report for Algiers, our next stop, was not promising but we would have to worry about that later.

'Let's go!' shouted Leo as he walked swiftly, trying not to run, from the refuelling office where he had paid cash for our petrol – we were carrying a fortune in dollars for our slush fund. We climbed aboard and slammed the hatches shut. I started up and taxied at a furious pace to the take-off position while Leo did the take-off check and got take-off clearance from the control tower. Without stopping we swung onto the runway, slammed on maximum power, belted down the runway and shot into the air like a startled pheasant, just as orange tinted the eastern sky. The Wright Cyclone engines snarled their displeasure at being subject to such cavalier treatment.

It is axiomatic in flying that when things go wrong they go wrong unexpectedly and suddenly. We were at a comfortable 8,000 feet following the North African coast and had just passed the Tunisian–Algerian border. It was warm and peaceful. Leo was dozing and I was trying to keep awake when, without warning from the instruments, there was a colossal bang from number three engine, followed by the unnerving crunch of metal fighting metal, severe vibration and, to cap it all, puffs of smoke. Number three engine's oil temperature and oil pressure gauges were, as one might say, rising and falling respectively. For a minute or two Leo and I were busy: number three throttle closed, press the feathering button, left rudder, mixture shut, fuel off, ignition off, open up number four engine, rudder trim to compensate the asymmetric power, a touch of elevator trim, more trim, close cowl flaps. We watched the propeller feather and stop with its three blades knife-edging into the airflow. But feathering did not stop the smoke. I poised my finger over number three's fire extinguisher button and raised an eyebrow at Leo. He hesitated – it would make a mess – before nodding. I pressed the button. For a few moments the smoke got worse as it mixed with steam and chemicals but under our anxious gaze it subsided, hiccupped and finally stopped. We fidgeted with the controls, getting the power setting and trim right and settled down on our three good engines before leaning back in our seats. The panic was over.

'What the hell was that?' wondered Leo. We concluded it was either the main crankshaft bearing seized or a broken connecting rod.

We were down to three engines. Though that was not a serious problem, as the B17 could fly all day on three, other damage might have been caused, particularly to the fuel or hydraulic systems and Algiers was still over two hours away. Above us lowering cloud reminded us that the weather at Algiers – low cloud and poor visibility in rain – might be a problem when trying to land on three engines. Despite our cargo of 'spare parts' we had to seek an alternative aerodrome. We were not worried. In order to refuel at Algiers our flight had been cleared at ministerial level in Paris. We looked at our maps. The nearest Algerian aerodrome was Bône, twenty miles away. At that time, during the ferocious height of the Algerian fight for independence against the French, it was a French Air Force base. After the 1956 Suez campaign, France and Israel were good friends and the Israeli and French Air Forces old comrades. Bône, with its military secrecy, could not be a better bolt-hole.

We called them up on the R/T, declared a Pan situation – a mild emergency – and requested permission to land. It was readily granted and we landed within fifteen minutes, escorted by two Mystère jet fighters in the air and an ambulance and fire-tender on the ground. We felt that they had over-dramatised the situation until we realised, as we parked in front of the control tower, that this was an aerodrome at war. Light bombers and fighters buzzed around the sky, landed, refuelled, re-armed and took off again. Uniforms everywhere reminded us that we were unshaven, un-washed and wearing mufti.

We unpacked our sponge bags, shut the hatches and asked to see the commanding officer. It took some time before we were under-stood. I do not speak French. Leo said he did but none of the Frenchmen believed him. A Jeep took us to the CO's office. I am not familiar with French badges of rank but, to judge from the gold braid and the rows of medal ribbons, the CO was very senior. It was obvious he felt so. Our appearance did not muster confidence.

He listened to our story as it was being translated by his aide. Disbelief spread across his features as we explained that we were on a secret flight authorised by the Israeli government, that the French government in Paris had cleared our flight and granted us permission to land and refuel at Algiers, that our cargo was also top secret, that we had lost an engine and now needed assistance to get a replacement engine from French or Israeli sources. Finally, a bath, a meal and a bed would not come amiss as we had not slept for 36 hours and had been flying almost non-stop for twelve.

The CO and his aide excused themselves and left the office. Half an hour later the aide returned and explained that he would take us to the officers' mess for a wash and brush-up and lunch, while the formalities were being attended to.

After a shave, shower and a delicious cold lunch we waited in the mess lounge for the aide to return. After two hours or so we began to get impatient. There was a lot to do if we were to get an engine delivered and installed.

Suddenly the mess door banged open and the aide walked in, accompanied by three soldiers armed with sub-machine-guns. The guns were pointed at us.

'You are under arrest,' the aide said flatly. 'You will come with me.'

We went with him, of course. It was the first time I had looked down the barrel of a sub-machine-gun pointed at me in earnest. It was daunting. We climbed aboard a mini-bus parked outside and were driven to the main hangar. Our Flying Fortress had been moved and was parked with its nose just inside the hangar with all the hatches gaping open. On the hangar floor, laid out in neat rows and covering a vast area, was our cargo. Bazookas, machine guns, mortars, grenades, small arms and ammunition. To one side were empty wooden crates and blankets and our forlorn-looking luggage, gaping open. I felt as though I had been stripped naked. 'Jesus Christ!' said Leo. It was fair comment. We were not yet alarmed, just annoyed. These people would soon be apologising, egg on their faces, once they had checked with their superiors in Algiers and Paris.

We were then driven to the military police headquarters in Bône. Flood-lighted and surrounded by sandbags, barbed-wire and sentries, it was a grim-looking building. We were escorted to separate rooms. There were bars on the windows, a table and two chairs and a glaring light hanging down from the ceiling, so shaded that it shone into my eyes as I sat down. Two armed guards stood behind me. My interrogator walked in and sat down opposite me. He adjusted the table and chair until I was fully floodlit and he was in the shadow. I assumed Leo was going through the same rigmarole. When he had settled down he did not say anything but just sat there appraising me. I was glad I had shaved and showered. I decided I would emulate him and just sat there looking back. He was short, badly dressed in dark civilian clothes, just like the Gestapo, and wore a loaded shoulder holster which he did not bother to conceal. He looked uncannily like Peter Lorre. I would not have been entirely surprised if Sydney Greenstreet had walked into the room. I discovered over the next few days that he smelled of deodorant in the morning, deodorant and garlic in the afternoon and deodorant, garlic and booze in the evening.

I broke the silence by asking what was this all about and were we being charged and if so with what. He replied, in fluent English but with a heavy accent, that Algeria was under martial law and that legal niceties had been temporarily suspended.

'Our flight', I said, 'has been authorised by the French and Israeli governments. This can be cleared up in five minutes if you telephone Algiers, where we had permission to land, or Paris.'

'We have telephoned Algiers, who telephoned Paris, but it is

Saturday and everyone in the Quai d'Orsay is away for the weekend except the duty officer. He knows nothing about you and suggested that we shoot you.'

I looked at him quickly to see whether he was being jocular. Perhaps he was, but he was to good an interrogator to show it.

'Why?' I asked.

'Because you are supplying arms by air to the Algerian rebels,' he replied. 'A capital offence,' he added.

So that was it. I again explained the background and purpose of the flight. He was not convinced. He said he had been advised that the condition of our Flying Fortress was such that it could not possibly fly across the south Atlantic, a point that most pilots might have agreed with, but I could not admit it and advised him not to judge sausages by their skins. The metaphor baffled him and it took some time before he grasped my point.

I then demanded to see the British Consul, but he reminded me that I was in no position to demand anything.

'Why are the arms wrapped in blankets?' he continued.

'Just wrapping,' I replied. 'Nothing sinister.'

'It is sinister,' he accused. 'They are wrapped to protect them from damage when you throw them out of the aeroplane to the rebels waiting in the desert.'

I asked him why, if we were supplying arms by air to the rebels, would we land here at a French Air Force base of all places when we had engine trouble, when we could have flown to anywhere in Europe on the remaining three engines? Alternatively, if for some inexplicable reason we were forced to land here, why did we not chuck the arms into the Mediterranean before landing? It was with some relief that I saw the first flicker of doubt in his rheumy, Gallic eyes but the questions continued. It was about 2 am and my eyes had not shut properly for two days when we adjourned for what was left of the night. He said that we were still under arrest, but that we were being accommodated under armed guard at an hotel. This news lifted my morale. Villains are rarely accommodated in hotels prior to being shot at dawn as it would disturb the other guests.

The hotel was pink-washed, small and simple. We were put in separate rooms. The bathrooms were not *en suite* and the guards posted outside our bedroom doors escorted us along the corridor, sub-machine guns at the ready, whenever we used the bathroom.

The next morning the interrogation continued. No, I am not Jewish. No, I am not receiving vast sums of money for the flight. No, I do not find it necessary to be anti-Arab merely because I suppport Israel. They have the same father, be he called Abraham or Ibrahim. Yes, I do believe the Algerians should be granted independence. Yes, I do read pornographic books if they are literate – someone had obviously found Henry Miller's *Tropic of Capricorn* in my luggage. Mid-morning the British Vice-Consul was shown in. He was languid and foppish and obviously thought I was a flaming nuisance. After questions about my welfare and whether I had any complaints, he passed me a packet of Players cigarettes. It was a nice thought and I inhaled deeply after the cautious puffs and coughs of Gauloises.

He then enlarged on the background to our situation.

The Algerians had been struggling for independence from French colonial rule since the mid-1920s. What had started with a mild protest movement was now a full-scale insurrection. It was not a gallant war. Only a few days before we landed at Bône, French aircraft had bombed and strafed Sisi Sakiet Youssef, a small village across the border in Tunisia a few miles east of Bône suspected of harbouring Algerian guerrillas, resulting in the deaths of 63 innocent Tunisian villagers. Not a single Algerian was among the casualties. The day we landed, a young woman had been executed in Algiers for terrorist offences.

The French colonialists and military in Algeria, led by General Salan, the commander-in-chief, and General Massu, commander of the notorious 10th division, had become disaffected and suspected that the Fourth Republic, weakened by the fall of Mollet's government, was preparing to grant independence to the Algerians. At the time we got involved General Salan's staff were planning mutiny and an airborne invasion of France to topple the French government and install General de Gaulle as President, who they assumed, incorrectly, would support their cause and deny independence to the Algerians.

It was not surprising that in such circumstances, when communications between Paris and Algiers were frosty and minimal, that the authorities in Paris failed to inform their counterparts in Algiers of our flight.

The Vice-Consul passed me a batch of French and English

newspapers. We were front page news. 'Arms Plane Briton Held,' said the *Daily Express*. 'Mystery Plane Case,' said *The Times*. 'Briton in Flying Fortress Arms Mystery,' said the *Mirror*. 'Briton In Arms Plane Held By the French,' said the *News Chronicle*, accompanied by photographs. I wondered what Associated Television's sales director would think. In the French newspapers there were wild theories about our flight. The arms were destined for Algerian rebels, said one. Another, that they were en route to the Moroccan rebels next door, who were waging their own war of independence against the Spanish. Another, that our flight had originated from Cairo, confirming Egypt's direct involvement in the Algerian rebellion. Finally, that the whole affair was a red herring designed to divert attention from the Algerian political crisis. I found out later that Israeli newspaper theories were even more bizarre.

I asked the Vice-Consul whether we were going to be shot. He replied that it was now unlikely. 'But', he added musingly, 'there was a moment.'

By now it should have been transparently obvious that we were telling the truth and that the telephone lines between Bône, Algiers, Paris and Tel Aviv had been humming to confirm this. Not a bit of it. The light still shone on my face and the questions still flowed. Despite orders from Paris that we were to be released immediately, we were held for another four days. Fortunately the guards were by now as bored as we were and no longer insisted on escorting us to the bathroom. We passed the time confined to our hotel bedroom, drinking local araq, playing gin-rummy and dallying with the chambermaids.

The explanation for the delay in releasing us from arrest was that the fiasco of our flight, and the resultant worldwide publicity, gave the disaffected military and colonialists in Algiers the opportunity of demonstrating to their superiors in Paris that their loyalty and obedience to metropolitan France was not to be taken for granted, and if there was any more nonsense about granting independence to Algeria they would take action and make a unilateral declaration of independence from France.

We were released from arrest without apology. The arms were confiscated by the Algerian authorities, who then ordered us not to continue our flight to South America but to fly the B17 back to

278

Israel after it had been repaired. These decisions were made in Algiers in defiance of the French government in Paris, who had ordered that we were to be permitted to continue our flight, with cargo, to South America.

We spent the rest of the day inspecting the engine – it was a broken connecting rod – and shouting down the telephone to the Israeli Embassy in Paris, arranging for a replacement engine and engineers to be flown from Israel.

That night Leo and I celebrated in Bône, now called Annaba. After drinking and belly-dancers, Leo and I wandered around the Arab quarter and the market, enjoying our freedom and revelling in the smell of spices, the oil lanterns and the soft, velvet touch of Mediterranean night. There were no tourists of course; this was long before package tours. The mood was broken when a squad of *poilus* stopped us and advised us not to wander around the Arab quarter after dark.

A C46 aircraft, another old friend, arrived from Israel the following day with a replacement engine and a team of mechanics from Bedek. Leading the team was Dov, the Dov of Bandar Abbas. 'Doctor Livingstone again, I presume,' he said with a grin as we shook hands. With typical Israeli efficiency the replacement engine was fitted to the Flying Fortress within a few hours and we were ready to go. None of us was in the mood for effusive farewells, and Leo and I climbed aboard the empty B17 after the most perfunctory of goodbyes to the French. After an uneventful ten-hour non-stop flight we landed back in Israel twelve days after we had departed.

The following day we attended a world's press conference chaired by Shimon Peres, later Prime Minister. The affair was finally put to rest when Premier Ben Gurion and the French government issued statements confirming that the French and Israeli governments had been aware of the purpose and destination of the flight and regretted that the authorities in Algiers had forbidden the flight to continue.

I wondered about that at the time. There was no point in the Algerian French not permitting us to continue to South America. They had no axes to grind there and they certainly did not need our consignment of arms. I suspected that the politically embarrassing world-wide publicity persuaded the Israeli authorities to drop the whole affair and get us back home before any more political damage was caused in South America, and colluded with the French in Paris to blame Algiers for confiscating the arms and turning us back. After all, *vide* Suez, France and Israel were quite experienced at mutual collusion.

My suspicions appeared to be confirmed when I discovered, nearly thirty years later, that the arms were ultimately destined for Batista's anti-Castro forces in Cuba. When I found that out I was glad we had been turned back. Had those arms reached Batista I would have bitterly regretted it. The whole affair was a murky episode of which I am not particularly proud. I should have asked many more questions before agreeing to join that flight.

I was a bit concerned about my notoriety as an alleged gun-runner when I returned to London, but Associated Television's offer of a job was still open. I put away my smelly leather helmet and goggles and white silk scarf for the last time and settled down.

Last Word

LIFE, MORE TRUE than art, rarely offers a neat and tidy ending to an autobiography, other than the deathbed. Meanwhile, I will gather the looser ends.

Now that I have reached, at three score and ten, Sunday breakfast-time in the week of my life, I have come to the conclusion that my days will end with a whimper rather than a bang. I have ventured down too many blind alleys, made too many enemies, suffered fools too ungladly and worshipped iconoclasm too gleefully to finish up other than a nobody, sans honours, sans riches, sans obituaries. I discovered too late that one should temper one's opinions with tact and disguise one's message in the presence of fools. That one can disagree without being disagreeable. That it is as important to win friends as to win arguments.

Some argue that we are the fruit of our free will. My mother would have said it was water finding its own level, but I suspect that fate has conspired here and there. Free will is like two falling leaves saying to each other in an autumn gale: where shall we go now?

That I never flew to El Dorado does not concern me, for I have never cared for or respected wealth or the wealthy, and one of the maxims of my youth, that private property is theft, still lingers in my values. Now that I have reached the stage when the future is much shorter than the past and things put off are put off forever, it is with some relief that I find, with most passions spent and ambition flown, I can accept my lot with equanimity. Looking back I have neither failed nor suceeded, the fate of most of us, but I have had more fun than most. Also, unlike most nobodies, I shall leave the world a better place than when I entered it because I helped found the State of Israel.

I fell in love for the first time, aged forty, with Sally, an upper-class waif aged twenty-three. When I first met her she was an ex-debutante, painfully thin, spotty and suffering from split hair ends. It was her voice and her giggle that captivated me. Within two years she late-blossomed into a well-built, lovely woman. Her father, High Sheriff of Sussex, Wykehamist, Oxford cricket blue, captain of Sussex county cricket team, company chairman and gentleman farmer of a thousand acres in East Sussex, had recently died, tragically young, aged forty-eight. His unfair untimely death devastated Sally, his eldest child. Her mother was a hopeless alcoholic, her two younger brothers and sister were at boarding schools. Her closest male relative, Uncle George Loveday, chairman of the Stock Exchange, was too distant a figure to be much of a surrogate father.

Sally and I both worked at Associated Television's head office at Marble Arch, in London. We joined the company at almost the same time. I had just returned from my swansong Algerian fiasco and was deeply tanned and a touch mysterious. We began an agonising on-off relationship, for I was old enough to know it was all wrong, lasting two years. The reader will have no difficulty imagining how welcome I was to her family; middle-aged, broke, married and working-class. I met George twice at his club in his justified attempts to warn me off. I was not overwhelmed by Boodles – the Prime Minister was having an aperitif at the next sofa – for most, if not all, of my malapropisms and solecisms were things of the past. I could now pass muster as a gent when I wanted to and I bought my suits from Savile Row, my shirts from Jermyn Street and my bowler, umbrella and shoes from St. James's Street.

To George's surprise I agreed with every word he said and his words were harsh. I explained that I was aware that I was a father-figure to Sally and had several times tried to break it off. Eventually Sally and I decided that she should go to Canada in a final attempt to sever our relationship. She was back within six months. I was divorced from Alice and married Sally. I am grateful that Alice was prepared to be friends with us both. George and I also became quite good friends.

At the age of forty-eight I begat my first child, a daughter, followed by another daughter two years later. Years later I got raised eyebrows from the Post Office counter-clerks when I queued up each month for my old age pension and the child allowances for the two girls. Few parents qualify for both simultaneously. Marrying late and surrounded by the persistent, youthful vitality of my children has kept me young. I think they too have gained from the age-gap, for my years have brought some wisdom.

My daughters are bright and attractive. Reflecting the paradoxes

31 Gordon Levett and his wife Sally, 1968

32 Gordon Levett sitting on the wing of an ex-101 Fighter Squadron Spitfire during a reunion at the Israeli Air Force Museum, Hazerim, April 1993

33 Same setting – different aircraft. This one is a Messerschmitt 109

of my life they both received a public-school education with the help of the Assisted Place Scheme, followed by both winning scholarships for two years' sixth-form boarding at boys' public schools. Both went to Cambridge and got good degrees, the elder economics at Trinity and the younger medicine at Pembroke. I have achieved more through my daughters, my *alter egos*, than through myself.

After nine years of fetid office politics, politics at which I was hopeless, at Associated Television I resigned at being passed-over for promotion. This was followed by twelve years' buying and running hotels. The last one, just outside Lydd airport, turned out a disaster. It was 1982 and we had just completed rebuilding and renovating the hotel on borrowed money when VAT doubled overnight, interest rates on our substantial bank loan went up to 22 per cent, Lydd-based Skyways Airline went bust and Lydd airport – our *raison d'etre* – closed. We just avoided bankruptcy by selling fast at a massive loss and finished up broke and homeless.

We became dependent upon social security and rented a council house which, five years later, we managed to buy on a 100 per cent mortgage. We have no capital and no career pension. I have no job and can't get one; too old. I occasionally earn a few paltry pounds writing aviation articles. Sally has a fulfilling job with a charity as director of fund-raising and PR and commutes to London. She says that she would rather do that than housework. I wear the apron strings. It seems to work – I was never a male chauvinist pig. We scrape by. Sally has become a Christian, but I am glad to say she still swears occasionally and does un-Christian things. I must be getting mellow at last because I don't mind too much occasionally finding an open Bible on the kitchen table. Not so long ago it would have gone out of the window.

It has taken a long time, but I am back where I started at the bottom of the pile and I have brought Sally down with me. It has also taken me a long time to find out what courage is. Sally, this flibbertigibbet born with a set of silver spoons in her mouth, has shown true courage over these years during our downward path. Not once by rebuke, by a murmur of regret, by the flick of an eyelash, by a sigh, has she shown resentment or blamed me for bringing her down from the ivory tower of wealth and privilege to social security handouts. Not once in over thirty years. That is guts and courage, not *Achtung* Spitfire! and *Dawn Patrol*. She not only has my love, she has my admiration.

My life has been a series of ups and downs in more senses than one but the good things have more than balanced the darker side. I have little on my conscience and I sleep easily. My memories are an atlas of travel and adventure in what, looking back, seemed a much larger and more gracious world. There are few things in my life that I regret and time has healed old wounds.

I am invited to Israel occasionally, where I don my VIP cloak and meet old friends, now Cabinet ministers and generals. Ezer is now President of Israel. I still feel at home there, but on every visit I am saddened that Israel, this tiny country the size of Wales, has never known a moment of peace in its entire forty-five-year history and is still under siege, with its borders, apart from the cold peace with Egypt, still front lines.

Like my father and my father's father and, no doubt, his father too, I will leave my children materially nothing, but they have already inherited a fortune born of my influence. I have broken the mould of ignorant generation begetting ignorant generation, of ignorance breeding ignorance in my family genealogy. Our two daughters have been brought up in a world of books and knowledge and liberal compassion and entered the groves of academe with style and confidence. I have achieved my ambitions through them. Both have benefited, as did my stepson Grahame (now a professor), from the deprivation and wasteland of my early youth, for I would not let it happen to them. On this I rest my case.